How to Expand & Upgrade PCs

Second Edition

Preston Gralla

201 W. 103rd Street
Indianapolis, IN 46290

How to Expand & Upgrade PCs, Second Edition

International Standard Book Number: 0-7897-2500-2

Library of Congress Catalog Card Number: 00-110465

Printed in the United States of America

First Printing: March 2001

03   02   01   4   3   2

Trademarks

Warning and Disclaimer

Associate Publisher
Greg Wiegand

Acquisitions Editor
Stephanie McComb

Development Editor
Nicholas J. Goetz

Managing Editor
Thomas F. Hayes

Project Editor
Tricia Sterling Liebig

Copy Editor
Megan Wade

Indexer
Kelly Castell

Proofreader
Maribeth Echard

Technical Editor
Chris Faust

Illustrators
Stephen Adams
Tammy Ludwig
Laura Robbins

Team Coordinator
Sharry Lee Gregory

Cover Designer
Anne Jones

Production Designer
Trina Wurst

Contents at a Glance

Introduction 1

Chapter 1
What's Inside Your Computer 4

Chapter 2
Installing a New Motherboard or CPU 22

Chapter 3
Adding Memory to Your PC 40

Chapter 4
Installing a New Power Supply 50

Chapter 5
Adding or Replacing an IDE Hard Drive 56

Chapter 6
Installing a Floppy Drive 72

Chapter 7
Installing a CD-ROM Drive 80

Chapter 8
Installing a DVD Drive 90

Chapter 9
Installing a SCSI Drive 100

Chapter 10
Installing a Removable Drive 112

Chapter 11
Installing a Tape Drive 120

Chapter 12
Installing a Keyboard and Mouse 128

Chapter 13
Installing a Joystick or Other
Gaming Devices 136

Chapter 14
Installing a Scanner 142

Chapter 15
Installing a Digital Camera 152

Chapter 16
Installing and Upgrading a Graphics
Card and Monitor 158

Chapter 17
Installing a NetCam 172

Chapter 18
Installing a Sound Card and Speakers 178

Chapter 19
Installing an MP3 Player 188

Chapter 20
Installing USB Devices 194

Chapter 21
Installing a Modem 204

Chapter 22
Installing a Printer 216

Chapter 23
Upgrading Notebook Computers 222

Chapter 24
Installing a Home Network 230

Chapter 25
Performing Computer Maintenance 240

Glossary 246

Index 252

Acknowledgments

A book as complex as this requires the hard work and dedication of many people—and people too numerous to list here have helped create it. Thanks to Stephanie McComb and Angie Wethington for trusting me with this project and for all the help along the way, as well as to Renee Wilmeth for getting it rolling. Development editor Nick Goetz did an extraordinary job whipping it into shape, working with the illustrators, and generally pulling off what seems to me to be magic in making sure this book came together. And, of course, thanks to the illustrators—Stephen Adams, Laura Robbins, Tammy Ludwig—this book is a visual experience, and without the beautiful illustrations, there would be no book.

Thanks also to Tricia Liebig, project editor; Maribeth Echard, proofreader; and Trina Wurst, layout technician, for putting on the finishing touches.

Several companies helped me with technical information and advice, so that I could make sure that the "how-it-works" type illustrations were correct. In particular, people from SONICblue, the makers of the Diamond Rio MP3 player (my personal favorite and the one I use all the time); and people from 3COM, the makers of the HomeConnect WebCam (another favorite, and one I use often) provided a great deal of useful help.

As always, thanks to my agent Stuart Krichevsky. And, of course, thanks always goes to my wife Lydia, and children Mia and Gabe who have grown used to having to carefully wend their way through my office, eyes glued to the floor, so they don't trip over tools, cables, monitors, keyboards, mice, and modems, as well as a computer lying on its side, its innards exposed and cables and other guts spilling out.

Special thanks go to Ron White, whose books and knowledge have provided inspiration as well as much raw—and finished—material for this book.

Finally, most of all, thanks go to hardware guru extraordinaire Chris Faust. Chris took apart computers and hard disks and add-in cards and anything else you could name, and took detailed pictures of them all with a digital camera so that they could be illustrated. He did it all with good grace and good humor. And he did a tech edit on the entire book to make sure all the details were right. It's safe to say that without Chris there would be no book.

Dedication

To do-it-yourselfers everywhere who know that the only way to do something right is to do it yourself.

Tell Us What You Think!

As the reader of this book, *you* are our most important critic and commentator. We value your opinion and want to know what we're doing right, what we could do better, what areas you'd like to see us publish in, and any other words of wisdom you're willing to pass our way.

As an Associate Publisher for Que, I welcome your comments. You can fax, email, or write me directly to let me know what you did or didn't like about this book—as well as what we can do to make our books stronger.

Please note that I cannot help you with technical problems related to the topic of this book, and that due to the high volume of mail I receive, I might not be able to reply to every message.

When you write, please be sure to include this book's title and author as well as your name and phone or fax number. I will carefully review your comments and share them with the author and editors who worked on the book.

Fax: 317-581-4666

Email: feedback@quepublishing.com

Mail: Greg Wiegand
            Que
            201 West 103rd Street
            Indianapolis, IN 46290 USA

Introduction

If you own a computer, you know all too well that things often go wrong with them. You wake up one morning, turn on the computer, and the thing simply won't start. Or, you can't install any new programs because your hard disk is full. You want to play a great new game, but you don't have the right graphics card.

And it's not just that things go wrong with them. You're always looking for ways to get your computer to do more, or you want to buy new equipment. Maybe you'd like to install a scanner, or a new modem, or a new hard disk.

Let's face it, computers cost a lot of money, and you want them to last awhile. So, upgrading and expanding them should be cheap and easy.

Too often they're not. You find yourself wading through technical manuals written in a language resembling Sanskrit. You find fast-talking salesmen getting you to buy equipment you don't need. Computer technicians charge an arm or a leg to do something like installing a hard disk—that's if you can even find someone to install it for you.

Those are the kinds of problems this book is devoted to—helping you expand and upgrade your computer yourself. You'll find that there's no need to hire someone to do it for you. Even if you've never picked up a screwdriver, you'll see that you can do it yourself.

Too often, books that offer advice on how to upgrade and expand PCs are written for people with advanced technical skills. This book is different. This book is written for everyone, at every skill level, not just those who already know what USB stands for. Whether you've never opened up your PC, or you're a pro at installing SCSI devices, you'll find it helpful. That's because this book takes a different approach to helping you upgrade and expand computers than do other books. It's devoted to the time-honored idea that a picture is worth a thousand words. So, I don't just tell you how to do something—I *show* you in easy-to-follow pictures and step-by-step instructions.

To make it even easier for you to expand and upgrade your computer, I also show you how computers and all their components work and how they fit together. So, before I show you how to put in a new hard disk, for example, I show you how the hard disk is connected to your computer, what cables to look for, and how the whole thing fits together.

Many people who buy this book may buy it for a single reason—for example, to learn how to install a scanner. But I hope that even if you buy it for that single reason, you'll soon gain enough confidence to install other devices, and to do computer repairs yourself. You'll be surprised how easy it is—and not only will you be saving money and getting a more powerful computer, you'll be having fun as well. And you'll have the satisfaction of knowing you did it all yourself.

This second edition of the book has been significantly expanded over the first edition. It will show you how to install all the newest technologies—everything from cable modems to MP3 players, WebCams, and even home networks.

How to Use This Book

You'll probably start using this book by turning to the chapter of the thing you want to repair or upgrade—a removable drive, a monitor, a graphics card. But before doing that, I suggest that you spend at least a little time perusing Chapter 1, "What's Inside Your Computer." It shows you all the tools you'll need for expanding and upgrading your computer, and shows you how to do basic things, such as opening the case and installing hardware drivers. And it gives a great look inside your computer and shows you how everything fits together, so you'll know what you're looking at when you see all those wires, cables, and chips.

In "How to" chapters, you will find the special tools needed for that particular task pictured just to the right of the title.

Most chapters start off with an illustration showing you how that peripheral or device works, and how it connects to your computer. It's a good idea to check out that illustration before reading the rest of the chapter, so you'll know what to expect ahead of time, and will know how everything fits together.

After that opening illustration, you'll find step-by-step instructions with clear illustrations describing how to repair and upgrade that particular computer component. Each of these step-by-step illustrations starts off by telling you what you'll need to accomplish the task—what tools and what software, if any software is required. Then, you'll read the steps themselves. At the end of the steps, you'll find something that you should pay particular attention to—"Watch Out!." It gives advice on common problems you'll face, and offers suggestions for making your upgrade or repair go easier.

So, take a deep breath, roll up your sleeves, turn to Chapter 1, and get to work. There's money to be saved, and new capabilities to add to your computer!

CHAPTER

What's Inside Your Computer

The Tools You Need   6

The Front of Your Computer   8

The Back of Your Computer   10

How to Open the Case   12

A Look Inside Your Computer   14

How to Set Jumpers and DIP Switches   16

Installing Hardware Drivers   18

Getting System Information and
Using CMOS Setup   20

BEFORE you start expanding and upgrading your PC, you first need to know exactly what's inside it—and what kind of tools you need for the job. In this chapter, you get an insider's look at your computer—a guided tour of every part of it and an understanding of what those parts do, how they fit together, and what you need to know about them before you get to work.

You also learn important basics such as working with hardware drivers, performing diagnostics on information about your system, and changing the computer's basic setup information. You also see all the tools you need to have at hand before opening your computer's case.

The Tools You Need

Nutdriver
Many screws used in a PC also have hexagonal heads, so a hexagonal-head nutdriver will work on them; in fact, they often work better because it surrounds the head of the screw, making it less likely that a slip will strip the screw head. A 1/4-inch nutdriver is your best bet because it's a standard size for computer equipment.

Screwdriver

You'll need some sort of screwdriver to open the cases of most PCs and to add or remove expansion cards inside the PC. Get both a Phillips screwdriver (middle) and a medium-size flathead screwdriver (left). Some computers also use special star-headed screws called Torque screws, so if your computer uses these special screws, you need a Torque screwdriver (right). Three-eighth-inch screwdrivers are best. Don't use screwdrivers with magnetic tips—they can damage your machine.

Pickup tool
Screws and other small objects have a nasty habit of falling into the insides of your PC—often in places where they can't be retrieved, such as between two expansion boards. With a pickup tool, you'll be able to grab them. You push the knob at one end of this flexible tool, and wire claws extend from the other end. You then surround what's fallen with the claws, slowly retract the knob, and the tool grabs the runaway screw.

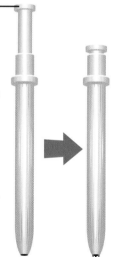

Small flathead screwdriver
You'll need a small flathead screwdriver about 1/8-inch across. You'll mainly use it to tighten cables attached to serial, parallel, and other ports. It is also helpful for removing memory chips and setting various switches.

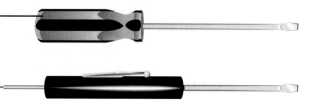

Tweezers
These are good for holding small objects and for changing settings on an expansion board. Get the cross-locked kind, pictured here.

Grounding wrist strap
Static electricity you pick up could seriously damage some components of your computer. To make sure you don't zap an electronic part, wear this. Wrap it around your wrist, and then attach the other end to a grounded piece of metal, such as a metal table leg.

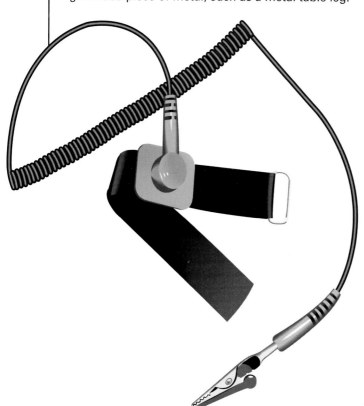

Needlenose pliers
A good, all-around tool for holding screws, getting objects that are too heavy for the pickup tool, or a hundred and one other things.

Chip puller
Good for extracting a processor when you want to replace it or for removing memory chips—although with the newer kinds of memory, you won't necessarily need this tool for that.

The Front of Your Computer

When you upgrade or repair your PC, you often will be working inside the case rather than outside it. But you also need to know what's on the front of your computer before working inside it.

CD-ROM or DVD drive
Here's where you put CD-ROMs or DVDs into your computer. For information on how to upgrade or repair a CD-ROM or DVD drive, turn to Chapter 7, "Installing a CD-ROM Drive," and Chapter 8, "Installing a DVD Drive." The actual drive is housed in a drive bay inside your computer.

Floppy drive
This drive accepts 3 1/2-inch floppies. Virtually no computers sold these days have a drive for 5 1/4-inch floppies. For information on how to upgrade or repair a floppy drive, turn to Chapter 6, "Installing a Floppy Drive." The actual drive is housed in a drive bay inside your computer. In an emergency, you can use the floppy drive to boot your computer.

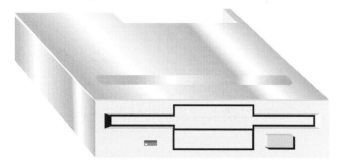

On/off switch
You use this switch to turn your PC on and off. Although your PC often will turn off automatically when you shut it down in Windows, you can use this switch to turn off your computer if it locks up for some reason. This switch is connected to the PC's power supply.

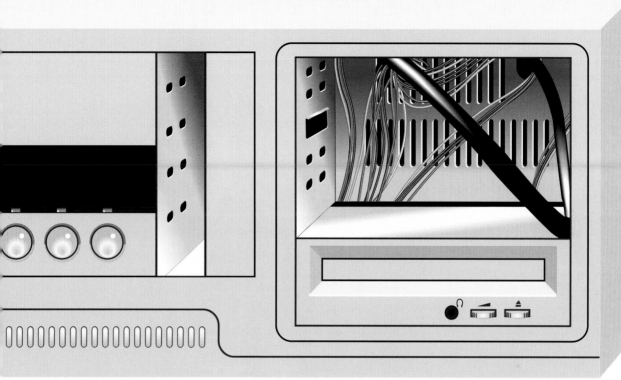

Reset switch

Use this switch to turn your computer off and then restart it. Use it only in case of an emergency; it's a better idea to shut down your computer in the normal manner, by using software or the on/off switch.

Drive bays

There is a specific space inside the case of your PC called a drive bay where you can put extra drives such as hard drives, CD-ROM drives, DVD drives, floppy drives, and other storage devices. You can't see these drive bays from the front of your computer, but you can when you take off its case. There are two types of drive bays: 3 1/2-inch bays and 5 1/4-inch bays.

Indicator lights

You'll find a variety of lights on the front of your computer that give you vital information about its operation. A power light tells you when the power is on; a hard disk light flashes on when the hard disk is being accessed; and a reset light goes on when the computer is reset.

The Back of Your Computer

On the back of your computer are a variety of plugs and ports where things such as your keyboard, mouse, printer, and other devices attach to your PC. Here's a look at what's most likely on the back of yours.

Mouse and keyboard ports
Your keyboard and mouse plug into ports that generally look exactly like each other. There is usually a small picture of a mouse next to the mouse port and a small picture of a keyboard next to the keyboard port. Sometimes the ports and plugs are color coded, to make it even easier to figure out where to plug in the keyboard and the mouse.

Universal Serial Bus (USB) port
These ports enable you to connect devices such as scanners to your computer. They also enable you to hook them up without having to open the case of your computer. Older PCs don't have USB ports, whereas newer ones usually have one or two. For more information on USB ports, turn to Chapter 20, "Installing USB Devices."

Parallel port
The printer plugs into the parallel port, sometimes called the printer port. Other devices, such as scanners, also plug into the parallel port. Your computer often calls the parallel port LPT, such as LPT1 or LPT2.

Game port
A variety of devices, such as joysticks, plug into the game port—a 15-hole female port usually attached to the portion of the sound card that sticks outside the back of your computer. On some machines, you might find two game ports: one on the sound card and one above either the serial port or the parallel port. It's best to use the sound card game port.

Video port
Your monitor plugs into the video port. In most cases, it is a 15-hole female port, which is for a VGA or Super VGA monitor. If you have an older computer, it might have an EGA port, which is a 9-hole female port. Other devices, such as projectors, can be attached to the video port as well.

Fan

Your power supply can get hot and needs to be cooled off. There's a fan in it that cools it off by blowing air out the back of the computer. There might also be other fans in your computer. These can be fan cards that plug into a expansion slot, are built into the case, or are on the microprocessor itself.

Power cord plug

Here's where you plug your power cord into your computer. The cord sends electricity from the wall outlet to the power supply inside your PC.

Serial port

Many different devices can plug into a serial port, such as modems and mice. Most serial ports are 9-pin and are a male connector—in other words, the pins stick up and plug into a female plug that has 9 holes in it. Some serial ports, however, are larger and have 25 pins in them. Serial ports are also called COM ports. Converters are available to convert a 9-pin port to a 25-pin port or vice versa.

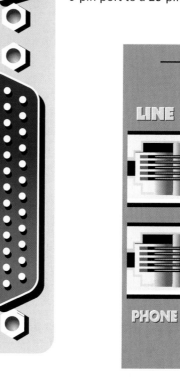

Modem jack

If your computer has an internal modem, it will have modem jacks, which a phone line can plug into to give you access to the Internet. A modem typically has two jacks, so if you want to share a phone line with your telephone, you can run a wire from the jack labeled phone to the telephone, and a wire from the other jack, labeled line, to the phone line.

How to Open the Case

To expand or upgrade almost anything, you have to get inside the case of your PC. Although there are variations in how you do this, you'll be able to open the case of just about every computer by following these steps.

1 Get Rid of Static Electricity

You often build up a static charge simply by walking on carpets and upholstery, especially during the winter months when the air is dry. You can destroy some PC components if you accidentally discharge static electricity onto them. Because of that, always get rid of any static charge you might carry before opening the case. One way is to use a grounding wrist strap. You can also touch a grounded object, such as the power supply of your PC.

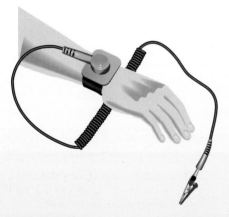

2 Turn Off Your PC

Before doing anything, you have to turn off your PC. If you try to upgrade or repair the computer while it's on, you could do damage to the computer as well as to yourself. Be sure to turn off anything attached to your computer, such as a printer or monitor.

3 Unplug the Power Cord

If you open the case of your PC while it's plugged in, you could hurt yourself or your computer, so unplug it first. The power cord usually plugs into the back of your PC. Unplug it from there, not from the wall or the power strip. If you unplug it from the wall or power strip, you could accidentally unplug the wrong device and end up opening your PC with the power cord still attached. You might find your monitor plugged into your power supply, so remove that as well.

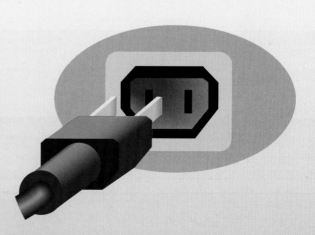

◳ Find the Screws on the Case

If you have a desktop model, usually three to five screws hold it in place. A minitower usually has six or more screws, and a full tower might have as many as eight or ten. In some instances, instead of screws, there are thumbscrews you can unscrew by hand. Many cases now have a snap-on front cover that when removed reveal the screws that hold on the cases. Some cases forgo these kinds of screws altogether and instead use one or more thumbscrews to hold it in place.

◴ Remove the Screws

You might need a Phillips screwdriver, a flat-head screwdriver, or a Torque screwdriver, depending on the type of screw. Better yet would be to use a hexagonal nutdriver if your screws have hexagonal heads. Be sure to place the screws in a safe place, such as a paper cup. You also might want to tape them to the case until you need them again.

◶ Remove the Case

You usually remove the case by sliding the cover toward the rear of the computer and then lifting it off its rails. After you've removed the case, you should ground yourself again before reaching inside to do whatever work you're planning. On some desktop PCs, the case slides out from the front instead of the back.

Watch Out!

- Remember to turn off any devices attached to your PC, as well as the PC itself, before opening the case.

- Be sure that you're grounded so that you don't damage any delicate internal components.

- When you remove the screws, put them nearby in a safe place, or tape them to the case after it's opened—you'll need them when you reattach the case.

A Look Inside Your Computer

Before you can upgrade or repair your PC, you have to know what's inside. Here's a roadmap to the major components and a brief explanation of what they do.

Microprocessor (CPU)

This is the brains of your PC, also called a CPU (central processing unit). It does most of the processing and computations. On many PCs, you can replace the micro-processor with a faster one—although the mother-board has to specifically enable the new, faster microprocessor to be plugged in at a specific speed. When you install a new CPU, you'll probably have to change jumper settings, as shown in the illustration on the following pages.

ROM BIOS chip

Short for read-only memory, basic input/output system. This holds the code necessary for starting up your computer and is also used for basic functions of receiving and sending data to and from hardware devices, such as the keyboard and disk drives. On occasion, in order to take advantage of new hardware or capabilities, you'll need to upgrade your ROM BIOS chip.

CMOS chip

This chip contains a record of the hardware installed on your PC. The CMOS battery supplies it with power so that the data will remain stored even when the computer is turned off. The CMOS chip remembers things such as the size and capabilities of your hard drive and other basic information about your computer.

CMOS battery

A small battery that provides power to the CMOS chip.

RAM (random access memory)

This is the memory where programs are run and data is stored while the data is being manipu-lated. When you turn off your computer, any information in RAM is lost. The more RAM you have, the more pro-grams you can run at once. It can also make applications run faster. The fastest RAM avail-able today is known as Rambus memory, or RIMMS.

RAM cache

This is memory that sits between your CPU and your main RAM. It is faster than main RAM. Information is shuttled here from main RAM so that it's available faster to the CPU.

Power supply
Provides power to your PC by converting the current from your wall outlet to the kind of power that can be used by your PC and all its components. Some power supplies also have a second plug for attaching your monitor.

Drive bays
These are where you put hard drives, CD-ROM drives, floppy drives, and similar add-ins.

Removable drive
Removable drives store data permanently like a hard drive or a floppy drive, but hold data on removable disks. These disks commonly hold several hundred megabytes of data or even several gigabytes of data.

Floppy drive
The floppy drive stores data in the same way as does a hard drive, but it stores information on removable disks that hold only 1.44MB of data. In an emergency, you can start your computer from the floppy drive.

Motherboard
This contains the main circuitry of the computer and provides the way in which all components communicate with one another. All components of a PC plug into the motherboard in one way or another.

Expansion slots
These hold the expansion cards, also called adapters, that expand how your PC can be used, such as video cards, disk controllers, and similar add-ins.

Ports
These let you plug in devices such as a keyboard, modem, printer, and mouse. Some ports are connected to the motherboard whereas others are connected to expansion cards.

How to Set Jumpers and DIP Switches

Sometimes you might come across expansion boards to put in your PC that need to be set in a certain way so that they'll work properly with your computer. In general, these kinds of boards are older, and you might not come across them. Many newer boards don't require manual settings.

If a board does require to be set manually, however, it will use things called jumpers and DIP switches. These are very small switches on the board, that when set in a certain pattern, tell the board how to work with your computer. This page shows you the most common kinds of jumpers and DIP switches and explains how to set them.

DIP Switches

DIP switches are tiny rocker or slide switches grouped in a plastic housing.

Most groups of DIP switches clearly identify the on and off positions. Not all do, though. If there are no clear markings, check the expansion card's manual.

DIP switches usually are found on motherboards and on older expansion cards. You need to flip the small controls on these switches on and off in order to configure the expansion card to work properly with your computer. A common kind is pictured here. Check your computer's owner's manual or piece of hardware you're installing to see the proper settings for these switches.

In this kind of DIP switch, you change the setting by pressing down on the high end with a pen, straightened paper clip, or similar narrow object that will let you change one switch at a time.

Jumpers

Jumpers are also used on motherboards and older expansion cards to configure the card so that it works properly with your computer. They're a primitive type of switch in which the circuit is completed by placing a small connector lined with metal so that the current can flow between two metal posts. This jumper is on.

To change a jumper's setting, grab the connector with tweezers or needlenose pliers. Pull it off and replace it so that it fits over two posts to turn the jumper on or over one post to turn it off.

When a jumper is turned off, the connector is positioned so that it fits over only one post. This jumper is off. ―――――――

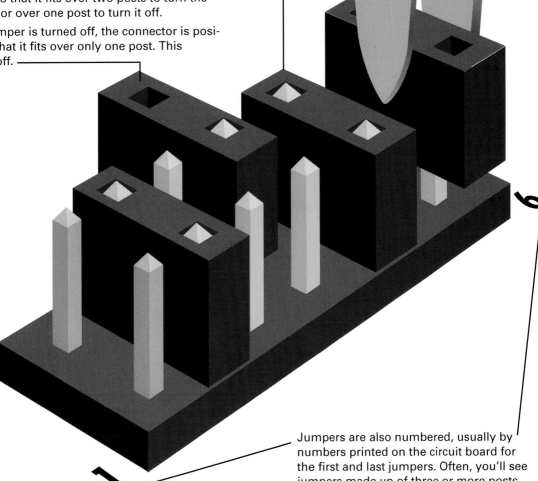

Jumpers are also numbered, usually by numbers printed on the circuit board for the first and last jumpers. Often, you'll see jumpers made up of three or more posts. You'll need to put the connector on just two of the posts in a certain way to give you the jumper setting you need.

Installing Hardware Drivers

Whenever you install a new piece of hardware, you also have to install what are called drivers. *Drivers* are software that mediate between your hardware and your operating system—they're what enable your hardware to work with the software in your computer.

You install drivers after you install the hardware. Until the drivers are installed, your new hardware won't work. With Windows, it's relatively easy to install drivers. Here are the steps to take, after you've first connected the hardware.

① Turn Your Computer Back On

Turn on the computer if you've had to turn the computer off during installation of the hardware. That way, the operating system should recognize that you've installed new hardware, if what you've added supports plug and play. If you didn't have to turn off the computer, or if the operating system didn't recognize that you added new hardware, tell the operating system to find your new hardware. Click the **Start** menu and choose **Control Panel** from the **Settings** menu. Then, double-click the **Add New Hardware** icon and follow the onscreen instructions.

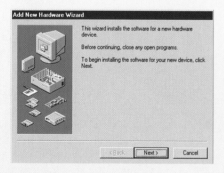

② Identify the New Hardware

Your computer will now search for the new hardware you've installed. This could take several minutes. At some point it might ask whether it should search for the hardware itself or whether you want to specify the hardware you've added. If you're absolutely sure of the hardware you've installed, you can specify the hardware. Otherwise, tell it to find it itself.

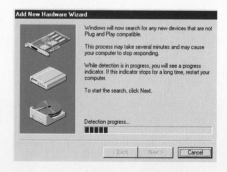

3 Put In the Driver Disk

After several minutes, the computer will identify the hardware you've installed. It will ask you whether you have a disk from the manufacturer that contains the driver. If you have that disk, put it into your drive, and then indicate the drive and subdirectory where it should look. If you don't have the disk, put in your Windows disk and tell it to find the driver on that disk.

4 Finish Installing the Driver

The operating system will find the driver and start to install it. Follow the directions onscreen to finish the installation. At each step, you'll click the **Next** button, until at the end, you'll click **Finish**. At this point, your new hardware should be ready to use.

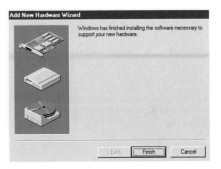

5 Confirm That the Driver Works

To confirm that the hardware has been installed properly, go back to the Control Panel and double-click **System**. Then, click the **Device Manager** tab. Click the small cross next to the kind of device that you've installed, such as a modem. If the driver has been installed properly, you'll see its name there—if it hasn't, you'll see an error message of some sort. Try installing the driver again by turning off your computer and then turning it back on.

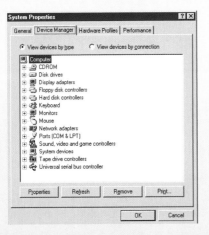

6 Check the Web for Newer Drivers

After you've installed a piece of hardware, it is a good idea to go to the hardware manufacturer's Web site, download any newer versions of the driver, and then install them.

Watch Out!

■ If you don't have a driver for the specific device you're installing, use a generic one from the Windows disk.

■ Check the manufacturer's Web site frequently as often as once a month to check for new drivers.

Getting System Information and Using CMOS Setup

When you expand or upgrade your PC, you often need to know vital information about its hardware and software. In some instances, it would be difficult, if not impossible, to find this information by opening the case and examining the hardware inside. And in almost all instances, it's easier to find out this information by using software built into your computer than it would be to open the case and examine the components. As you'll see here, there are several ways to get system information. Also, when you expand or upgrade, you'll often have to tell your computer to recognize the new component, such as telling it to recognize a second floppy disk that you've installed. In that instance, you'll use what's called the CMOS (Complementary Metal-Oxide Semiconductor) screen.

◼ Use the Microsoft Diagnostic Utility

If you have version 5.0 of DOS or later, you probably have a utility called the Microsoft Diagnostic Utility. This free utility gives you important information about your computer, such as how much memory you have installed, your DOS version, and more. Run the utility before doing any upgrades so that you know what's inside your system. The utility probably will be located in your DOS directory and has the filename MSD.EXE. To run it, type **C:\MSD** or **C:\DOS\MSD**.

◼ Use the Windows Device Manager

Many Windows computers don't have MSD.EXE. Windows offers a similar utility called the Device Manager. To get to it, right-click **My Computer** and choose **Properties**. The main screen gives you basic information, such as how much memory you have installed and the kind of processor you have. For detailed information about your system, click the **Device Manager** tab. From here, you'll be able to see detailed information about any component in your PC.

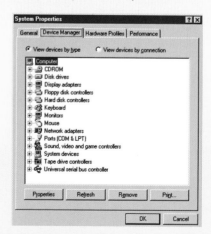

3 Use Microsoft System Information

In addition to the Device Manager, Windows 98 has a useful utility offering a quick overview of your computer. It's called the Microsoft System Information utility. It will report on all the basic information about your system, such as the processor, the size of your hard disk, and details on your hardware and software components. To get to this utility, click the **Start** button, choose **Accessories** from the **Programs** menu, and then choose **System Information** from the **System Tools** menu.

4 Understand What Is in the BIOS

Your computer has a chip in it that holds all the basic information about your computer and its components, such as the type and size of your hard disk and floppy disks, and similar vital information. The chip is called the BIOS chip. You can upgrade the BIOS chip by replacing it. If you have a flash BIOS, you can upgrade it merely by installing a new piece of software. When you add some new hardware, you might need to replace your BIOS because older BIOS chips might not work with the new hardware.

5 Use the CMOS Setup Screen

When you install certain components, such as a hard disk, you need to tell the BIOS about them. You do that by using the CMOS screen. You get to the CMOS screen by pressing a special key when your computer starts. The key you press varies according to your computer, but often is the Delete (Del), F1, or F2 key. Read your computer's documentation to find out how. Also watch your computer as it boots up because there is usually a screen telling you which key to press. (Note: Many components, such as modems or scanners, don't require that you change your CMOS.)

6 Choose Options on the CMOS Screen

To tell your BIOS about new components, follow the onscreen directions. You'll usually choose from a series of menus and options instead of typing in information. After you've told the BIOS about your new components, save the information by following the directions onscreen, exit the CMOS setup, and your computer will recognize the components. On most CMOS screens, you can get help for any function by highlighting that option and pressing the F1 key.

Watch Out!

- Keep a written record of your BIOS information from the CMOS screen in case you need to reinstall your hard drive, or if something goes wrong and deletes the information.
- Change things in the CMOS screen only if you are absolutely sure that the settings you're changing are accurate.
- Be sure that you save the information in your CMOS setup screen before exiting; otherwise, the new information won't take effect.

CHAPTER

Installing a New Motherboard or CPU

How Motherboards and CPUs Work   24

Before Upgrading Your CPU   26

How to Install a CPU   28

Before Installing a New Motherboard   30

How to Remove Your Old Motherboard   32

How to Install a New Motherboard   34

How to Install a New Battery   36

How to Install a New BIOS   38

IF you're not happy with your PC's performance, but don't want to spend the money to buy an entirely new PC, you can upgrade its motherboard or its CPU. The CPU is essentially the brains of the PC—the faster the CPU, the faster your computer will run. Some motherboards don't allow CPU upgrades, however, and some cases don't allow you to put in a new motherboard. Check your system documentation to see about your CPU.

The motherboard also affects your system's performance. If you buy a fast, new CPU, it might not give you as much a speed boost as you want, because the motherboard's old bus could slow it down. A motherboard with a faster bus will ensure that your new CPU runs as fast as it possibly can.

This chapter shows you how you can upgrade your PC's CPU and motherboard. It also tells you how you can replace the system BIOS and the PC's clock. An old BIOS might not support some of the newer hardware available, so if you have an old system, it's a good idea to put in a new BIOS. And buying a new clock will ensure that your computer's vital CMOS information doesn't vanish.

How Motherboards and CPUs Work

Battery
Your system's CMOS needs a way to be powered, even when the computer is turned off. So, a battery on the motherboard sends a steady stream of electricity to the system's CMOS, even when your computer isn't on. CMOS contains basic information about your computer, such as the kind of hard disk it has. If power went off to the CMOS, it would forget all that information. Older batteries might eventually run out of power. They can be replaced with a new battery. In some instances, you won't be able to replace the battery, but these batteries have been designed to live long after your motherboard's lifetime.

BIOS chip
The basic input/output system handles the most basic tasks of your computer, such as configuring hard disks, transferring data to and from the keyboard, and similar tasks. The BIOS is contained on a BIOS chip on the motherboard. The BIOS can be upgraded by installing special software if it's a flash BIOS, or by removing the chip and putting in a new one if it's not a flash BIOS.

Ports
Parallel and serial ports are either directly connected to the motherboard, or are attached to the motherboard via ribbon cables. This allows data to be sent to and from printers, modems, and similar devices.

Slots
Devices communicate with each other via slots on the motherboard's bus. These slots allow devices, such as graphics cards, internal modems, sound cards, network cards, and others, to plug into the bus.

Motherboard
This is attached to the computer's case by a set of screws. The motherboard, however, shouldn't touch the case itself, so plastic spacers or standoffs sit between the screw and the case, holding the motherboard a fraction of an inch away from the case.

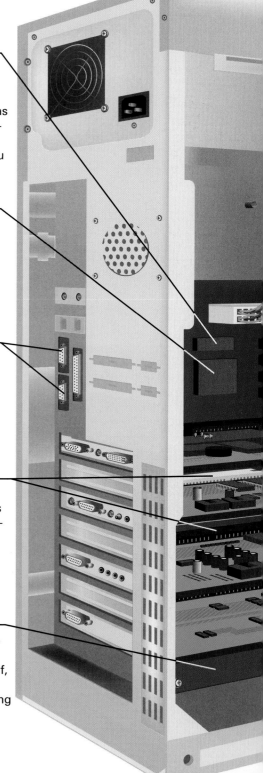

RAM

The motherboard holds the computer's RAM (random access memory) in memory sockets. There are many different kinds of memory sockets to accommodate the many different kinds of memory. Common ones include single inline memory modules (SIMMs), dual inline memory modules (DIMMs), and RIMMs. You'll have to buy the specific memory type (such as DIMMs) to match the memory socket on your PC. So, DIMMs will fit only into a DIMM socket, for example.

Storage devices

Hard drives, floppy drives, and CD-ROM drives attach to a controller on the motherboard via ribbon cables. On older motherboards, the controller is found on an add-in card in a slot. Data travels back and forth between the storage devices and the CPU and other computer components along these ribbon cables.

CPU

The central processing unit, such as a Pentium II, Pentium III, or Celeron chip, is what performs all the computer's calculations and is essentially the brains of your PC. The CPU fits into a CPU socket or slot. You'll have to buy the specific CPU to match the socket or slot on your PC. So, if you have a type of socket or slot that can accept only a Pentium chip, for example, you won't be able to put a Pentium II into it.

Before Upgrading Your CPU

Upgrading your CPU is a bit like giving your PC a brain transplant. It can be a tricky task, but often the most important part is the things you need to do *before* actually doing the upgrade. You need to figure out what kind of CPU your motherboard can handle, what kind of CPU will physically fit in your system, and what kind you'll want to buy. Here's what to do before doing the upgrade.

❶ Back Up Your Hard Disk

Because upgrading your CPU can potentially lead to problems, it's always a good idea to back up your hard disk so that you have a copy of all your programs and data should something go wrong. You can use the Windows Backup feature to do this. Click the **Start** menu, choose **Programs**, **Accessories**, and then **System Tools**. From the System Tools menu, choose **Backup** and follow the instructions.

❷ Determine Your CPU Type

The CPU you now have will help determine what kind of CPU you can upgrade to. To figure out what kind of CPU you now have, check your system case and your system's BIOS. Often, a small sticker on the outside of your case will identify what processor your computer uses, such as a Celeron, Pentium II, or Pentium III (all made by Intel). When your PC boots up, before your operating system starts, your BIOS might flash information telling you the kind and speed of processor inside your PC.

❸ Look Inside to Find Your Processor

The processor usually is a large square chip or a large rectangular case sticking up from the motherboard. Usually stamped on the CPU in large type are the manufacturer and chip types (such as an Intel Pentium II). There are often markings that tell you the chip speed—frequently, the last three numbers in a long string. So, A80503166 would tell you that the chip runs at 166 megahertz. Copy down the codes and check the Intel Web site for further chip information.

4 Determine Your CPU Socket Type

Pentium IIs, Celerons, and some Pentium IIIs are fitted via a slot 1 design, pictured here. A retention mechanism and sometimes support brackets hold the chip. Many Pentiums and 486s use a ZIF socket, where a small lever removes the CPU. There are four types: socket 3, socket 5, socket 7, and socket 370. If it's a socket 7, that will be imprinted on the socket. The CPU might also be attached via a low-insertion force (LIF) socket, in which many small pins on the bottom of the CPU fit into a grid of holes in the socket.

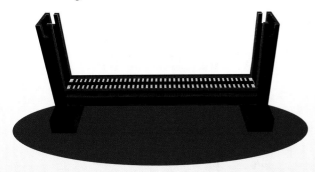

5 Determine Your CPU Upgrade

You'll often be able to upgrade to only a specific speed and make of processor. Check your system documentation. You'll usually be able to upgrade 486 processors to a Pentium OverDrive processor. Pentium processors usually are upgradable with Pentium OverDrive processors and Pentium OverDrive processors with MMX. Whether you can upgrade also depends on whether your system's bus speed can handle the new, faster chip speed. Sometimes, you can set jumpers to make the motherboard handle a faster speed.

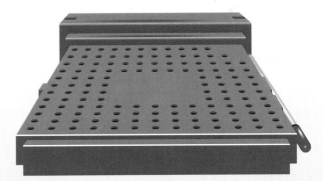

6 Consider Upgrading Your BIOS

Your BIOS might not be able to handle your new CPU. Because of that, consider upgrading your BIOS before you install a CPU, especially if you have an older computer. Turn to the section "How to Install a New BIOS" later in this chapter to upgrade a BIOS.

Watch Out!

- Don't "overclock" your system by setting it to run faster than its rated speed. Intel and other chip manufacturers warn that doing so can damage your motherboard, particularly because it might overheat.

- Check your computer's manual to see what kind of CPU you can upgrade to.

How to Install a CPU

After you've taken basic precautions, such as backing up your hard disk, and you've decided what CPU you'll buy, it's time to do the upgrade. You'll remove your old CPU and put the new one in its place, making sure to attach a cooling fan if it needs one. Here's how to do it.

▉ Turn Off Your Computer

Before you can install a new CPU, you have to turn off your computer and then let it cool down. First turn it off, and then unplug the power cord. Ground yourself, take off its case, and let the CPU cool for about 10 minutes if you've been running your computer. CPUs can get hot when they run, so be sure it's cooled down before handling it.

▉ Remove the CPU from ZIF Socket

How you remove the old CPU will be determined by what kind of socket it is in. Many Pentiums and 486s are in a ZIF socket, in which a small lever removes the CPU. If it's in a ZIF socket, push the small lever away to the side of the CPU, and then lift up the lever. That pushes the CPU from its socket. You can then easily lift the CPU out by hand.

▉ Remove the CPU from a LIF Socket

LIF sockets have no handle, so the best way to remove a CPU from one is to use a CPU extraction tool or a chip puller. A chip puller looks like tongs. Put the tongs under each side of the CPU and pull the chip up firmly but carefully. You might need to tip the CPU slightly to one side and then the other to remove it. Be careful not to tilt it too much to one side, or you could break a pin. If you have to move it from side to side to get it loose, remember to pull the chip straight up to remove it.

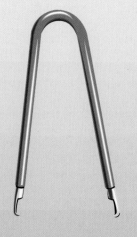

4 Remove the CPU from a Type 1 Slot

Before you can remove the CPU from the type 1 slot, you first have to disconnect the CPU cooling unit from the power source. (CPU cooling units, also called heat sinks, prevent chips from overheating.) After you disconnect the heat sink, unclip the heat sink support if your CPU has those supports. Finally, release the processor from the motherboard and lift out the CPU. You do this by applying pressure to the tabs on each side of the chip to unlock it, and then gently pulling it straight up.

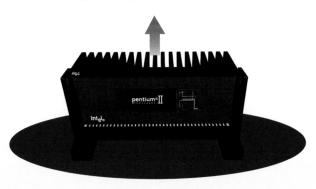

5 Install the New CPU

Put the upgrade CPU into the now-empty slot on the motherboard. Align pin 1 on the processor with pin 1 on the socket. If it's a ZIF socket, pin 1 is on the corner that lacks the corner pinhole. Align the CPU's pins with the socket's holes and slowly lower the CPU into the socket, making sure that all the pins are lined up properly. When it's lined up, press down slowly until the CPU is all the way into the socket. Connect a cooling fan, if one came with your new CPU.

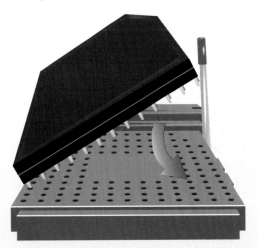

6 Turn On Your Computer

Because things can go wrong when installing a CPU, turn your computer on before putting the case on, in case you need to reseat the CPU. After everything is working properly, you can close the case and begin using your new, faster CPU.

Watch Out!

- Verify that your motherboard is capable of handling the increased clock and bus speed of a faster CPU.
- Make sure that the new CPU you buy will fit into your existing CPU slot.
- Check that your existing BIOS can handle your new CPU. If not, upgrade the BIOS first.
- Be careful when removing your old CPU to remove it gently so that you don't break a pin.
- Make sure that pin 1 on your new CPU aligns with pin 1 on the CPU slot.
- If a CPU cooling fan didn't come with your CPU, buy one.

Before Installing a New Motherboard

If installing a new CPU is like giving your PC a brain transplant, installing a new motherboard is like giving it a new skeleton, nervous system, heart, and lungs. It's one of the most intricate things you can do when expanding or upgrading a PC. But you'll find it's worth it, because when you have a new motherboard, you'll be able to run your computer faster because it has a faster bus speed, you can put in a faster CPU, and you'll be able to expand it in other ways as well. Set aside several hours before replacing your motherboard so that you can take your time, and troubleshoot any problems along the way.

1 Buy a Motherboard That Fits

Motherboards come in several different form factors. Buy one that will fit into your computer's case. Newer computers tend to conform to the ATX form factor. Check your system's documentation or call the manufacturer to see whether your motherboard is an ATX one. If so, buy an ATX motherboard. If it's not, call the system manufacturer to get its specifications for when you buy a new one. If you can't find a motherboard to fit your case, buy a new case.

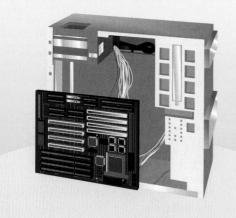

2 Decide on Motherboard Specs

Different motherboards have different specifications: They can handle different amounts of memory, can run at different bus speeds, have a different number of slots, and might or might not have an integrated controller where you can plug in devices such as your hard and floppy disks. Buy a motherboard that can handle the fastest CPU, has the fastest bus speed, can accommodate the most memory, and has the most ports. If you're planning to use your old CPU, buy a motherboard that will work with it.

3 Decide If You Need a New CPU

Generally, when you buy a motherboard, it won't have a CPU on it—although they are available. It's a good idea to replace your CPU when buying a motherboard, because the motherboard alone might not give much of a performance boost.

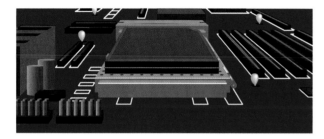

4 Back Up Your Hard Drive

Installing a new motherboard on your PC can be a tricky task, so make sure that you've saved all your data and programs, should something go wrong.

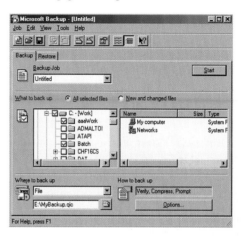

5 Copy Your CMOS Information

You'll want to keep a copy of things such as your type of hard drive, and similar information, in case that information isn't automatically recognized when you install the motherboard. Get to the CMOS screen by pressing a special key when your computer starts. The key you'll press varies from computer model to model, but often is the Delete (Del) key or the F1 or F2 keys. To find out how to access your CMOS, read your computer's documentation. For more information, turn to Chapter 1, "What's Inside Your Computer."

6 Diagram Your Old Motherboard

As you'll see, many different cables, wires, and connectors attach to the motherboard. To make sure that you'll put them all correctly on your new motherboard, it's a good idea to draw a diagram and write notes as you take out your old motherboard. Then, you can refer to it when installing your new motherboard.

Watch Out!

- Make sure that your case has enough slot openings to accommodate the number of slots on the motherboard you buy.

- If you buy a new case and a motherboard, buy the case from the same place where you buy the motherboard so that you're sure the motherboard will fit inside the case.

- If you're going to replace the CPU, make sure that your motherboard can accommodate the CPU you plan to buy, such as a Pentium II, Pentium III, or a Celeron chip.

How to Remove Your Old Motherboard

Removing your old motherboard can be a delicate piece of surgery. You have to remove all the connectors, such as from the power supply and disk drives, and you have to take out all the add-in cards from their slots. If you plan to reuse the CPU and RAM, you need to remove those as well. And there are a variety of other cables and connectors you have to unplug before removing the motherboard. If you want more in-depth information about removing cables and connectors, turn to Chapter 4, "Installing a New Power Supply," Chapter 5, "Adding or Replacing an IDE Hard Drive," and Chapter 6, "Installing a Floppy Drive."

1 Turn Off Your PC

After you turn off your computer, unplug the power cable, open the case, and ground yourself or use an antistatic wrist strap. You want to make sure that you don't carry any static electricity that might harm anything inside your computer. As you remove cables and connectors, make a diagram so that when you plug everything back into your new motherboard, it will all be in the right place.

2 Remove the Connectors and Devices

Unplug your mouse, modem, monitor, keyboard, and other devices connected to your PC or motherboard. Note which serial devices are connected into COM1 or A and COM2 or B, so you can reconnect them in the same way on the new motherboard. You won't need to remove the ribbon or power connectors.

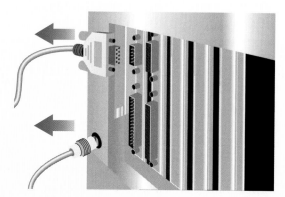

3 Remove All Cards from Their Slots

Cards are held in place by small Phillips-head screws. Unscrew each, and then pull out the cards by holding the card at each end and pulling them up and out. Put the cards in a safe place and keep the screws—you'll need them to attach the cards to your new motherboard. You will probably find a small cable that connects from your CD-ROM drive to your sound card or to the audio connector on some video card. You can leave these connected, or you can take them out when removing the card from the motherboard.

4 Remove the RAM You Will Reuse

RAM is commonly packaged in units called SIMMs. SIMMs are held onto the memory slots by metal holders or plastic tabs on each side of the SIMM. Gently press both tabs outward and the SIMM will be released. A good way to do this is to use two small flathead screwdrivers—use them to press the tabs outward until the SIMM is released. If metal tabs hold in the SIMM, it is often easier to use your thumbnails instead. Put the SIMMs in a safe place where they won't be damaged by static.

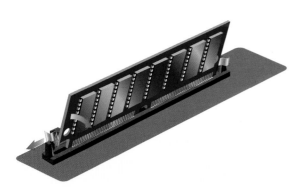

5 Unplug Connectors and Cables

Ribbon cable runs from your motherboard or from a controller card to devices such as your floppy drive and hard disk drive. Unplug the ribbon's connectors from the motherboard or controller card, but leave the ribbons plugged into the devices such as the hard disk and floppy drives. Next, unplug the ribbon cables connecting the motherboard to the serial and parallel ports. Finally, unplug the cables that run from the power supply to internal devices and the motherboard.

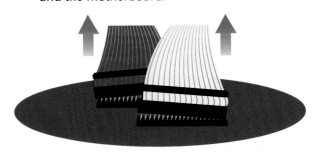

6 Remove the Old Motherboard

Motherboards typically are held in place by screws and plastic standoffs that sit between the motherboard and the case. First, unscrew the screws. Next, remove the standoffs. Pinch their tops with a pair of needlenose pliers and push them through their holes, or lift the motherboard up to release them. You now should be able to remove your motherboard. Hold its edges and pull it straight off the computer.

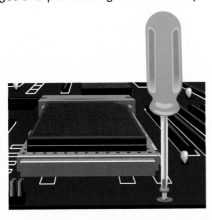

Watch Out!

- When you remove cards, make sure you put them in a place where they won't be harmed by static electricity.
- Look for screws that need to be removed under the power supply or behind disk drives.
- When removing the old motherboard, don't use too much force.
- After you unplug parallel and serial cables, put masking tape on them and label them to make sure that when you put them back, you put them in the proper place.
- Check your new motherboard's manual to see whether it requires that power supply cables be plugged in differently than when they were attached to your original motherboard.

How to Install a New Motherboard

After you've chosen the motherboard you want to install, made a diagram of where your components plugged into your old motherboard, and removed the old motherboard, it's time to install the new motherboard. Exceedingly important in this procedure is that you attach the connectors properly and tightly. Give yourself several hours for installing the new motherboard.

❶ Screw In the New Motherboard

Start by pushing the plastic standoffs into the holes of the motherboard where you had previously taken them out. This will keep the motherboard from touching the case. Then, fit the new motherboard into place. Screw it in, but be careful not to screw it in too tightly or you'll crack the motherboard. To ground the motherboard, use at least two screws to hold in the motherboard.

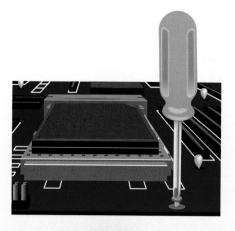

❷ Install the CPU

If your new motherboard didn't come with a CPU, you'll have to install it—turn to the earlier section, "How to Install a CPU."

❸ Install RAM on the Motherboard

Put RAM onto your motherboard. Because it's a new motherboard, it will be some form of SIMM, DIMM, or RIMM. Make sure that you align pin 1 of the RAM (it has a notched corner) with pin 1 on the RAM socket. Typically, you'll put the bottom of the SIMM into the socket at a 45-degree angle, and then push it back up to lock the SIMM with tabs. For more information on how to install RAM, see Chapter 3.

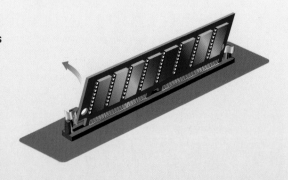

4 Connect Cables and Connectors

Connect the cables from the power supply to the motherboard and to devices such as disk activity lights and on/off switches. Also connect the floppy and IDE connectors from your motherboard to your floppy drive, hard drive, CD-ROM drive, and similar devices. Be sure to connect them in the same way that they were connected initially to your motherboard or controller card. Be sure to match up pin 1 correctly. Then, attach the serial and parallel port cables.

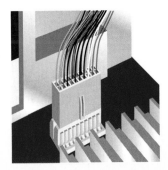

5 Install the Cards

Put the cards you've removed back into the motherboard's slots, and screw them in with the Phillips-head screws. If one of the cards was an IDE controller card, do not reinstall that card if your motherboard has a controller built into it. By installing the old controller card, you might cause problems with the existing controller.

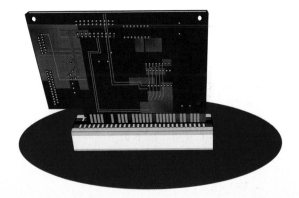

6 Connect the External Devices

Plug back in your mouse, your modem, your monitor, your keyboard, and anything else connected to your PC or motherboard. Then, plug you computer back in, turn on your monitor, and turn on your PC. As Windows recognizes the change in hardware, it might take you several reboots before everything is working properly. You might need to go into the CMOS settings to get it all to work. Before you close the case, you want to make sure that everything works. Then, if everything works fine, put the case back on.

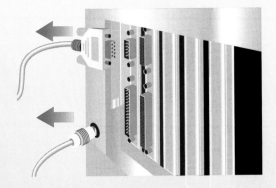

Watch Out!

- Be sure the black wires are together when aligning the two power connectors on the motherboard.

- When in doubt, follow the user's manual for connecting power and LED cables to a new motherboard.

- If possible, buy a motherboard with an ATX form factor. It's a standard and will be easier to add components and to upgrade.

- Remember to put plastic spacers between the motherboard and the case so that the motherboard doesn't touch the case.

How to Install a New Battery

Your computer's battery doesn't provide power to run your computer—your power supply does that. Instead, the battery keeps the proper time and date, even when your computer is turned off, and it powers the CMOS so that the CMOS can maintain important information about your computer such as the kind of hard disk it has.

If your battery fails, or even gets low, worse things can happen to your computer than merely forgetting the time and date—because the CMOS wasn't supplied with the proper amount of power, it might not even recognize that you have a hard disk in your computer. You might get an error message telling you that you have **Invalid Configuration Information**. Here's what you should do to replace your battery.

1 Write Down CMOS Settings

You're going to need this information after you install your battery, because you're probably going to have to restore your CMOS settings after installing your battery. Get to the CMOS screen by pressing a special key when your computer starts. The key you'll press varies according to your computer, but often it is the Delete (Del), F1, or F2 keys. Read your computer's documentation to find out how. Also watch your computer as it boots up, because there is usually a screen telling you which key to press.

2 Turn Off Your Computer

After you turn it off, remove the case and ground yourself, or wear an antistatic wrist strap. You'll want to be sure to get rid of any static electricity so that you don't zap any of your computer's circuitry.

3 Find Your Computer's Battery

Some batteries are AA or AAA alkaline batteries in a battery pack attached to the motherboard via wires. Others are watch-type batteries. Another type of battery, a real-time clock battery, is small, black, and rectangular, and doesn't look like a battery at all, as you can see in the following figure. It usually says **DALLAS** and **REAL TIME** on it, and has a picture of a clock. It's often located near the CPU. Real-time clock batteries can last up to 10 years, so they probably will never need to be replaced.

4 Take Out the Old Battery

Take note of how it's attached to the motherboard so that you'll know how to install a new one. Each battery is removed differently. You remove the real-time clock by using a chip puller to grab it at both ends and gently rock it until it loosens and you can pull it out. If you don't have a chip puller, grasp the chip with your thumb and forefinger and rock it until it loosens, and then remove it. If it's soldered into the board, you might not be able to remove it without causing damage.

5 Insert the New Battery

Place the battery precisely where the old one was. Especially make sure that the + and – sides are facing properly.

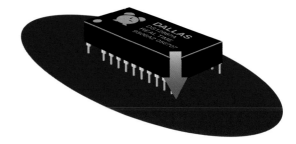

6 Turn On Your Computer

First, put the case back on, plug the computer in, and then turn it on. Don't be alarmed when your computer starts up if you get an error message about your system's CMOS settings. In any case, go into your CMOS settings and restore them to what they were originally. You might be lucky and your settings might not have been changed. But in many cases, they will have changed, and you'll have to put them back to what they were originally.

Watch Out!

■ Match your new battery to your old one—it'll have to fit into the location where your old battery is now plugged in.

■ When you take out your old battery, pay attention to how it's connected. That way, you'll know how to put in the new one.

■ Double-check to see that you've put the + and – connections in the proper place on the motherboard.

How to Install a New BIOS

Your computer's BIOS (basic input/output system) sits on a chip on your motherboard. It determines vital things about your computer, such as how large a hard disk your computer can handle. An old BIOS won't be able to recognize many of today's newest peripherals.

If you have a "flash" BIOS, you can upgrade your BIOS by running a piece of software. If you don't have a flash BIOS, you'll have to buy a new BIOS chip. When you buy, have at hand the make and model of your computer, as well as any information that comes onto your screen about your BIOS when you start your computer.

1 Flash Upgrade BIOS

If your BIOS is flash upgradable, it means that you don't need to remove your old BIOS and install a new one—you'll be able to upgrade it using a piece of software. Go to the manufacturer's site and download the software for upgrading your BIOS. You'll run the software you downloaded to install the flash upgrade. But before installing it, be sure to read and print out the instructions on the Web site for downloading and installing the upgrade.

2 Turn Off Your Computer

If your BIOS isn't flash upgradable, you'll have to take it out and install a new one. Turn off your computer, unplug it, remove the case, and then ground yourself or wear an antistatic wrist strap. You'll want to be sure to get rid of any static electricity so that you don't zap any of your computer's circuitry.

3 Look for Your System's BIOS Chip

Your system might have from one to five BIOS chips. They usually are small chips with a stick-on label (sometimes the label is shiny and silvery-looking) and usually have the word BIOS printed on them, as well as several other numbers. If there's more than one chip, they might have something such as BIOS-1, BIOS-2, and so on printed on them. Be sure to write down where each of those chips go. When you install your new BIOS chips, they're going to go in precisely those places.

4 Take Out Your Old BIOS Chip

The easiest way to remove the chips is by using a chip puller. Use it to grab the chip at both ends and gently rock it until it loosens and you can pull it out. If you don't have a chip puller, try grasping the chip with your thumb and forefinger and rocking it until it loosens and then removing it. You can also use a small screwdriver to pry out the old chip by first prying up one end and then prying up the other until it's loose enough to take it out of the socket.

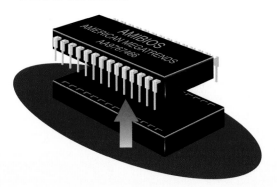

5 Put In Your New BIOS Chips

If you have more than one chip, put the chips in the same order as your original ones. Make sure that the notched end of the chip lines up with the notched end of the socket. Before putting in each chip, be sure that the pins are straight. If they're not, you can use needlenose pliers to straighten them. Line up the pins on one side of the chip with the holes in the socket, and then with the other side. When both sides are lined up, push down with your thumb on the chip until it's firmly seated in the socket.

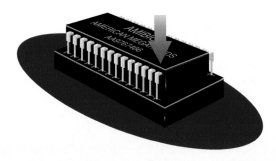

6 Get Your Computer Going Again

Put the case back on your computer, plug in the computer, and turn your computer on. Your BIOS should now work automatically. If you compare what the bootup screen said before you installed the BIOS with what it says now, you'll notice that the date has changed, along with the name of the BIOS manufacturer, if you acquired your BIOS from a new manufacturer. The CMOS won't change, unless the new BIOS adds some kind of new feature not previously available, such as giving you the choice of letting you boot from an IDE or SCSI drive.

Watch Out!

- If your BIOS is flash upgradable, you won't need to install a new BIOS—just download an upgrade from the maker's Web site.
- When removing the BIOS, be careful not to twist it or pull too hard so that you don't break off any pins.
- Seat the new BIOS firmly before closing up your PC.

C H A P T E R

3

Adding Memory to Your PC

How Memory Works   42

Recognize the Different Kinds of Memory   44

Determine What Memory You Need   46

How to Add or Replace Memory   48

ONE of the easiest and cheapest ways to make your computer run faster is to upgrade it by adding more memory, called random access memory or RAM. If your PC seems sluggish, especially when you run several applications at once, you might be in line for a memory upgrade. When your computer doesn't have enough memory, it can't hold all your programs and data in RAM, so it has to take some of those programs and data and put them temporarily on your hard disk. Your hard disk is much slower than RAM, causing your computer to work sluggishly. If your computer is constantly reading from your hard disk, you might be in line for a RAM upgrade. RAM doesn't cost very much these days, and is getting less expensive all the time. Because of that, you should consider buying and installing the maximum amount of RAM that your computer can hold—it's an inexpensive way to make it run faster.

How Memory Works

1 RAM (random access memory) is put on your computer using RAM chips placed into special slots. When your computer is turned off, RAM is empty—unlike a hard disk, it can't store data unless the RAM is powered by electricity.

2 When you turn your computer on, electricity flows from the power supply to the motherboard. Because the RAM is directly attached to the motherboard, it gets electricity from the motherboard. When RAM is powered by electricity, it can store data.

3 When you want to open a program or open a file, you issue a command with your keyboard or mouse. The operating system takes that command and sends it to your CPU.

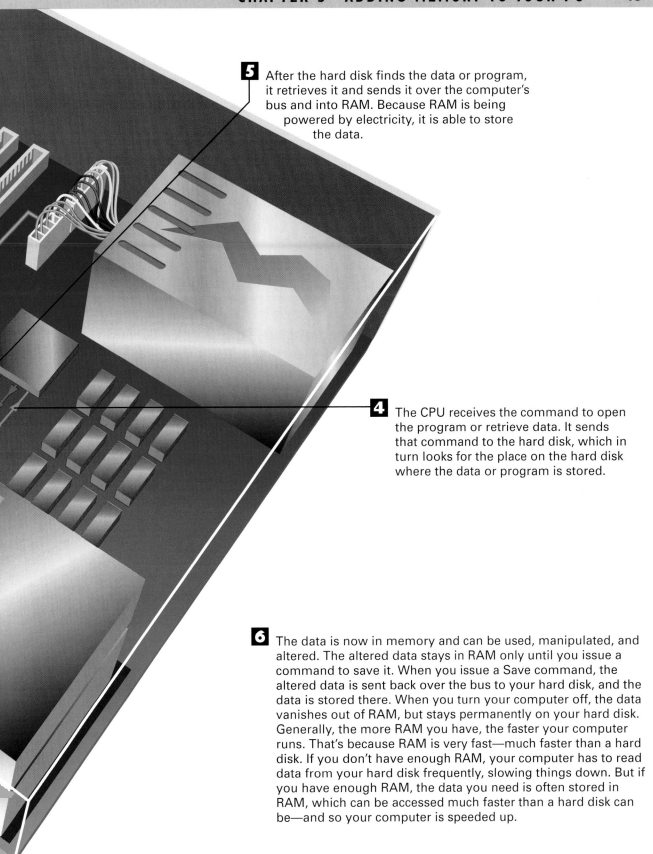

5 After the hard disk finds the data or program, it retrieves it and sends it over the computer's bus and into RAM. Because RAM is being powered by electricity, it is able to store the data.

4 The CPU receives the command to open the program or retrieve data. It sends that command to the hard disk, which in turn looks for the place on the hard disk where the data or program is stored.

6 The data is now in memory and can be used, manipulated, and altered. The altered data stays in RAM only until you issue a command to save it. When you issue a Save command, the altered data is sent back over the bus to your hard disk, and the data is stored there. When you turn your computer off, the data vanishes out of RAM, but stays permanently on your hard disk. Generally, the more RAM you have, the faster your computer runs. That's because RAM is very fast—much faster than a hard disk. If you don't have enough RAM, your computer has to read data from your hard disk frequently, slowing things down. But if you have enough RAM, the data you need is often stored in RAM, which can be accessed much faster than a hard disk can be—and so your computer is speeded up.

Recognize the Different Kinds of Memory

RAM comes in many different kinds of configurations and types—and runs at many different speeds, as well. Before you upgrade, you need to know how to spot the different types. Pictured here are the different types of RAM, including the older-style DIPs and newer SIMMs, DIMMs, SDRAM, and Rambus memory (often called RIMMs).

1 Dual Inline Packages (DIPs)

If you have an older computer, it might use an older kind of memory called a dual inline package (DIP). DIPs plug directly into their own sockets on the motherboard. It's difficult to find DIPs today because they're old. They come in pairs or sets of eight.

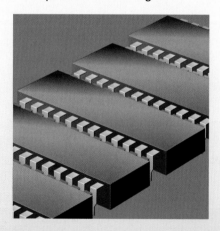

2 Single Inline Memory Modules

SIMMs (Single Inline Memory Modules) plug into long, matching sockets on your motherboard. SIMMs have more capacity than DIPs. Typically, a motherboard has several banks of SIMM sockets into which you plug SIMMs. SIMMs come in 30-pin and 72-pin formats. 30-pin SIMMs usually have less capacity than 72-pin, and often come with capacities of 256K, 1MB, 2MB, and 4MB. 72-pin SIMMs come in 1MB, 2MB, 4MB, 8MB, 16MB, and 32MB.

❸ DIMMs, SDRAM, and Rambus

DIMMs (Dual Inline Memory Modules) look much like SIMMs, but they come in a 168-pin format. They are usually a faster and higher-performance memory than SIMMs, and are used in Pentium PCs. They come in capacities ranging from up to 64MB and beyond. Newer kinds of memory, Synchronous DRAM (SDRAM), and Rambus memory (often called RIMMs), run even faster, and also come in capacities up to 64MB and beyond.

❹ ECC Versus Non-ECC

A SIMM or DIMM usually has nine chips of memory on it. Eight of those chips are used for the memory itself. The ninth chip is called a parity chip. The parity chip is used for error checking, to make sure that the other chips aren't making any errors. Some computer systems require parity chips, whereas others do not. In newer kinds of memory, such as SDRAM and Rambus, you don't refer to parity or nonparity—instead you refer to error correcting code memory (ECC) or non-ECC. Check your PC or motherboard's manual to see which kind of memory your PC requires.

❺ Memory Comes in Different Speeds

The faster the memory, the faster a computer operates. Memory comes rated at different speeds, and the faster the memory, the more it costs. Memory speed is measured in nanoseconds, and the lower the nanosecond rating, the faster the memory. For example, a 60-nanosecond chip is faster than an 80-nanosecond chip. Be sure that the memory you buy is as fast as the memory you're replacing. Many newer, faster Pentiums come with SDRAM and Rambus memory RAM that run much faster. Rambus memory can run at 600Mhz, 700Mhz, and 800Mhz, whereas SDRAM runs at 100Mhz or 133Mhz—the speed of the system bus.

Watch Out!

- You can use memory with parity chips on a computer that doesn't require parity chips. Memory without parity chips, however, won't work on a computer that requires parity chips.

Determine What Memory You Need

The most difficult part of upgrading your computer's memory is figuring out the specific kind of memory you need—and knowing how much memory you can add in what kind of configuration. Here's what you need to know.

1 How Much Memory You Have

There are several ways to see how much memory you have. When you first start your computer, you see information flash by on the bootup screen, including how much memory there is. If you have Windows, there's an even easier way. Right-click the **My Computer** icon and choose **Properties**. The screen shows how much memory you have. In some cases, this screen might not accurately report how much memory, so it's safer to look at the information in the bootup screen.

2 Determine If You Need ECC or Non-ECC

As explained in the previous illustration, some computers require parity memory or ECC memory. Check your system's documentation or motherboard manual—or head to the manufacturer's Web site or call technical support to see whether yours requires parity or nonparity memory, or ECC or non-ECC memory.

3 Determine the Kind of Memory

Check your system documentation to see what kind of memory you have. Alternatively, open the computer case and look. Look inside at the memory chips. See what kind of memory is in the bank. SIMMs have either 30 or 72 pins. DIMMs, SDRAM, and Rambus are larger and usually have 168 pins. Many motherboards have 30-pin and 72-pin banks of memory, or 168-pin banks. You can sometimes use a combination of the banks. To be absolutely sure about what kind of memory you need, check your computer or motherboard documentation.

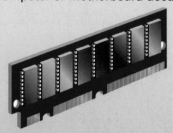

4 Determine the Memory Speed

Get memory at least as fast as the memory in your PC. Check your system documentation or call technical support to find out how fast the memory in your PC is.

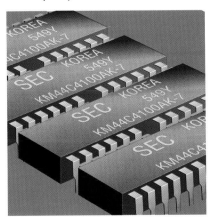

5 Determine the Configuration

Your computer has a set of memory slots, and the motherboard can handle a maximum amount of memory. To find out the maximum amount, check the manual or the manufacturer's Web site, or call technical support. Some computers can handle memory modules only in certain configurations—and because of this, you might have to throw away your existing memory and buy all new memory. For example, some computers can use four 4MB SIMMs and three 8MB SIMMs for a grand total of 64MB. Some computers, however, require eight 8MB SIMMs to get the job done. However, computers with SDRAM or RIMM memory usually don't have this problem.

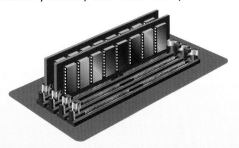

6 Determine If You Need Proprietary Memory

Although many computers accept memory chips from a variety of manufacturers, some computers accept memory only from the manufacturer of the computer. If that's the case, you have to buy the memory from the manufacturer. Proprietary memory typically costs more than other types of memory.

Watch Out!

■ Double-check that the memory you're buying is of the right type and configuration for your PC.

■ Buy the fastest memory that your computer can handle. Check the system or motherboard manual for information.

How to Add or Replace Memory

After you've figured out the kind and type of memory you need to put into your computer, and the configuration of RAM chips, the hardest work is done. But you still have to open the case, take out the old memory, and put in the new. Here's how to do the final steps in a memory upgrade.

1 Locate the Memory Sockets

Memory sockets are long sockets with some or all the sockets occupied by memory modules. First turn off your computer, unplug it, ground yourself or wear an antistatic wrist strap, and remove the case.

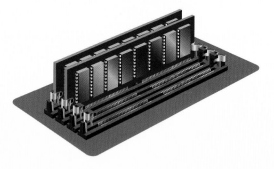

2 Remove the SIMM Modules

In order to upgrade memory, you might have to remove existing SIMMs. The SIMMs hold on to the memory slots by metal holders or plastic tabs on each side of the SIMM. If they're held in place by plastic tabs, gently press both tabs outward and the SIMM is released. A good way to do this is to use two small flathead screwdrivers—use them to press the tabs outward until the SIMM is released. If instead there are metal tabs holding the SIMM in, you can use the small screwdrivers, although it is often easier to use your thumbnails.

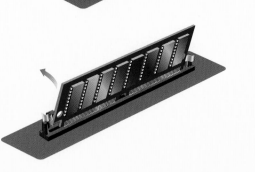

3 Install the SIMM Modules

Locate the notch on the SIMM; it enables memory to be installed in only one way. Match up the notch to the module. You usually tilt the SIMM at a 45-degree angle, push gently until it goes into the slot, and then tilt it upward to an upright position. Often you hear a small click as it fits into place. For other SIMMs, press them straight in first, and then down at an angle. The bottom of the SIMM should completely fit into the slot and should be perfectly level before pulling or pushing the SIMM upward from the 45-degree angle.

4 Remove the DIMMs, SDRAM, and RIMM Modules

DIMMs generally are easier to remove than SIMMs. DIMMs have tabs on each side, often made of plastic. Push down on these tabs at the same time, and the tabs push the DIMM out of its socket. SDRAM and RIMM modules are removed similarly, except in some instances a RIMM module might have a terminator that attaches to the motherboard. If it does, remove the terminator.

5 Install the DIMMs, SDRAM, and RIMM Modules

DIMMs have two notches on the bottom that match the DIMM socket. Align the slots properly with the socket. Press down evenly across the top of the DIMM until the tabs on each side of the DIMM slip up into place. SDRAM and DIMM memory is removed similarly, except that in some instances with RIMM modules you will have to attach a terminator to the motherboard. Check your documentation.

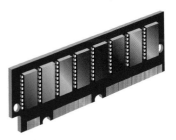

6 Turn On the Computer

Your computer might automatically boot into the CMOS screen, and the BIOS will automatically recognize the new memory. You have to exit the CMOS screen for the settings to take effect, and your computer might then reboot. If, when you first turn on your PC, you get an error message, bring up the CMOS screen, and the BIOS will automatically recognize the new memory. Exit the screen and save the CMOS settings for them to take effect.

Watch Out!

- Be sure that the memory you buy matches the kind of memory that your computer can accept.
- Don't buy slow RAM—you might save a few dollars, but you slow your system down.
- If your computer requires proprietary memory, you have to buy special memory for it, usually from the manufacturer.
- Be sure that when you plug the RAM modules in, they're fitted snugly into their sockets; otherwise, they won't work.

CHAPTER

Installing a New Power Supply

How Power Supplies Work   52

How to Install a Power Supply   54

WITHOUT a power supply, there is no PC. This little-thought-of work-horse takes the power from your wall outlet and transforms it into much lower-voltage direct current that can be used by your PC. It routes that current to all your PC's components so they have the power to run—think of it as your computer's energy plant. If you have a bad power supply, don't even think of getting it repaired. They're inexpensive enough that you should buy a new one instead. And never try to open the power supply or fiddle around with its insides, because even when it's turned off and unplugged it holds electricity, and you can hurt yourself badly.

It is often hard to know when you need a new power supply. But if your PC simply refuses to turn on and no electricity comes into it, you need a new one. And, if the fan stops running and you can't feel air coming out of the back of your PC, you probably need a new one as well.

If you notice signs like these, before getting a new power supply, be sure that it's connected tightly to the motherboard. If the connection is loose, it appears that the power supply has gone bad—when in fact, you only need to reseat the connection.

How Power Supplies Work

Fan
As the power supply operates, it produces heat. To make sure that the power supply doesn't overheat and become damaged (or damage your computer's components), there is a fan built into the power supply that cools it off, blowing hot air out of the rear of the computer. Be sure the fan is always running. If it stops, replace the power supply immediately.

Power supply
Your PC's power cord plugs directly into the power supply. The power supply transforms its 110-volt alternating current (AC) into a lower-voltage direct current (DC) that can be used by your computer's components. Power supplies can provide from 100 to 300 watts of electricity. When you buy a new one, get one that produces at least 250 watts, so you can power all your computer's components and future upgrades.

Motherboard
Many different-colored wires run out of the power supply and bring power to your computer's components. Several of these wires attach to the motherboard and supply power to the motherboard and the components that are plugged into it. The wires are usually black, yellow, and red, which make them easy to identify. In your computer, make note of the exact way that the cables are connected to the motherboard. The two black sides of the power connectors are always together when connecting to the motherboard. When you install a new power supply, you need to reconnect them in the same way.

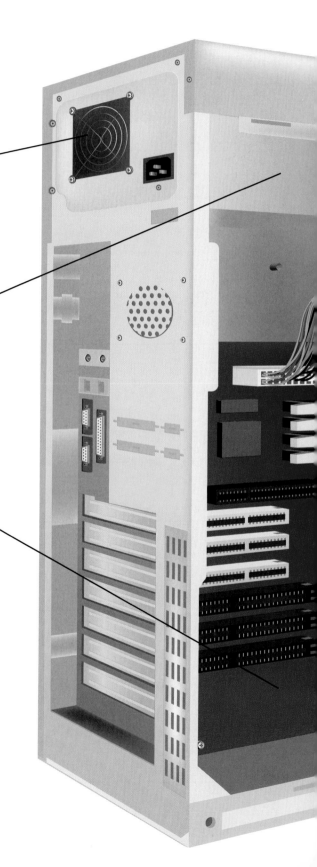

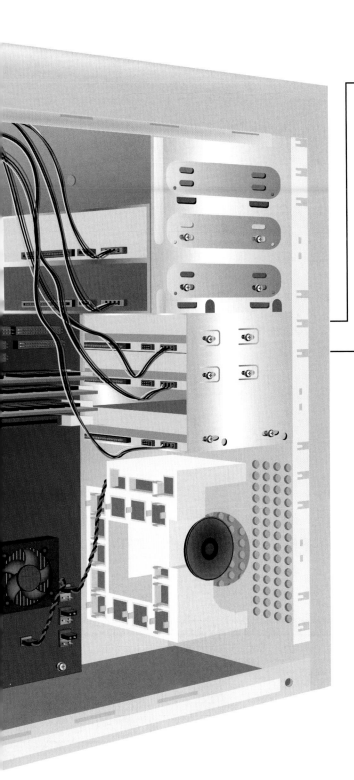

LED indicators

Other wires run to various drives on your computer, such as the hard drive, floppy drive, and CD-ROM drive. You might see a small red-and-black wire that connects to the front of the case that supplies power to LED readouts there. (Only some cases have these readouts.) If you have one of these readouts and want it to still be active, be sure your new power supply has one of these wires.

Power switch

A set of wires also runs to the on/off switch on the front of your computer. They carry the signals that tell the power supply to turn on or off. Some power supplies attach to the on/off switch via wires, whereas the on/off switch is a part of other power supplies. When you install a new power supply, you have to be sure to connect these wires the exact same way that they're connected on the old power supply—if you don't, you could blow the power supply the first time you turn it on. Sometimes these wires are all the same color. In that case, when you install a new power supply, hold the new switch next to the old one, pull the wire out of one and connect it in exactly the same place on the new switch. That way you'll be sure that the wires are connected in the exact same way. In instances where the power switch is found on the motherboard, the power supply will have a small wire that connects to the "power switch" pins on the motherboard.

How to Install a Power Supply

Replacing a power supply is a relatively simple matter. First, you turn off your PC and open its case, being careful to first discharge static electricity, as seen in Chapter 1, Lesson 4. Then, you disconnect all the cables that run from it to your computer's components, being careful to draw a diagram so that you know how to reattach everything. You then take out the old power supply, put in a new one, and reconnect all the cables.

1 Unplug Motherboard and Drives

Power connectors connect the wires from the power supply to different parts of your computer. Unplug the power connectors from the motherboard, which are usually the largest. Pull the connectors straight up and then tilt them at an angle to remove them so that you don't damage their plastic teeth. If you have an ATX connector, it has a small plastic clip on it. Pull away the plastic clip, and then pull up on the connector. Wires also run from your power supply to your PC's drives. Pull these power connectors off.

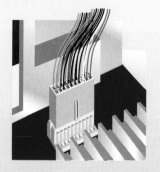

2 Unplug the Power Switch

If the on/off switch is built directly into the power supply, you don't need to do anything. If it's not built in, four colored wires run from the power supply to the switch. Remove the wires from the switch with needlenose pliers, if need be. These might be all the same color. If they are, when you install a new power supply, hold the new switch next to the old one, pull the wire out of one and connect it in exactly the same place on the new switch. That way you connect them in the same way as in your old power supply.

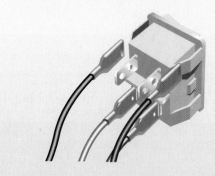

3 Remove the Power Supply's Screws

Often, four screws hold the power supply in place. Don't confuse the screws that hold the power supply in place with the screws that hold the fan onto the power supply. The screws that hold the power supply in place are on the outside of the case, whereas those that hold the fan onto the power supply are on the power supply itself.

▲ Remove the Power Supply

It should slide out relatively easy. Sometimes there are clips on the front of the power supply that secure the power supply to the case, so you might have to first slide the power supply forward to clear the clips, and then lift it out of the case. Some computer cases have a small plate built in and the power supply fits on top of that plate.

▲ Slide In the New Power Supply

Touch a grounded metal object first to discharge static electricity, or use a wrist strap. If your power supply is secured by clips, you have to slide it forward into them before screwing the power supply back in. Check the back of the power supply to make sure the switch there is set to 110 volts, if you're in the U.S., or to 220 volts, if you're in a country that uses 220 volts. After you slide in the power supply, screw it in.

▲ Reconnect the Power Connectors

Following the diagram you drew when you took out your power supply, reconnect all the connectors. Be careful when plugging in the connectors, especially the power switch, which is the heavy cable running from the power supply. Make sure that no cables are lying across or on top of any fans or your microprocessor. After you plug in your computer and turn it on, your system should start up. You should hear the power supply fan go on, and all your components should work.

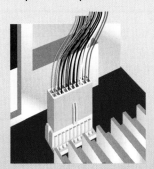

Watch Out!

- Don't put a screwdriver or poke around inside the power supply, even when it's not plugged in—you could get a nasty electric shock.
- Match your new power supply to your existing one—match the size and screw hole placement, and if yours has an on/off switch on it, the new one must have one, too.
- Before turning on your new power supply, be sure that its switch is set to 110 volts if you're in the U.S. and to 220 volts if you're in a country that uses 220-volt power.

CHAPTER

5

Adding or Replacing an IDE Hard Drive

How an IDE Hard Drive Works   58

How to Know When to Upgrade   60

Before Installing a Hard Drive   62

How to Install a Controller Card   64

How to Add a Second Hard Drive   66

How to Replace Your Existing Hard Drive   68

How to Format and Partition a Hard Drive   70

TO a certain extent, your hard drive *is* your computer. It's where you store all your data, all your files, and all your programs.

There are many reasons you might need to add or replace a hard drive. You might be running out of hard drive space, or the hard drive might be continually reporting errors, which might mean that it's time for a replacement. Or you might simply want a new hard drive that's faster and holds more data than your current one. You have the option of either replacing your existing hard drive, or adding a second one.

There are several ways that a hard drive connects to the rest of your computer, notably via an IDE/EIDE connection or a SCSI connection. The most common kind of connection is via IDE/EIDE, and that's what we cover in this chapter. To install a SCSI drive, turn to Chapter 9, "Installing a SCSI Drive."

To add a new hard drive to your computer, you first have to take some safety precautions and prepare your PC. Next, open your computer's case, slide the new hard drive in, and connect it via cables to your PC. (If you're replacing your old hard drive, instead of adding a second one, you have to first take your old hard drive out.) After you put your new hard drive in, you have to tell your computer to recognize it, and then prepare the new hard drive so it can be used. The number of hard drives you can add depends on your BIOS, the number of drive bays, and available power connections. Check your system manual for information.

This chapter shows you everything you need to know, starting with an illustrated tour of how your hard drive works.

How an IDE Hard Drive Works

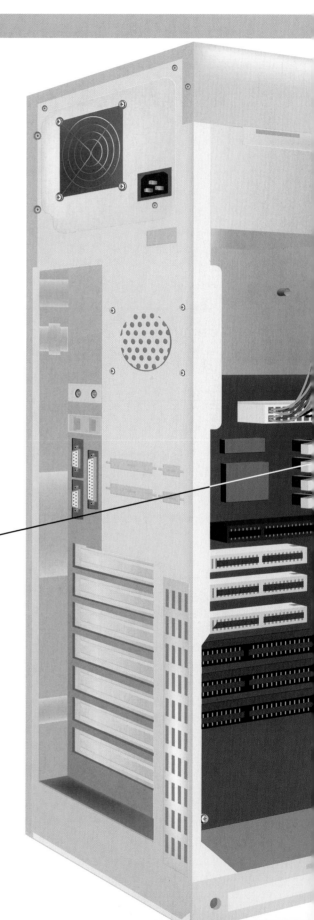

Ribbon cable
The controller sends and receives information to and from the hard drive via a 40-pin ribbon cable. A connector at each end of the cable plugs into the hard drive and into the controller. Some ribbons are marked with a different color to indicate the first pin. Knowing this makes it easier to connect them.

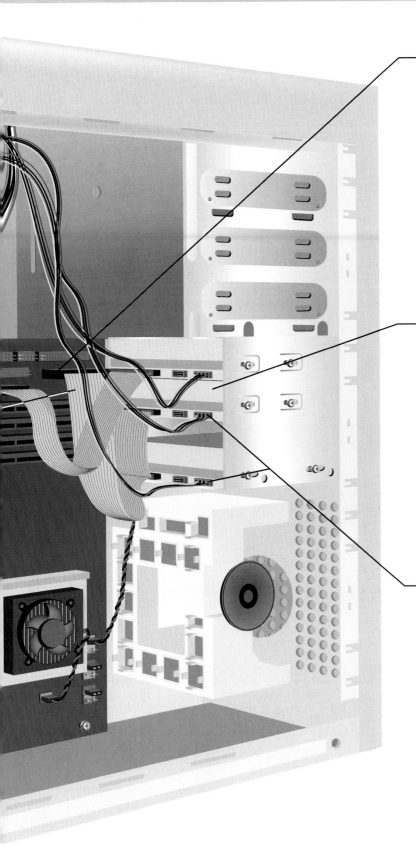

Controller
A controller inside the computer sends instructions back and forth between your PC and the hard drive, sending information to be stored, or asking for information to be retrieved. Sometimes the controller is on a separate board, although usually it is on the motherboard itself. There are several different kinds of controllers, such as IDE/EIDE and SCSI. A hard drive with a SCSI controller is usually faster than one with an IDE/EIDE controller, although SCSI controllers and hard drives are more difficult to install.

Hard drive
The hard drive, inside its sealed metal housing, fits into a drive bay on a computer. Drive bays come in 3 1/2-inch and 5 1/4-inch sizes, as do hard drives. Magnetized platters in the hard drive store the data, and spin at high rates of speed—up to 10,000 revolutions per minute. Read/write heads move across the spinning platter to retrieve and store information. The space between the read/write heads and the spinning platters is minute so that data can be read accurately—typically less than the width of a human hair, at 2/100,000 of an inch.

Power connection
The hard drive gets its power from the power supply. It connects to the power supply by a cable and universal connector that plugs into the hard drive.

How to Know When to Upgrade

It's fairly easy to know when to add a new hard drive or replace your old one—when you're running out of hard drive space, or when your existing hard drive is showing signs that it might be headed for a crash.

The larger decision is whether to replace your old hard drive with a new one, or instead to add a second hard drive. Follow the advice on these pages before deciding what to do.

■ Insufficient Drive Space Message

You can get these kinds of messages even when it appears that you have enough hard drive space to install new software. Often, during the installation process, more hard drive space is used than is eventually needed for the completely installed software. So, when you get this kind of message, it means it's time for a new hard drive. To hold you over until you get a new hard drive, delete unneeded files to free up space.

■ Run Troubleshooting Software

Continuing to get disk errors even after you've run troubleshooting software, such as hard drive utilities, might mean your hard drive is about to go bad. It might be time to replace it. By replacing it as soon as possible, you might be able to salvage some data before you lose everything that is on the drive.

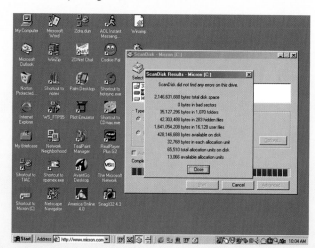

■ Your Hard Drive Slows Your PC

An old, slow hard drive can make your computer perform sluggishly. It takes a long time to load and save your programs and files. You can make your computer faster by upgrading to a new, faster hard drive. If you frequently see your hard drive light flash when you load programs and open and save files, and there's a delay when they load or open, your hard drive might be slowing down your PC.

4 When to Add a Second Drive

It's more difficult to replace a hard drive than it is to add a second one. When you replace a hard drive, you have to back up your entire hard drive, and you have to copy everything on it to a new hard drive. If you're happy with the performance of your hard drive, add a second one instead of replacing your existing one.

5 When to Replace a Hard Drive

Although it's more difficult to replace a hard drive than it is to add a new one, if your old hard drive is going bad, the best thing to do is get rid of it and replace it with a new one.

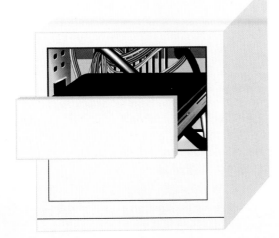

6 Buy the Largest Drive You Can

It's surprising how quickly hard drive space gets eaten up by programs and data. Hard drives are relatively inexpensive. Buy the largest one that you can afford.

Watch Out!

- Don't go for the least expensive hard drive. This is a vital part of your machine, and its performance can dramatically alter how well your computer works.
- Check your computer and hard drive documentation to make sure your new hard drive will work with your old one.

Before Installing a Hard Drive

Before you start to install your hard drive, there is a set of precautions you should keep in mind and some steps you should take to prepare your PC for your new hard drive. Here's what to do.

1 Back Up Your Hard Drive

Before installing a new hard drive, back up the data from the old one. This is especially important if you're replacing your hard drive instead of adding a second one. You might want only to back up your data (the data files you want to keep, such as word processing documents), or you might instead want to copy the operating system and your programs. Back up your hard drive to a tape drive, a Zip drive, or similar removable media.

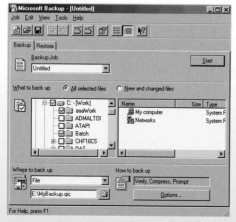

2 Create a Bootable Floppy

If you use Windows, you also need to make a bootable floppy disk. To do that, put a disk in your floppy drive. Get to the Control Panel by double-clicking **My Computer** and double-clicking the **Control Panel**. Next, double-click **Add/Remove Programs** and click the **Startup Disk** tab. From the tab, click **Create Disk** and follow the instructions.

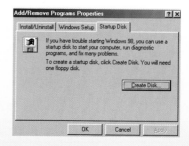

3 Check Your BIOS Settings

To install a second hard drive, you need to know your BIOS settings for your current hard drive. And if you're replacing your hard drive, it's generally a good idea to have these handy, in case something goes wrong with the installation and you must reinstall your old hard drive. Go to the CMOS screen and write down all the information it contains about your hard drive. For information on how to get to the CMOS screen, turn to Chapter 1.

4 See What Size Drive Bay Is Free

You need a drive bay free for your new hard drive. And you want to make sure that your new hard drive can fit into your existing drive bay. Turn off your computer, unplug it, ground yourself, take off the case, and see what drive bay you have free. Hard drives come in 3 1/2-inch and 5 1/4-inch sizes, so be sure your bay accommodates the drive you buy. You can fit a 3 1/2-inch hard drive into a 5 1/4-inch bay by getting a special adapter kit, but a 5 1/4-inch hard drive won't fit into a 3 1/2-inch bay.

5 Determine If You Need Mounting Rails

Some hard drives are mounted inside bays via mounting rails or adapter kits. Look at how your current hard drive is mounted to see whether you need a kit or rails. If you're mounting a 3 1/2-inch drive into a 5 1/4-inch bay, you need an adapter or rails.

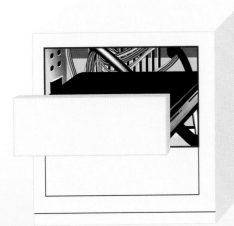

6 Get a Two-Drive Ribbon Cable

You connect your hard drive to your PC with a ribbon cable, and if you're putting in a second hard drive, you have to be sure that you have a ribbon cable that supports two drives. If you don't have one on your hard drive, one might come with your new hard drive. If it doesn't, be sure to buy one.

Watch Out!

- Be sure that you have a drive bay that can accommodate a new hard drive.
- Record your BIOS information before taking out your old hard drive or installing a new one.
- Always make a boot disk before installing a new hard drive or adding a second one.

How to Install a Controller Card

Your hard drive connects to a controller card or directly to your motherboard. Ribbon cable runs from that card or motherboard to your hard drive, and a connector at the end or in the middle of the cable plugs into your hard drive. The ribbon cable commonly has several connectors. However, if those connectors are already plugged into devices such as hard drives or CD-ROM drives, you might need to put in a new controller card.

▌1▐ Do You Need a Controller Card

If you're taking out your old hard drive and using a new one, you'll probably be able to use your existing controller card, or be able to connect your new hard drive to the motherboard. Controllers can support multiple hard drives, so even if you're adding a new hard drive, you probably won't need to install a new controller card. However, if you have more than four devices, such as hard drives and CD-ROM drives, hooked up to a controller, you might need to install a new controller card.

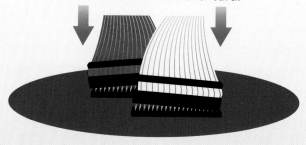

▌2▐ Turn Off Your PC

You install the controller card into an empty slot on the motherboard. After you take off your computer's case, look on the motherboard and locate an empty slot.

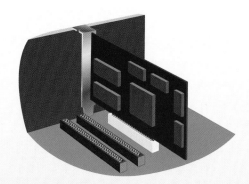

▌3▐ Unscrew the Flap over the Slot

In order to fit the card into place, you're going to have to take off the small metal flap protecting the slot. The flap is held in place by a small screw. Take the screw off (it's usually held in place by a Phillips screw) and take off the flap. Put the screw in a safe place—you're going to need it in order to secure the card you're putting in.

4 Align the Card in the Slot

Make sure the connectors on the card line up properly with the slot where you are putting the card.

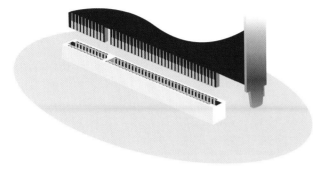

5 Gently Push the Card into Place

Use two hands, and applying gentle, even pressure, push the card down into the slot. After the card is in place, press down firmly to make sure that it's all the way into the slot. If it's not pushed all the way into the slot, your new hard drive won't work.

6 Screw the Card into Place

To make sure that the card won't come loose, screw it into place. You use the same screw that you took off the metal flap—and you screw the card into the same place where the metal flap was screwed in.

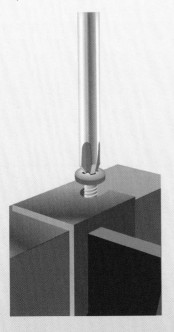

Watch Out!

- Be sure the controller card is seated firmly—if it isn't, your new hard drive won't work.
- Don't press too hard when putting in the controller card, or you could damage the card or the motherboard.

How to Add a Second Hard Drive

In most cases, when you put a new hard drive in your PC, you're going to keep your existing hard drive. That way, you have extra storage space—and it's easier to add a second hard drive than it is to take out your old hard drive and replace it with a new one. Follow these steps for adding a second hard drive to your PC. Before you install the drive, turn off your PC, open the case, and ground yourself.

1 Match the Drive and Bay

It's best to match the size of your hard drive to the size of your drive bay. So, for example, a 3 1/2-inch disk should go into a 3 1/2-inch disk bay. However, you can install a 3 1/2-inch drive into a 5 1/4-inch bay if you first install mounting brackets. Follow the directions for screwing them in. After they're installed, you can install your hard drive onto the brackets.

2 Install Your Hard Drive into the Bay

First, carefully slide the new drive into the bay or onto the mounting brackets. Make sure that its back end, with the various ports and connections, is facing inside the computer. And then, screw the drive into the bay. Connect all the screws so that the hard drive is held firmly in place. Don't overtighten or strip the screws, though.

3 Connect the Data Cable

The data cable, a wide ribbon cable, runs from your controller to your hard drive. If there is no free connector on the cable, you have to buy a new one. (If you have more than four devices connected to the controller, you might need a new controller.) In either event, connect the ribbon cable connector to the 40-pin slot on the hard drive. The ribbon cable has a stripe on one side of it, indicating that that side of the cable plugs into pin 1 on the hard drive connector—the pin closest to the power supply connector.

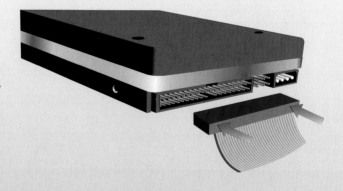

4 Connect the Power Supply

Your hard drive needs power in order to work, so you're going to have to connect it to your power supply. The power supply cable has a connector on the end of it, which is usually four sockets encased in a small sheath of white plastic. Plug that into the connector on your hard drive.

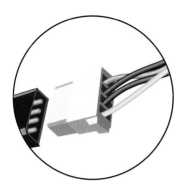

5 Set the Jumpers

You can make your new hard drive either a master or a slave. Because you have an existing hard drive, set it to be a slave by setting the jumpers on the back of the hard drive. Check the hard drive documentation for how to set the jumpers properly.

6 Set CMOS and Format the Disk

Before you can use your hard drive, you have to tell your computer about it by changing the CMOS settings. And you also have to format the hard drive so it can be used by your computer. For information about changing CMOS settings and formatting your hard drive, turn to the section "How to Format and Partition a Hard Drive," later in this chapter.

Watch Out!

- Be sure that you have a spare connector on your ribbon cable to attach to the new hard drive.

- If you have more than four devices attached to your controller, you might need to get a new one.

- You won't be able to use your new hard drive until you change the CMOS settings, partition it, and format it.

How to Replace Your Existing Hard Drive

When you replace your old hard drive with a new one, you first take out the old drive, then put in the new one, and finally put the operating system and other necessary files onto your new hard drive.

Before you can install the new drive, you have to open the case and ground yourself. Turn to Chapter 1, "What's Inside Your Computer," for more information on opening the case.

1 Disconnect the Cables

First, disconnect the data cable, the wide ribbon cable that runs from your motherboard or controller card to the hard drive. Hold the connector as close to the hard drive as possible and pull it off firmly but gently. Then take off the power cable, which has a smaller connector usually made of white plastic. Pull it off. Be aware it's usually more difficult to take off than is the data cable.

2 Slide the Hard Drive Out

Take off the screws that hold the hard drive in place. They might hold the hard drive into a drive bay or they might hold the hard drive onto rails or brackets inside the drive bay. The hard drive should slide out relatively easily after you've unscrewed it. If it doesn't, you've probably missed a screw.

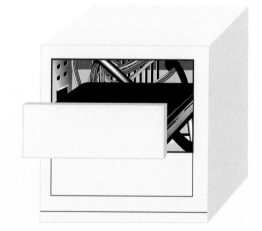

3 Slide In the New Drive

If your new drive has the same physical dimensions as your old hard drive, you simply slide it right into place. However, if you're installing a 3 1/2-inch hard drive into a 5 1/4-inch bay, you have to first screw in mounting brackets. After you slide the drive in, connect all the screws so that the hard drive is held firmly in place. Don't overtighten or strip the screws, though.

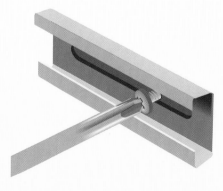

4 Connect the Data Cable

Take the data cable that you unplugged from your old hard drive and plug it into the proper place on your new hard drive. You'll notice that the ribbon cable has a stripe on one side of it. That indicates that that side of the cable plugs into pin 1 on the hard drive connector—the pin closest to the power supply connector.

5 Connect the Power Supply

Take the power cable that you unplugged from your old hard drive and plug it into the proper place on your new hard drive. The power supply cable has a connector on the end of it, which usually is four sockets encased in a small sheath of white plastic. Plug that into the connector on your hard drive.

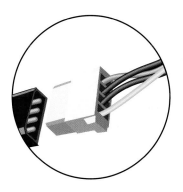

6 Set CMOS and Format Disk

Before you can use your hard drive, you have to tell your computer about it by changing the CMOS settings. And you also have to format the hard drive so it can be used by your computer. For information about changing CMOS settings and formatting your hard drive, turn to the section "How to Format and Partition a Hard Drive," in the next section.

Watch Out!

- You won't be able to use your new hard drive until you change the CMOS settings and format it.

- Be sure to use rails or an adapter kit if your new hard drive doesn't fit into your drive bay.

How to Format and Partition a Hard Drive

Physically installing your hard drive is only the first part of the process of installing a hard drive. After you've made the proper physical connections, you have to tell your computer to recognize the hard drive, partition it (divide it into pieces), and finally format it so that it can be used. On the other hand, you can keep it as one large drive and skip the partitioning step.

If your computer comes with special software, use it and skip this section.

■ Run CMOS to Recognize the Drive

Press whatever key you need to for entering CMOS information. (See Chapter 1 for more information on how to do that.) Often, CMOS will recognize your new hard drive and you won't have to do anything more to the BIOS. If it doesn't, you have to choose the hard drive in CMOS, and then enter information about the hard drive's cylinder, heads, and sectors. Check the hard drive's manual or manufacturer's Web site for this information. Save and exit the CMOS menu in order to put the settings into effect.

■ Boot from a Floppy

When you exit CMOS, the computer should restart if you're replacing your hard drive. Put in the boot floppy that you've prepared before it restarts. If you are using Windows 95, Windows 3.1, or DOS, you see a prompt that looks like this: **A:\>**. If you're using Windows 98, you get a startup menu, asking you whether you want to start the computer with or without CD-ROM support. Choose **CD-ROM support**. In Windows 98, a RAM drive will be created. Write down the letter of the RAM drive; you'll need it later on.

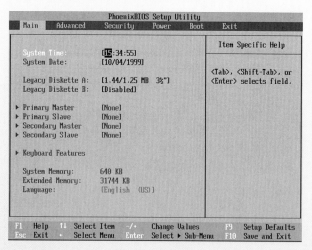

3 Partition Your Hard Drive

You can have a single partition, or can divide your disk into separate drives. To partition your hard drive, type **FDISK** at the DOS prompt and follow the instructions. If you're replacing your old hard drive with a new one, be sure to choose "Create DOS Partition" and then "Create Primary DOS Partition." If you're adding a second hard drive instead of replacing your old one, you see the option "Change Current Fixed Disk Drive." Choose that, and then choose to create a Logical DOS partition to make your new drive D: (or E:, if you already have a D: drive). If you're partitioning your C: drive into several partitions, you *must* set the primary partition to "active."

```
                  MS-DOS Version 6
                Fixed Disk Setup Program
          (C)Copyright Microsoft Corp. 1983 - 1993

                     FDISK Options

Current fixed disk drive: 1

Choose one of the following:

1. Create DOS partition or Logical DOS Drive
2. Set active partition
3. Delete partition or Logical DOS Drive
4. Display partition information


Enter choice: [1]




Press Esc to exit FDISK
```

4 Format Your Hard Drive

If you're replacing an old hard drive with a new one, you will need to restart your computer, so leave in your boot floppy. After it reboots, type **Format C: /S** at the DOS prompt to format your new hard drive, and put the DOS operating system onto it. With Windows 98, the operating system files are copied to your new hard drive from the RAM drive that Windows 98 previously created. Assuming that the RAM drive was letter D, type the following to format your hard drive and put basic operating system files onto it: **D:\Format C: /S**. If you're not replacing your old hard drive from the DOS prompt, type **Format D:** (or whatever letter your second drive will be). If you've created separate partitions instead of just one, format each of them in turn.

5 Reinstall Your Operating System

If you're replacing an old hard drive with a new one, you have to reinstall your operating system. To do that, get your Windows disks and reinstall Windows onto your new hard drive. If you're not replacing your old hard drive, and are only adding a second one, you won't need to put the operating system onto it.

6 Copy Backed-Up Data and Files

After you've confirmed that the hard drive is working properly, copy all the data and files that you've previously backed up to your new hard drive.

Watch Out!

- All the cable connectors should be tight.
- When plugging the ribbon cable into your new hard drive, be sure that the side with the stripe lines up with pin 1 on the hard drive—the pin nearest the power connector.
- If you're installing a second hard drive, double-check that you've set the jumper settings on the drives properly so that one is the "master" and the other is the "slave."
- If you're replacing your old hard drive, when you format your new hard drive, be sure to use the /S parameter—that will add system files to the new hard drive so that it's bootable.

CHAPTER

Installing a Floppy Drive

How a Floppy Drive Works   74

How to Remove Your Old Floppy Drive   76

How to Install a New Floppy Drive   78

FLOPPY drives aren't as important today as they used to be, considering that much software is distributed on CD-ROMs. However, they're still useful, especially when you're exchanging data with someone. Floppy drives receive electricity from the power supply, and send information to and from the computer via a ribbon cable.

Replacing a floppy drive is relatively easy. You take out the old drive by first taking off the ribbon cables and power cables, unscrewing the drive, and sliding it out. Then, you put the new one back in place, reconnect the cables, and screw it in. If you're adding a second floppy drive, you'll have to use a second set of ribbon cables and power cables, and you'll have to go into your system's CMOS screen and tell it to recognize the new drive.

How a Floppy Drive Works

Power supply
The floppy drive is powered by
the computer's power supply.
Cables attach the floppy drive to
the power supply and bring power
to the drive.

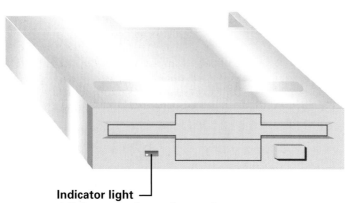

Indicator light
A light on the front of some floppy drives lights up
when data is being accessed from the drive.

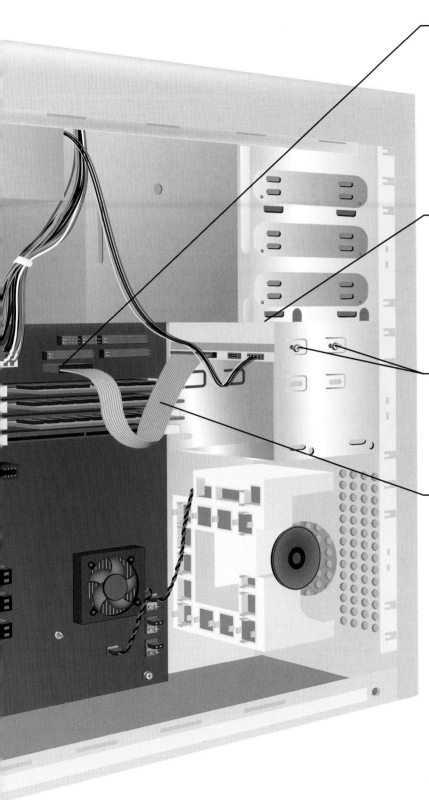

Controller
When data is read or written to the disk, the floppy drive's controller board receives information from the motherboard, and sends signals to the drive's circuit board. The circuit board then controls the movement of the floppy disk, and of read/write heads located inside the floppy drive. The controller can either be an add-in board, or can be built into the motherboard itself.

Read/write heads
When floppy drives store data, read/write heads move along the surface of the disk until they find an empty spot to place the data. When the drives are looking for data, the read/write heads move along the surface of the disk, until they find the data being looked for, and then read the data.

Mounting screws
Floppy drives sit in a computer's drive bay and are secured by mounting screws on the front or sides of the drive. Mounting rails sometimes are used if the floppy is a much smaller size than the bay.

Ribbon cables
The motherboard communicates with the floppy drive by sending and receiving information along a set of ribbon cables that run from the motherboard or an add-in card plugged into the motherboard to the floppy drive.

How to Remove Your Old Floppy Drive

Before you can install a new floppy drive, you have to take out your old one. This set of instructions tells you how. If you are installing a second floppy drive instead of replacing an old one, turn to the next illustration.

1 Turn Off Your Computer

After you turn it off, unplug it so that you won't receive a shock when you're working inside. And make sure to wear an antistatic wrist strap, or to first discharge static electricity so that you don't damage anything inside your PC.

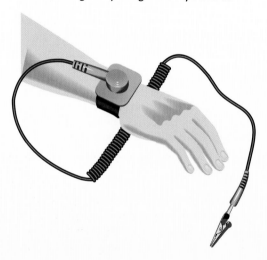

2 Remove Case

Look for the screws that hold the case in place and remove them with a Phillips screwdriver, a flathead screwdriver, or a hexagonal nutdriver if your screws have hexagonal heads. Be sure to place the screws in a safe place, such as a paper cup. You also might want to tape them to the case until you need them again.

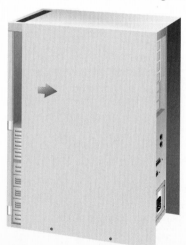

3 Remove the Ribbon Cable

A flat ribbon cable runs from the motherboard or a controller card to the floppy disk. Data runs back and forth along this cable. A plug connects the cable to the floppy disk. Remove the cable from the drive by pulling it straight off. It should come off easily.

4 Remove the Power Cables

Power cables run from the power supply to the floppy drive, supplying it with power. These cables are attached to the floppy drive by connectors. Pull the connectors off the drive. It might take more force to pull these off than it did to take off the ribbon connectors.

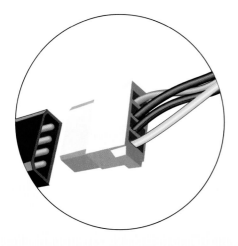

5 Take Off the Mounting Screws

Some drives are held onto the computer by small rails that slide into your computer, along with the floppy drive. If your drive uses rails, the mounting screws will be on the front of the drive. If it doesn't use rails, the mounting screws will be along the sides. Unscrew the mounting screws and keep them in a safe place.

6 Slide the Drive Out

Now that all the cables are off and the mounting screws are taken out, the drive can be taken easily out of the computer. Simply slide it out the front of the computer, toward you. It should come out easily.

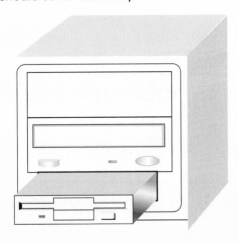

Watch Out!

- When you take off the case, put the screws in a safe place because you'll need them to put the case back on.
- Be careful not to strip the heads off the drive's mounting screws.
- It will require more force to remove the power cable than it will to take off the ribbon cable.

How to Install a New Floppy Drive

After you've taken out your old floppy drive, install a new one by simply sliding it into the spot where the old one was and reattaching the cables. If you're installing a second floppy drive, you'll have to look for an extra set of ribbon cables and power cables. In many cases, the ribbon you're using has an extra connector, so you can use that. After you install the drive, you'll use the CMOS setup screen to tell your computer to recognize the new floppy.

1 Match the Drive Size to the Bay

Drive bays and floppy drives generally come in three sizes: three-inch, five-inch, and bays that require mounting rails. It will be easiest if you match the size of your floppy drive to the size of your drive bay, although it's possible to mount a three-inch drive into a five-inch drive bay.

2 Slide In the Floppy

If you're installing a three-inch floppy into a five-inch bay, you might need to use rails.

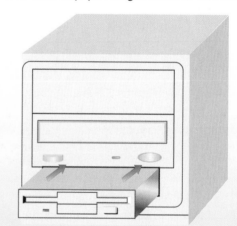

3 Attach Cables

Attach the ribbon and power cables to the drive. The ribbon cable has two sets of connectors—one at the end, and the other in the middle. If you're installing drive A, use the connector at the end; for drive B, use the middle one. Ribbon connectors usually can be plugged in only one way. If yours can go in both ways, be sure that the colored edge of the ribbon cable attaches the number 1 on the drive connector. When installing the power supply cable, be aware that it will fit into the drive in only one direction. Be careful not to force it.

4 Add a Second Floppy

If you're not replacing a floppy drive, but instead are adding a new one, there are a few things you should keep in mind. First, when you plug in the ribbon cables, use the spare connector that's not already used (it probably will be the one for the B drive, in the middle of the ribbon). For the power cables, look for spare cables coming out of the power supply, and use those.

5 Secure the New Drive

You'll have to use screws either on the front of the drive, if you're using mounting rails, or on the side of the drive, if you're not. Be careful not to overtighten so that you don't strip the screws.

6 Test the New Drive

Before putting your case back on, it's a good idea to make sure the new drive works. Your computer should start with no problem. If you've added a new drive, you'll have to change your computer's CMOS setup screen to recognize it (see Chapter 1 for information). Put a floppy disk into the drive and try saving and reading data to it. If the drive doesn't work, check that the cables are all plugged in properly and the connections are tight. When everything checks out, screw the computer's case back on.

Watch Out!

- Try to match the size of your new floppy drive to the size of your drive bay.

- If your old floppy was attached using mounting rails, either use those when sliding in your new drive, or buy a set of new rails.

- When attaching ribbon cables to the new drive, be sure that the ribbon connectors are attached to the correct ends of the drive connector.

- If your new drive doesn't work when you start your computer, be sure that all the cables are plugged in properly and the connections are tight.

- If you're installing a second floppy drive, you'll have to tell your computer to recognize the drive by using the CMOS setup screen.

CHAPTER

Installing a CD-ROM Drive

How a CD Drive Works 82

Before Installing a CD Drive 84

How to Install a New CD Drive 86

How to Replace Your Existing CD Drive 88

NO PC is complete without a CD drive. These drives play multimedia software, such as games, entertainment software, and similar programs. But they do more than that—most software is installed from CDs, not floppy disks. And they can also play music CDs, as well.

A CD drive needs an interface to connect to your PC. The most common kind is an IDE/EIDE, which can be found on an IDE/EIDE card, directly on the motherboard, or on a sound card installed on your system. However, you can also connect a CD drive to your PC with a SCSI interface. For information on installing a SCSI device, turn to Chapter 9, "Installing a SCSI Drive."

When buying a CD drive to install, consider what's called a CD-R drive or a CD-RW drive. These drives allow you to create CDs as well as play them, so that you can, for example, make copies of your music CDs. You can also use them to make backups of data and programs on your computer. A CD-R drive lets you write data once to a CD, whereas a CD-RW drive will let you rewrite data many times to it. (If you need a new CD-ROM, you might not want to get a CD-R/RW as your only CD, as these drives are pretty slow when it comes to the ROM part—especially when it comes to gaming.)

You'll often notice a number or series of numbers next to a CD drive, such as 16X, 32X, or 40X. That refers to the speed of the drive—in general, the higher the number, the faster the drive. The X refers to how many times the transfer rate of the drive is faster than the original CD standard. CD-R and CD-RW drives will also list the numbers that tell you how fast you can copy data to CDs using the drive.

You install a CD drive by putting it into an empty drive bay, attaching power cables and a data cable to it, and then attaching it to your sound card via a cable. If you're replacing your existing drive, you'll first take out the old drive, being careful to note all the connections so that you can connect the new drive in the same way as the old drive was attached.

How a CD Drive Works

Controller
An IDE/EIDE or SCSI controller inside the computer sends instructions back and forth between your PC and the CD drive, instructing the CD drive to send data to the PC. In most cases, the computer uses the same controller for the hard drive and for the CD drive—and the controller can be either on a separate card or directly on the motherboard. Some older CD drives used a proprietary card, but these days it's best to stick with an EIDE or SCSI controller for ease and compatibility.

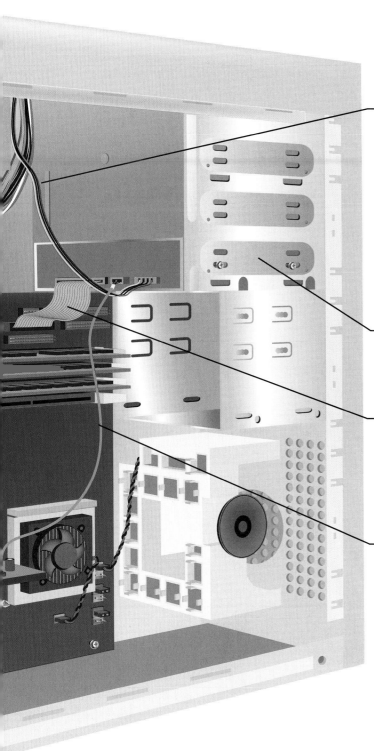

Power connector
The CD drive gets its power from the power supply. It connects to the power supply by a cable and 4-pin connector that plugs into the drive, similar to the ones that plug into your hard drive. If you have no free connectors, you can buy a Y cable, which will split one connector into two, so that you can use the second connector. But be careful not to overload your power supply with too many peripherals.

CD drive
The CD drive fits into a drive bay on a computer. Most CD drives fit into 5 1/4-inch bays. Screws hold the drive in place inside the bay.

Ribbon cable
The controller sends and receives information to and from the drive via a 40-pin ribbon cable, if you're using an IDE/EIDE controller. A connector at each end of the cable plugs into the CD drive and into the controller. A SCSI or some type of proprietary controller might use a 32-, 50-, 68-, or 72-pin cable.

Audio cable
Because CDs include sound and music as well as other kinds of data, they need to send sounds to the PC's sound card. They send data over an audio cable that attaches to the sound card. The sound card, in turn, sends the sound and music to the PC's speakers.

Before Installing a CD Drive

Before you start to install your CD drive, there's a set of precautions you should take, and some steps you should take to prepare your PC for your CD drive.

1 Create a Bootable Floppy Disk

You should make a bootable floppy disk. If you use Windows, put a disk in your floppy drive. Then, get to the Control Panel by double-clicking **My Computer** and double-clicking the **Control Panel**. Next, double-click **Add/Remove Programs** and click the **Startup Disk** tab. From the tab, click **Create Disk** and follow the instructions.

2 Verify That You Have a Free Bay

You'll be installing your CD in a drive bay inside your PC. You'll probably need a free 5 1/4-inch drive bay because many CDs are that size. The drive bay has to have an opening to the front of your PC. If you don't have a free drive bay, you can install an external CD drive that connects to your parallel port. Unless you are installing a CD drive that connects externally through a special card such as a SCSI card, these external CD drives are quite slow.

3 Check for a Free Power Connector

Your CD drive needs to get electricity from your power supply. Check to see that you have a spare power cable running from the power supply with a free connector at the end, and that the cable can reach to where you'll be putting in the drive. If there is no free connector, you can buy a Y cable, which will give you an extra connector. Disconnect one of your other cables, plug it into the Y cable, and you'll then have two plugs—one for whatever you disconnected and another for your CD drive.

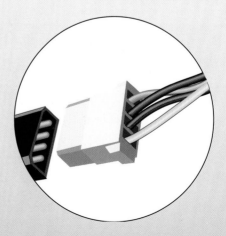

4 Determine the Type of Controller

Your CD drive connects to your computer through an IDE/EIDE controller, although some use SCSI. Match the drive to the controller. Check to see whether there is a space on your existing IDE controller to connect a CD drive. On some PCs, the IDE/EIDE interface is on the motherboard; on others, it's on an add-in card. If you have a sound card, there also might be space on your sound card. If you have a SCSI controller, turn to Chapter 9, "Installing a SCSI Drive."

5 Check the Ribbon Cable Length

You attach the CD drive to your controller via a 40-pin ribbon cable. Make sure that the ribbon cable will reach from the controller to where you'll be installing your CD drive. Most IDE/EIDE controllers are two separate controllers that enable you to connect four different devices: two devices on each ribbon "chain." Each chain has one "master" device, and if there's a second device, it is a "slave." These priority levels are set using jumpers or switches. If your hard drive is the master and you want to connect the CD on the same cable, the CD needs to be set as a slave. If the hard drive is the master and you want to connect the CD to the secondary controller (using its own cable), the CD needs to be set as a master.

6 Check for a Sound Card

Because CDs play music and sound, you need to attach your CD to a sound card. So, if you don't have one, you need to install it. For information on how to install a sound card, turn to Chapter 18, "Installing a Sound Card and Speakers."

Watch Out!

- Make sure that your CD drive uses the same kind of interface (IDE/EIDE, SCSI, or proprietary) as the controller in your PC.
- If you're attaching your CD to a controller that already has a device such as a hard disk on it, make sure that the "master" and "slave" settings on each are set properly.

How to Install a New CD Drive

If you don't have a CD drive yet, you'll certainly want to install one. Follow these instructions for installing a new CD drive in your computer. If you already have a CD drive and are replacing it, turn to the next section. For information about opening the case, turn to Chapter 1, "What's Inside Your Computer."

▌1 Set the Drive Switches

A CD drive can be either a "master" or a "slave." If you're connecting the CD drive to the same cable attached to your boot hard drive, you need to set the CD as a slave. If you're connecting it to the secondary controller, using its own cable, it should be set as a master. Check your CD documentation to see how the DIP switches or jumpers should be set. Turn to Chapter 1 for information on how to set DIP switches and jumpers.

▌2 Slide the Drive into the Bay

Find an empty drive bay and slide your CD drive in. It should slip easily into the bay. Then, screw in the drive.

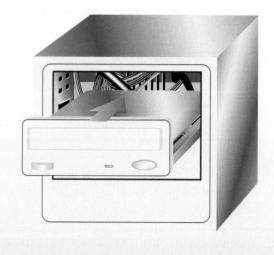

▌3 Connect the Cables

Connect the data cable—the wide, 40-pin ribbon cable that runs from an IDE/EIDE card, motherboard, or a sound card—to your CD drive. The ribbon cable has a stripe on one side of it, indicating that it connects to pin 1 on the CD drive. Next, connect a power cable from your power supply to your CD drive. The power connector will be notched, as will the space on the CD for it, meaning it can be plugged in only one way.

4 Attach the Audio Cable

In order for your computer to play CDs, it needs to connect to the sound card. You connect a cable from your sound card to a port on your CD drive. Two kinds of connectors can be used between a CD drive and a sound card. One is a large connector with a clip; the other is a small white connector with no clip. Make sure that you get the proper connector for your sound card and CD drive. If you don't connect the CD to the sound card, you won't be able to play audio CDs.

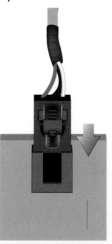

5 Close the Case

After checking that everything is secure, close up your PC, plug the power cable back in, and turn it on.

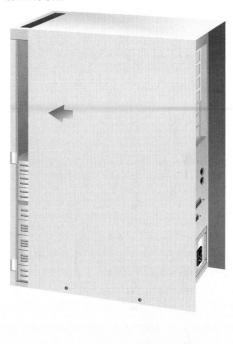

6 Install the Software Drivers

If you run Windows, when you restart your computer, your CD should be recognized automatically. If you're currently running DOS or an earlier version of Windows, instead run the installation software that came with your CD drive to install the proper drivers, so that your CD drive will work.

Watch Out!

- When closing your case, be careful that no ribbon or power cables are hanging out the side. Most of the time you won't notice them until after you have jammed or crimped the cable.

- Check to see that all cable connectors are tight before putting the case back on your PC.

- When plugging the ribbon cable into your CD drive, make sure the stripe lines up with pin 1.

- Before placing the CD drive into its drive bay, make sure that you've set the jumpers properly to be a "master" or a "slave."

- If you have an Ultra ATA 66 or 100 hard drive, don't attach a CD to the same cable on which they are connected. If you do, the hard disks may run at half their normal speed.

How to Replace Your Existing CD Drive

If you have a CD drive that's gone bad, or an older CD drive that runs at a relatively slow speed, you're going to want to replace your existing drive with a new one. It's very much like putting in a new drive, except that you'll first have to take out your old one. You'll want to use your existing cabling to make it easier to install the drive.

To start off, you need to open up the case. For information about opening up the case, turn to Chapter 1.

1 Check Your Current Drive Setup

The CD attaches to your computer via a wide, 40-pin ribbon cable. That cable might attach to a sound card, an IDE/EIDE card, or to the motherboard itself. The CD drive also attaches via an audio cable to the sound card and via a power cable to the power supply. Write down precisely where each cable goes so that you can attach your new CD drive in the same way.

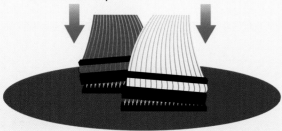

2 Take the Drive out of the Bay

You're going to put your new CD drive in the same place where your current one now sits, so you'll first need to take the old one out. Unplug all the cables from the CD drive, and then unscrew the drive and take it out of the drive bay.

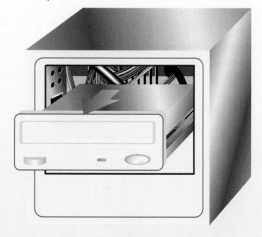

3 Set the Drive Switches

A CD drive can be either a "master" or a "slave." Because you're replacing an old CD drive with a new one, you should set this new drive the same way that the old one is set—either as a master or a slave. Check your CD documentation to see how to set the CD to be the master or the slave. Turn to Chapter 1 for information on how to set jumpers and DIP switches.

4 Slide the Drive into the Bay

First, slide the drive into the drive bay. You need to secure the CD drive by screwing it into the drive bay or railings. Then, attach the cables. You want to attach these in the same way as they were attached in your old drive. The ribbon cable has a stripe on one side of it, indicating that it connects to pin 1 on the drive, labeled with a small "1." Connect the power supply cable to the drive, via a connector on the end of the cable. Finally, attach the audio cable to the CD drive.

5 Close the Case

After checking that everything is secure, close your PC, plug the power cable back in, and turn it on.

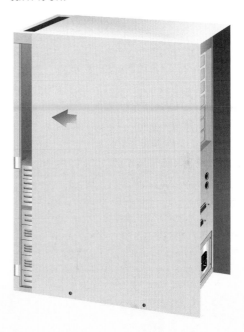

6 Install the Software Drivers

If you run Windows, when you restart your computer, your CD should be recognized automatically. If you're running DOS or an earlier version of Windows, instead use the installation software that came with your CD drive. Run that to install the proper drivers so that your CD drive will work.

Watch Out!

- Check to see that all the cable connectors are tight before putting the case back on your PC.

- When plugging the ribbon cable into your CD drive, make sure that the side with the stripe lines up with pin 1 on the CD drive—the pin should be labeled.

- Before placing the CD drive into its drive bay, make sure that you've set the jumpers properly to be either a "master" or a "slave."

- When closing your case, make sure that no ribbon or power cables are hanging out the side. Most of the time you won't notice them until after you have jammed or crimped the cable.

CHAPTER

Installing a DVD Drive

How a DVD Drive Works   92

Before Installing a DVD Drive   94

How to Install a DVD Drive   96

DIGITAL *Versatile Discs (DVDs)* have become the next revolution in multimedia computing. These disks can hold the equivalent of many CDs, and their multimedia capacities far outstrip anything available on CD. The animation they can play, and the quality of their music, are much more realistic than what you can get on a CD.

With a DVD drive, you not only can run DVDs made for computers, you can also watch movies recorded on DVDs. You'll be able to watch those movies on your PC, or on a TV, by hooking a TV up to your computer. And many newer DVD drives can run CD-ROMs, Photo CD and CD Plus, as well as DVDS.

Installing a DVD drive is much like installing a CD-ROM drive. You put it in an empty drive bay, and then attach it to your PC via an IDE/EIDE interface, which can be found on an IDE/EIDE card or directly on the motherboard. Some DVD drives can also be hooked up via a SCSI interface. When installing a DVD drive, you also have to install a DVD decoder card, and then hook the drive up to that. In some cases, you may have a graphics card that has a decoder already on it, so you won't need to install a separate decoder card. Check your graphic card's documentation to see whether yours has a DVD decoder on it. It's possible to install a DVD without a decoder, but then you won't be able to watch DVD movies on your PC, and you may not be able to see some movie scenes in DVD games. So, it's best to install a decoder.

If you have an older PC, be sure before buying a DVD drive that your computer has enough horsepower and other system capabilities to play DVD titles or to install a DVD drive. Check with the DVD manufacturer for system requirements.

How a DVD Drive Works

Graphics card
Some decoder cards attach to your existing graphics card, whereas others don't. You have to check your drive's documentation to see whether yours needs to attach to your graphics card or not. Some graphics cards include DVD decoders built into them. And for a number of graphics cards, you can buy a special DVD decoder daughterboard to plug into the card.

Decoder card
A DVD drive can play DVD movies and computer DVDs. In order for the drive to play movies, it requires a decoder or decoder card. The decoder card also makes the video display smoothly. This decoder is a separate device from the SCSI or EIDE controller and requires a separate connection to your computer. This decoder card doesn't replace your normal graphics card, so, if you have a graphics card, you use it along with the decoder. Your monitor plugs directly into the decoder card. If your graphics card includes a DVD decoder on it, however, the monitor stays attached to the graphics card because then no separate decoder is needed.

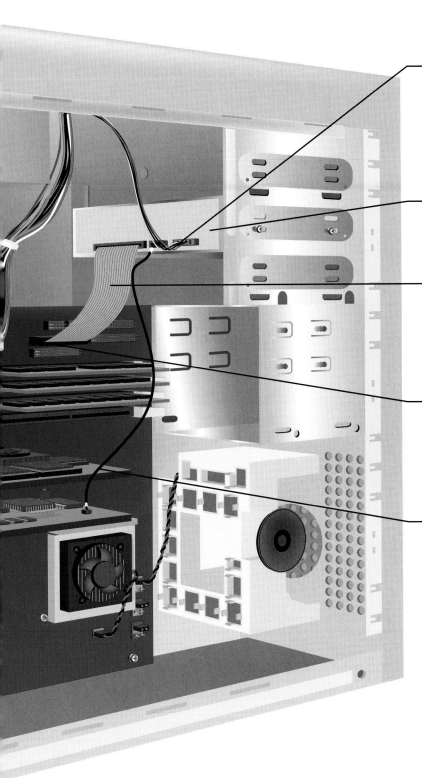

Power connector
The DVD drive gets its power from the power supply. It connects to the power supply by a cable and connector that plugs into the drive. The power connector is notched so that it can be connected only one way. Use the larger 4-pin connector for power.

DVD drive
The DVD drive fits into a drive bay on a computer. Most DVDs fit into five-inch bays.

Ribbon cable
The controller sends and receives information to and from the DVD drive via a 40-pin ribbon cable. A connector at each end of the cable plugs into the DVD drive and into the controller.

Controller
IDE/EIDE or SCSI controllers inside the computer send instructions back and forth between the components of your PC and the DVD drive, instructing the DVD to send data to the PC and receive instructions from it.

Decoder cable
The DVD drive often connects to a DVD decoder card via a cable. The decoder card makes the video display smoothly, among other features, and also allows you to play DVD movies on your computer. The decoder cable looks different from a normal ribbon cable that connects to the SCSI or EIDE controller. It may look like a standard CD audio cable or like a small ribbon cable.

Before Installing a DVD Drive

Before you start to install your DVD drive, there's a set of precautions you should take—and some steps you should take to prepare your PC for your DVD drive.

1 Create a Bootable Floppy

If you use Windows, you should make a bootable floppy disk. This will allow you to boot from the floppy disk if things go awry. First, put a disk in your floppy drive. Next, get to the Control Panel by double-clicking **My Computer** and double-clicking the **Control Panel**. Double-click **Add/Remove Programs** and click the **Startup Disk** tab. From the tab, click **Create Disk** and follow the instructions.

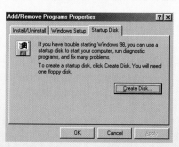

2 Verify You Have a Free Bay

You'll be installing your DVD in a drive bay inside your PC. You'll probably need a free five-inch drive bay because many DVDs are that size. The drive bay has to have an opening to the front of your PC to allow the disk tray to eject from the machine.

3 Verify You Have a Free Power Connector

Your DVD drive gets electricity from your power supply. Check to see that you have a spare power cable, that there's a free connector at the end of it, and that the cable and connector can reach to the drive. If there is no free connector, you can buy a 'Y' splitter, which will give you an extra connector. You disconnect one of your other cables, plug it into the Y cable, and you then have two plugs—one for whatever you disconnected and another for your DVD drive.

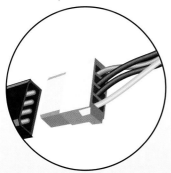

4 Determine the Type of Connector

Your DVD drive connects to your computer through an IDE controller, although some use SCSI. You need to match the drive to the controller. Check to see whether there is a space on your existing IDE controller to connect a DVD drive. On some PCs, the IDE interface is on the motherboard; on others, it's on an add-in card. If you have a sound card, there also may be space there, although the connector on some sound cards won't work with all DVD drives. If you have a SCSI controller, turn to Chapter 9, "Installing a SCSI Drive."

5 Check the Ribbon Cable Length

You attach the DVD drive to your controller via a 40-pin ribbon cable. Make sure that the ribbon cable will reach from the controller to where you'll be installing your DVD drive. If you're connecting to a SCSI controller, it will be a 50-, 68-, or 72-pin SCSI connection.

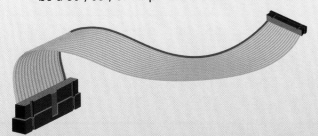

Watch Out!

- When connecting a power supply cable, use the larger 4-pin power connector, which is notched so it can connect in only one way.
- Make sure that your cables can reach from your power supply and controller to where your DVD drive will be.

How to Install a DVD Drive

After you've prepared your PC for putting in a DVD drive, you're ready to start installing it. First, though, you have to install a DVD decoder board in your PC. (In some instances, though, you can connect directly to your graphics card. Check your graphics card documentation.) After you've installed the DVD decoder card, you'll put the drive into a bay, hook up all the connectors, close up the case, and install the necessary software. You first have to open the case and ground yourself. For information on how to do that, turn to Chapter 1, "What's Inside Your Computer."

◼1 Find an Empty Slot

Look for an empty slot inside your PC. The slot should be a PCI slot. Check your system's documentation if you're not sure whether yours has one. After you find an empty slot, unscrew its metal placeholder. When you unscrew the placeholder, be sure to keep the screw because you'll need it in order to install the DVD decoder board.

◼2 Install the DVD Decoder Card

Position the card above the slot and using both hands, press down firmly but carefully until the card is seated securely into the slot. Then, screw in the mounting screw that holds the card in place.

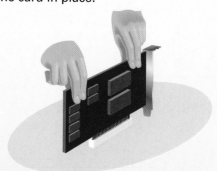

◼3 Connect the Sound Card Cable

Each DVD kit and decoder card is different. Yours may or may not require that it be attached to a sound board. Check your documentation and if it does, attach the cable from the DVD decoder card to your sound card.

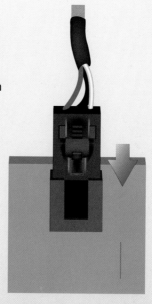

4 Connect Your Monitor

Some DVD decoder cards must be connected to your existing graphics card. Check your DVD drive's documentation. If it does, disconnect the monitor cable from your graphics card. Next, connect one end of a cable provided with the kit to the "VGA in" port on the DVD board, and connect the other end to your graphics card (in the spot where the monitor used to plug in). Then, connect the monitor to the DVD's "VGA out" port. If your DVD decoder board doesn't require a connection to your graphics card, don't do anything.

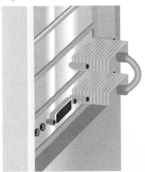

5 Set the Drive Switches

You'll need to tell the DVD drive whether it's the primary drive (a "master") or a secondary drive (a "slave"). You may set it with jumpers or DIP switches. Check your DVD documentation to see how to do it.

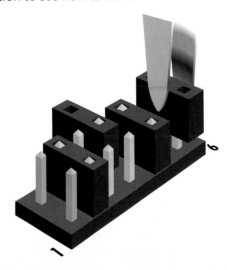

6 Slide the DVD Drive into the Bay

Find an empty drive bay and take off the front panel protecting it. You should be able to easily slide the DVD drive into the bay. It will probably need a five-inch bay. If you need to attach railings to the drive to hold the DVD drive in place, first install them, and then screw the drive into the railings.

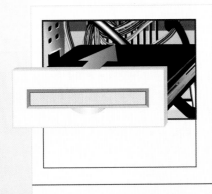

7 Connect the Data Cable

The data cable is the wide, 40-pin ribbon cable that runs from an IDE card, the motherboard, or a sound card, and connects to your DVD drive. The ribbon cable has a stripe on one side of it, which indicates that it connects to pin 1 on the DVD drive. There will be a small "1" indicating the pin on the DVD drive. Pin 1 is generally found next to the power connector; if not, check the system's documentation. Connect the ribbon cable to the drive.

8 Connect the Power Supply Cable

Your DVD drive gets power from the power supply. Locate a free power cable from the power supply. The power supply cable has a connector on the end of it, which usually is four sockets encased in a small sheath of white plastic. The connector will be notched and connect only one way. Plug that into the power connector on your DVD drive.

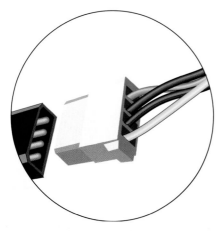

9 Connect the Decoder Card

Connect the DVD drive to the DVD decoder card by using the cable supplied with the DVD drive kit. It's possible that there might be more than one cable, depending on your kit. Check the documentation.

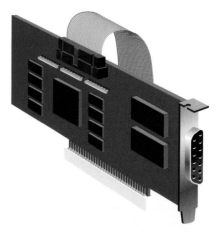

10 Attach Speaker and TV-Out Cables

One of the DVD's main benefits is that its sound quality is much higher than that of CD-ROM drives. So, you can use surround sound speakers with your DVD drive. You can also play DVDs on your computer and run them through your TV so that you can watch DVD movies. Attach the speaker cables and TV-out cables to the DVD decoder drive via the connections on the back of the card. Depending on your drive, you may instead run via a cable from the drive to the video card (if it has an onboard decoder) and then from the video card to the sound card.

11 Close the Case

After checking that everything is secure, close up your PC, plug it in, and turn it on.

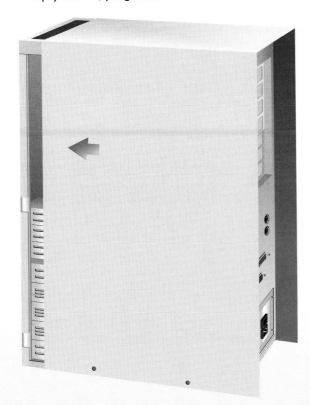

12 Install the Software Drivers

Depending on the version of Windows you have, when you start your computer, Windows may recognize that you've added new hardware. Follow the directions onscreen, inserting the manufacturer's disk when it asks you to. After that, you may need to install more software from the manufacturer's disk. Check for SETUP.EXE, INSTALL.EXE, or a similar file on the disk, and read the installation directions. Windows may instead simply boot and show the DVD drive as a new CD drive. In that case, simply install the player software from the manufacturer's supplied disk.

Watch Out!

- Be sure that all the cable connectors are tight before putting the case back on your PC.

- When plugging the ribbon cable into your DVD drive, be sure that the side with the stripe lines up with pin 1 on the DVD drive. The pin should be labeled.

- Make sure that you know whether you need to attach your DVD decoder card to your graphics card. If you do, follow the directions carefully for hooking it up.

- If you want to play DVD movies, make sure the DVD player comes with software for doing that.

CHAPTER

Installing a SCSI Drive

How SCSI Works   102

Before Installing a SCSI Drive   104

How to Install a SCSI Controller Card   106

How to Install a SCSI Device   108

How to Install Multiple SCSI Devices   110

HARD drives, CD-ROM drives, scanners, and other devices need some way to connect to your computer's motherboard. One of the ways to provide that connection is with a SCSI (small computer system interface). SCSI provides very high throughput, so the equipment you connect will run quite fast. A SCSI drive can transfer data at up to 160 megabytes per second, whereas EIDE drives are limited to a maximum of 33 megabytes per second. You can also connect from 7 to 15 devices to a single SCSI controller in daisy-chain fashion, depending on your controller; each device is connected in an unbroken chain to the next. That's the good news. The bad news is that it's more difficult to install SCSI devices than it is to install other kinds of devices.

You'll install SCSI devices by first installing a SCSI controller, and then connecting each device in turn. This chapter shows you everything you need to know about it.

How SCSI Works

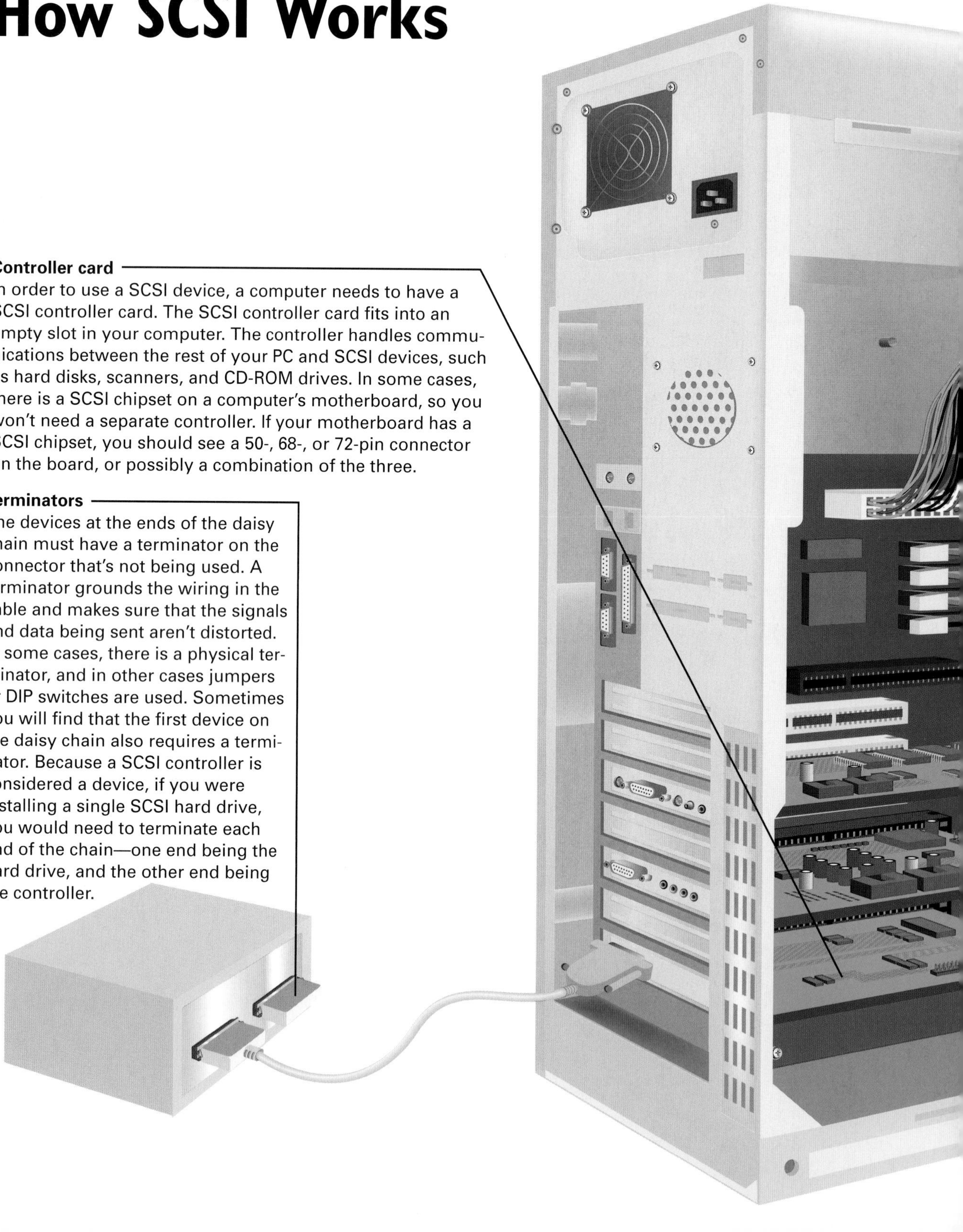

Controller card

In order to use a SCSI device, a computer needs to have a SCSI controller card. The SCSI controller card fits into an empty slot in your computer. The controller handles communications between the rest of your PC and SCSI devices, such as hard disks, scanners, and CD-ROM drives. In some cases, there is a SCSI chipset on a computer's motherboard, so you won't need a separate controller. If your motherboard has a SCSI chipset, you should see a 50-, 68-, or 72-pin connector on the board, or possibly a combination of the three.

Terminators

The devices at the ends of the daisy chain must have a terminator on the connector that's not being used. A terminator grounds the wiring in the cable and makes sure that the signals and data being sent aren't distorted. In some cases, there is a physical terminator, and in other cases jumpers or DIP switches are used. Sometimes you will find that the first device on the daisy chain also requires a terminator. Because a SCSI controller is considered a device, if you were installing a single SCSI hard drive, you would need to terminate each end of the chain—one end being the hard drive, and the other end being the controller.

SCSI ID number

Each device on the daisy chain needs to have a unique SCSI ID number. This SCSI ID number uniquely identifies the devices so that they can be recognized by the controller and computer, and used properly. Some devices require that they use certain ID numbers. You assign SCSI ID numbers different ways for different devices. Often, jumpers or DIP switches are used to set the ID numbers. In the case of a SCSI controller, the ID number, termination, and other features are usually set through an onboard BIOS.

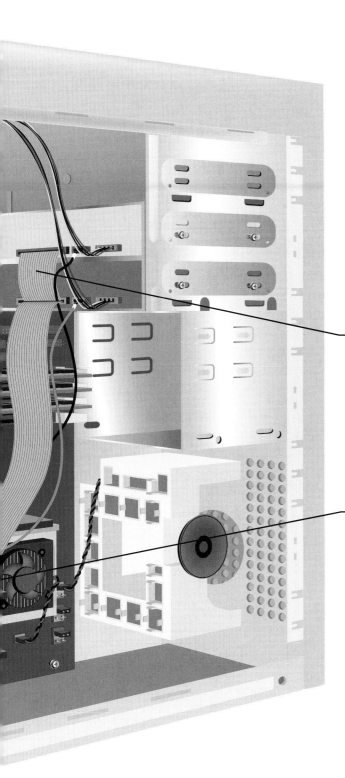

Daisy chain

Up to seven devices can be handled by a single SCSI controller. The devices are attached in daisy-chain fashion—they're attached to one another via a series of cables that start from the controller and go to each device in turn. Each device, including the controller, is assigned a number from 0 to 7 (or 0 to 15, if it is "wide" SCSI) to make it unique on the chain. It also requires that the devices at the beginning and end of the chain have "terminators" on them.

SCSI cable

SCSI devices are attached to the other devices in the daisy chain by sets of SCSI cables. A SCSI cable from another device in the daisy chain attaches to the incoming port of each SCSI device. Another SCSI cable attaches to the outgoing port on the device, which connects to the next SCSI device on the daisy chain. The three most commonly used connector types are 50-pin, 68-pin, and 72-pin.

Before Installing a SCSI Drive

Installing a SCSI drive or other device sometimes can be a frustrating experience. But if you prepare yourself properly, you should be able to install it with a minimum of fuss. Before you install a SCSI device, take these steps:

1 Determine If You Need SCSI

It's more difficult to install a SCSI device and controller than it is to install an IDE/EIDE. Before installing, make sure you need SCSI. You need SCSI if you require fast, hard-disk throughput, and if you plan to add several new devices to your computer, SCSI makes it easy to add new devices because you can daisy-chain them.

2 Back Up Your Hard Drive

You don't want to lose all the data on your old hard disk, so before installing a new hard disk, back up the data on the old one. This is especially important if you're replacing your hard disk instead of adding a second one. You may want to only back up your data, or you may want to copy the operating system, all your programs, and your data. Back up your hard disk to a tape drive, a Zip drive, or similar removable media. You back up your hard disk with backup software (Windows includes this).

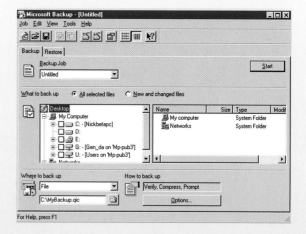

3 Create a Bootable Floppy

If you use Windows, you should also make a bootable floppy disk. To do that, put a disk in your floppy drive. Go to the Control Panel by double-clicking **My Computer** and double-clicking the **Control Panel**. Next, double-click **Add/Remove Programs** and click the **Startup Disk** tab. From the tab, click **Create Disk** and follow the instructions.

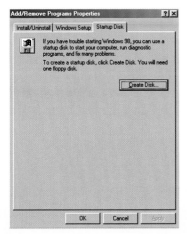

4 Verify You Have a Free Drive Bay

If you're going to install a hard disk or similar internal device inside your PC, you need a free drive bay. Make sure that your new hard disk or other internal device can fit into your existing drive bay. Hard drives come in three-inch and five-inch sizes, so make sure your bay will accommodate the drive you buy. You can fit a three-inch drive into a five-inch bay by getting a special adapter kit, but a five-inch hard disk won't fit into a three-inch bay.

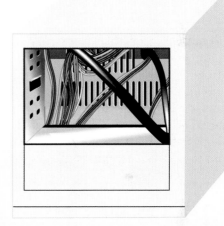

5 Check Your BIOS Settings

If you're installing a hard disk, you'll need to know your BIOS settings for your current hard disk. That way, if something goes wrong during the installation, you can easily reinstall your old hard disk. Go to the CMOS screen and write down all the information it contains about your hard disk. For information on how to get to the CMOS screen, see Chapter 1, "What's Inside Your Computer."

6 Verify You Have a Free Slot

A SCSI device needs to attach to a SCSI controller. You're going to install the SCSI controller before installing a SCSI hard disk or other device, so make sure that there's a free slot on the motherboard for it. It's best if you install a SCSI controller to a PCI slot.

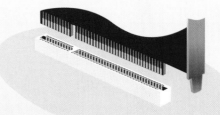

Watch Out!

- Make sure your controller card is the same type as the free slot on your motherboard.

How to Install a SCSI Controller Card

Before you can install a SCSI device in your computer, you first need to install a SCSI controller card. In some ways, it's like installing any other card—you open up your PC, find an empty slot, and install the card in it. But in other ways, it's much more difficult because you have to set SCSI IDs and put on a terminator. Before installing a SCSI controller card, open your case and ground yourself. For details on how to do it, turn to Chapter 1.

◼ Set Jumpers or DIP Switches

Check the documentation for your SCSI controller and motherboard and see whether you have to set any jumpers or DIP switches. If you need to set them, set them now. Turn to Chapter 1 for more information on setting DIP switches and jumpers. Often, though, most controllers are changed via the onboard BIOS.

◼ Find an Empty Slot

Your SCSCI controller card goes in an empty slot on the motherboard. In order to fit the card into place, you have to take off the small metal flap protecting the slot. The flap is held in place by a small screw. Take the screw off (it's usually held in place by a Phillips screw) and take off the flap. Put the screw in a safe place—you're going to need it to secure the card you're installing.

◼ Install the Card into the Slot

Align the card in the slot, making sure that the connectors on the card line up properly with the slot where you're putting the card. Using two hands, apply gentle, even pressure, and push the card down into the slot. After the card is in place, press down firmly to make sure that it's all the way into the slot. If it's not pushed all the way into the slot, your new hard disk won't work.

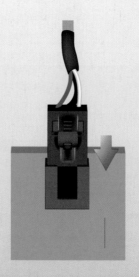

4 Screw the Card into Place

To make sure that the card won't come loose, screw it into place. Use the same screw that you took off the metal flap; you'll screw the card into the same place where the metal flap was screwed in. In some special SCSI controllers, you may also have to connect a power cable to it from your power supply. If you don't have a free cable, you can buy a Y connector to split the cable into two connectors.

5 Verify SCSI ID Numbers

SCSI devices have unique ID numbers, from 0 through 7 (or 0 through 15 in the case of wide SCSI). Most SCSI controller cards are set by default to 7. It's generally good to keep the default, but if you want to change it, you can change it by setting jumpers or DIP switches, or some other kind of control. Check the card's documentation for how to do it. Write down on a slip of paper the SCSI ID that you've assigned to the controller card, even if you've accepted the default of 7.

6 Put a Terminator on the Card

Most SCSI controllers allow seven devices to be attached to one another in daisy-chain fashion. The device at the end of the chain needs to have a terminator on it, and in many cases, the device at the beginning needs a terminator as well. A terminator will come with your SCSI card, or else you might set it via a DIP switch. You can also set the terminator via the CMOS. Check your documentation to see how to set yours.

How to Install a SCSI Device

After you put the SCSI controller in, it's time to install your first SCSI device. Installing any SCSI device is relatively the same. In this example, we look at installing a SCSI hard drive—your primary hard drive, the one you boot from. I'll assume that you've already taken out your hard drive. Keep in mind that installing a SCSI DVD or CD drive follows the same process. For more information about taking out hard drives and installing new ones, turn to Chapter 5, "Adding or Replacing an IDE Hard Drive."

■ Set the SCSI ID

Each SCSI device must have a unique ID number, from 0 through 7 (or 0 through 15 in the case of wide SCSI). The usual ID for a boot drive is 0, so set it at that. In a few cases, the number might be different, so check your documentation. You'll often set the number via jumpers or DIP switches. Check your documentation. Write down the ID number on a slip of paper, along with the SCSI ID for your controller card, to refer to when you install other SCSI devices. That way, you'll ensure you don't accidentally assign two devices the same SCSI ID.

■ Terminate the Device

SCSI allows seven devices to be attached to one another in daisy-chain fashion. The device at the end of the chain needs to be terminated. You terminate a device by plugging a terminator into it; the terminator usually goes onto the device itself, and usually not onto its cable or connector. Sometimes, you don't physically plug in a terminator but instead set a special jumper. Your documentation will show you exactly how to terminate the device. In some cases, the device at the beginning of the daisy chain needs to be terminated as well. Check your documentation.

3 Install the Drive into the Bay

If your new drive has the same physical dimensions as your old hard drive, you'll simply be able to slide it right into place. However, if you're installing a three-inch hard disk into a five-inch bay, you'll have to first screw in mounting brackets. Connect all the screws so that the hard drive is held firmly in place. Don't overtighten or strip the screws, though.

4 Connect the Controller Cable

For your new hard disk to work, it needs to be connected to your SCSI controller. Using the cables supplied with the card or the hard disk, attach the cables to the hard disk and to the connector.

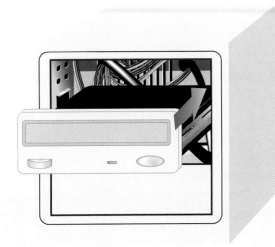

5 Connect the Power Cable

Take the power cable and plug it into the proper place on your new hard disk. The power supply cable has a connector on the end of it, which is usually four sockets encased in a small sheath of white plastic. Plug the cable into the connector on your hard disk. Use the larger 4-pin connector that is notched so it will connect only one way.

6 Format the Hard Disk

Turn on your PC with the boot disk in the floppy drive so you can boot from it. Before you can use your hard disk, you'll have to format it so that it can be used by your computer. For information about formatting your hard disk, turn to the section "Formatting and Partitioning Your New Hard Drive," in Chapter 5. If you've removed an IDE drive, you may have to go into your CMOS settings and tell the CMOS that the IDE drive has been removed.

How to Install Multiple SCSI Devices

SCSI controllers are useful not just because SCSI devices are fast—SCSI also allows you to daisy chain 7 or 15, in cases of wide SCSI, devices on a single controller. Here's how to do it. This assumes that you've already installed a SCSI controller and another SCSI device, as outlined in the previous sections.

■ Check Existing SCSI ID Numbers

SCSI devices are daisy chained from one to another. They each need to be identified with a unique SCSI ID, from 0 to 7 (or 0 through 15 in the case of wide SCSI). Before you start to install an existing device, know what IDs your other SCSI devices use. The best way to accurately determine the ID number is to physically look at the device itself. By utilizing software and other diagnostic methods, you will not necessarily know whether two devices are conflicting over the same ID number.

❷ Set the New Device's SCSI ID

The SCSI ID can be set in different ways, such as via jumpers, DIP switches, or some other kind of control (such as an onboard BIOS for a controller). Check the device's documentation to see how to set the ID. Make sure you choose an ID that isn't in use yet. Some devices require that they be set to a particular SCSI ID. Check to see whether your device has that requirement; if it does, use that ID. If another device already has that ID, change the ID of the other device, and then set the SCSI ID of the device you're adding.

❸ Physically Install the Device

If it's an internal device, unplug the computer, take off the case, ground yourself or wear an antistatic wrist strap, and install the device following the manual's instructions or instructions elsewhere in this book. If it's an external device, unplug the computer and install the device following the manual's instructions or instructions elsewhere in this book. Make sure that you attach power supply cables to it, if it's an internal device.

4 Attach It to the Daisy Chain

After you've installed the SCSI device, it's time to connect it to an existing SCSI device. You attach a device to the daisy chain via SCSI cables. Make sure the cables you use match the connector's pin width of your existing devices. If the external device will be in the middle of the daisy chain, it will connect to two SCSI devices. That means that you'll have to connect one SCSI cable to the incoming port of the device you're adding, and connect one SCSI cable to the outgoing port of the device. The ports should be labeled. You then connect the SCSI cables to the other devices. If you're putting a new device into the middle of the chain, make sure it's not terminated— many devices come terminated by default. Internal devices need only one connection.

5 Terminate the External Devices

SCSI requires that devices at each end of the SCSI daisy chain have terminators on them. If you're installing an external device at the end of the daisy chain, you'll have to put a terminator on it. Most external SCSI devices have two ports on the back. Put a terminator on one of those ports and the SCSI cable connected to another SCSI device on the other port. In some cases, you won't have a physical terminator, but instead will set your device to be a terminator by using a DIP switch. Check your documentation to see which yours uses.

6 Set Internal Terminators

If you're installing an internal device, and it's going to be at the end of the chain, you'll have to use a terminator as well. Internal devices usually set terminators by using a DIP switch. Not all do, however; some come with a plug that can be used as well.

Watch Out!

- If you're installing a device in the middle of a SCSI chain, make sure it's not terminated, because most new devices are terminated by default.
- Make sure that each SCSI device gets its own unique ID so that there are no conflicts.
- If you're installing a bootable SCSI hard drive, its ID should be set to 0 in almost all cases. Check the drive's documentation.
- Make sure the controller termination is set correctly for internal and external chains.
- Make sure you get the same type of connector for your devices and controller (50-, 68-, or 72-pin), although there are converters/gender changers, which are expensive.

CHAPTER

10

Installing a Removable Drive

How a Removable Drive Works **114**

How to Install an External Zip Drive **116**

How to Install an Internal Zip Drive **118**

IF you're looking to back up your hard disk, or to share large amounts of data with other people or computers, the best thing you can do is install a removable drive. These removable drives enable you to store hundreds of megabytes of data—or even a gigabyte or more of data—onto a single floppy-size disk or other medium.

There are several popular kinds of removable drives, but the most popular ones are made by Iomega. Iomega's best-known drive is the Zip drive, which can hold up to 250 megabytes of data, depending on the model. The Jaz drive can hold even more data, up to 2 gigabytes' worth. Other companies make removable drives, notably SyQuest.

This chapter shows how to install Zip drives. Jaz drives install similarly, so if you need to install one of those, this chapter is still a good starting point.

How a Removable Drive Works

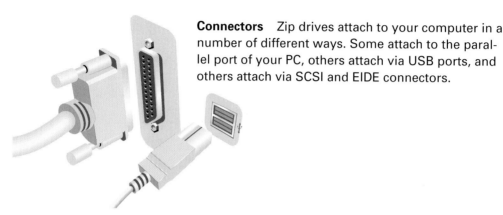

Connectors Zip drives attach to your computer in a number of different ways. Some attach to the parallel port of your PC, others attach via USB ports, and others attach via SCSI and EIDE connectors.

Zip disk
A disk for an Iomega Zip drive looks much like a floppy disk. It's about the same size, although slightly thicker. But the Zip drive can hold many more times the capacity of a normal floppy disk—up to 250 megabytes.

Cookie Inside the disk is a magnetic-coated Mylar disk called a cookie. It's protected by a hard plastic shell, with a metal plate that slides open to give read/write heads access to the cookie. The cookie is coated with special magnetic particles that allow it to hold more data than a normal floppy drive. The heads on a Zip drive are much smaller than those on a floppy drive, which allows more data tracks to be used per inch, also increasing the disk's storage capacity.

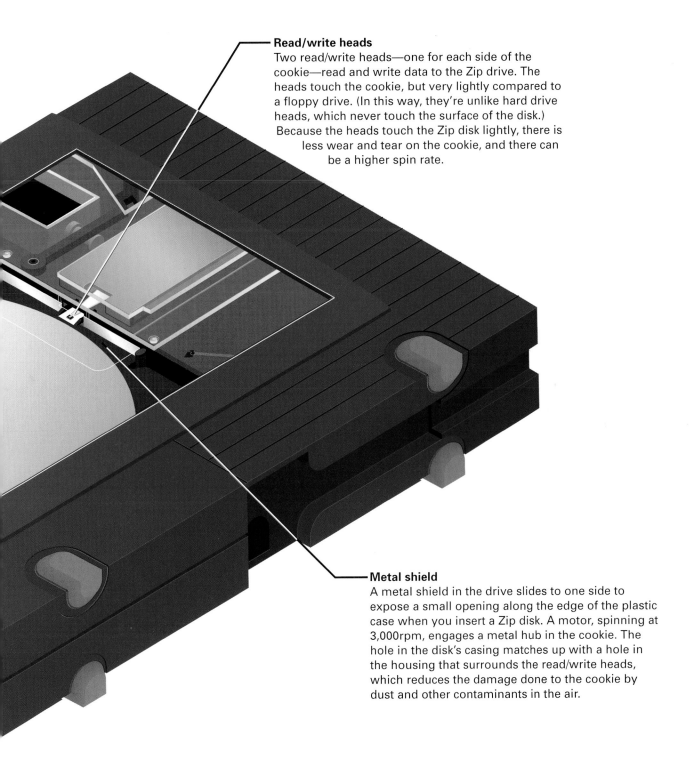

Read/write heads
Two read/write heads—one for each side of the cookie—read and write data to the Zip drive. The heads touch the cookie, but very lightly compared to a floppy drive. (In this way, they're unlike hard drive heads, which never touch the surface of the disk.) Because the heads touch the Zip disk lightly, there is less wear and tear on the cookie, and there can be a higher spin rate.

Metal shield
A metal shield in the drive slides to one side to expose a small opening along the edge of the plastic case when you insert a Zip disk. A motor, spinning at 3,000rpm, engages a metal hub in the cookie. The hole in the disk's casing matches up with a hole in the housing that surrounds the read/write heads, which reduces the damage done to the cookie by dust and other contaminants in the air.

How to Install an External Zip Drive

One of the least complicated ways to install a Zip drive is to install one on your parallel port. Then, when you want to transfer data to or from the drive, data is sent over your parallel port. If you want to use a printer, you'll also have to install a special pass-through cable, provided with the drive. When installing a parallel port Zip drive, it's a good idea to first turn off all power to your computer and its peripherals, including the printer and monitor. If you have a printer, unplug the printer cable from the PC's parallel port, but keep the cable plugged into your printer. For information on how to install a USB Zip drive, see Chapter 20, "Installing USB Devices."

1 Connect Cable to the Zip Drive

A cable will come with your Zip drive. Look for the end of it marked "Zip," and connect it to the Zip connector on the back of your Zip drive.

2 Connect the Other End to the PC

The parallel port is what your printer plugs into and is usually larger than the serial port on your PC. It is often labeled with a picture of a printer.

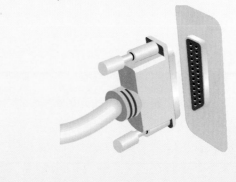

3 Attach Your Printer

To use your printer as well as your Zip drive, you need to attach the cable provided to the pass-through connector. Attach the supplied cable to your Zip drive, and then attach the other end to your printer. You'll now be able to use your Zip drive as well as your printer.

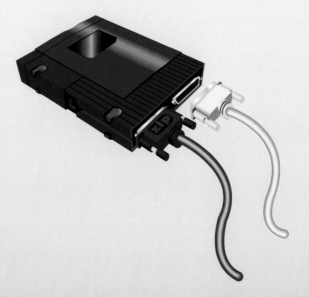

4 Connect the Power Supply

The Zip drive connects to a normal wall outlet or a power strip. After you've connected it, turn it on.

5 Turn On Your PC

When you turn on your PC, Windows automatically starts up.

6 Install Drive Software

Put the Zip CD-ROM in your CD drive. When you do this, it should automatically start the installation software. If it doesn't, run **Setup.exe** from the disks or CD-ROM supplied with the Zip drive. When you install the software, you'll install everything you need to use the Zip drive, and your computer will automatically recognize the Zip drive.

Watch Out!

■ Keep the Zip drive power on when you use your printer—it has to be powered in order for the pass-through connector to work.

■ Check to make sure that the power supply connector is plugged tightly into the Zip drive.

■ If you are having difficulty printing after installing the external Zip drive, your printer might not be compatible with the pass-through port. Refer to the owner's manual.

How to Install an Internal Zip Drive

If you prefer, you can install an internal IDE Zip drive instead of installing it externally via your parallel port. Installing it is much like installing other drives. Precisely how you install it will vary slightly depending on how your hard disk and CD drive are installed in your computer (and, even on whether you have a CD drive). In this instance, we'll assume that you're installing a Zip drive into a computer that has a hard drive and a CD drive, and that each of those drives are attached to their own "channel" on the controller. If your setup is different from this, check your Zip drive's documentation on how to install it.

Before installing the drive, unplug your PC, turn it off, remove the cover, and discharge any static electricity by touching the power supply. Turn to Chapter 1, "What's Inside Your Computer," for more details.

1 Check the Drive Jumpers

You install the Zip drive as a slave to the existing CD drive, which is a master. The Zip drive should come from the factory set as a slave, but to make sure, check the jumper settings. To be set as a slave, there should be no jumper blocks on the back of the drive, as pictured here.

2 Install the Drive into the Bay

You install the drive into an empty bay. Locate an empty bay, remove its panel cover, and slide the Zip drive in. Your bay might require that the drive use mounting rails, so install those now, if they're needed. After the drive is securely in the bay, screw it in.

3 Remove Cable from the CD Drive

Your CD drive connects to the IDE controller on the motherboard via a wide, 40-pin ribbon cable. Disconnect that cable from the CD drive, and then disconnect the cable where it connects to the IDE controller on the motherboard. Put the cable aside; you won't need it.

4 Connect the Cables

You now connect both your Zip drive and your CD drive to the controller on the motherboard with the 40-pin ribbon cable supplied with your Zip drive. Look for the end of the cable farthest from the middle connector, and then plug that end into the controller. Plug the ribbon's middle connector into the CD drive and the final connector into the Zip drive. In all cases, make sure that Pin 1 on the connector, indicated by a stripe on the cable, connects to Pin 1 on the drive or controller.

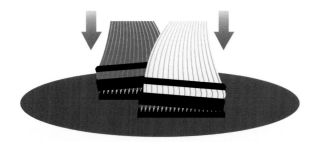

5 Connect the Power Supply

Your Zip drive needs power in order to work, so connect it to the power supply. The power supply cable has a connector on the end of it, which usually has four sockets encased in a small sheath of white plastic. Plug that into the connector into the Zip drive.

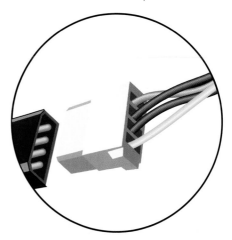

6 Install the Drive Software

Put the Zip CD-ROM into your CD drive. When you do this, it should automatically start the installation software. If it doesn't, run **Setup.exe** from the disks or CD-ROM supplied with the Zip drive. When you install the software, you'll install everything you need to use the Zip drive, and your computer will automatically recognize the Zip drive.

Watch Out!

- It's best to install your Zip drive to the secondary IDE channel—not the same one that your hard drive is on.

- Your CD drive should be set as a master. Check its documentation to make sure it's set that way.

- Make sure all the cables are connected tightly.

C H A P T E R

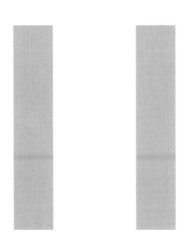

Installing a Tape Drive

How a Tape Drive Works   122

Before Installing a Tape Drive   124

How to Install a Tape Drive   126

IN some ways, running a PC is like walking a tightrope—you never know when your hard disk will crash and you'll be left without a safety net.

Think of tape drives as your safety net. You copy your entire hard disk to them so that if your hard disk or PC crashes, you'll always have a copy of your data and programs.

Installing a tape backup drive is relatively easy, and in many ways is like installing a floppy disk drive. A tape backup drive fits inside a drive bay inside your computer and sends and receives data via a controller. It often comes with its own proprietary controller, which you'll need to install. (There are, however, also IDE/EIDE and SCSI tape drives and even some that run off the floppy controller.) You attach a tape drive to a controller, hook it up to the power supply, install drivers, and then run tape backup software. After you do that, you're close to having a safety net when you compute: You'll actually have to use the tape drive to do backups to make sure that you're safe.

How a Tape Drive Works

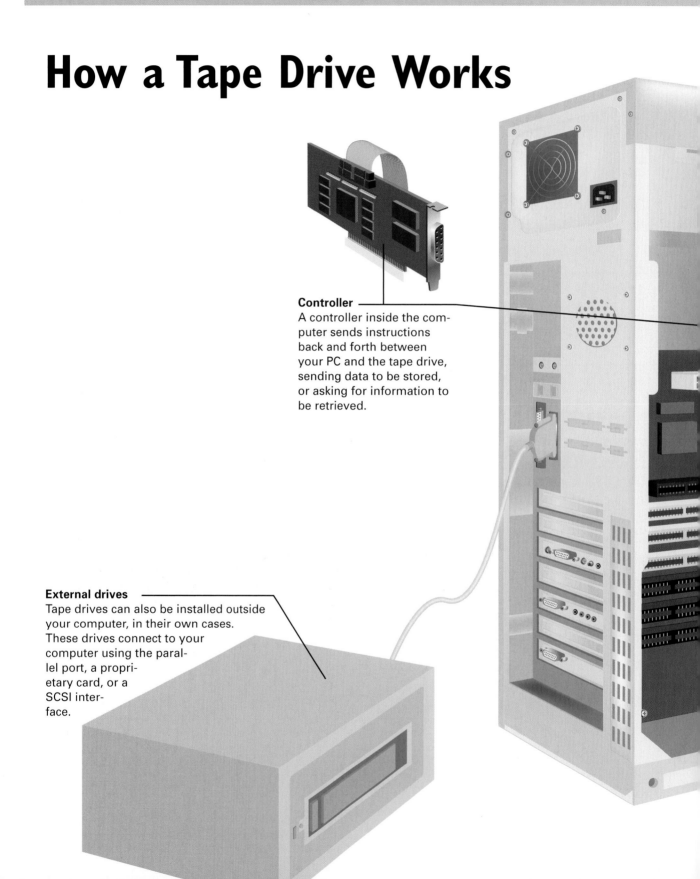

Controller
A controller inside the computer sends instructions back and forth between your PC and the tape drive, sending data to be stored, or asking for information to be retrieved.

External drives
Tape drives can also be installed outside your computer, in their own cases. These drives connect to your computer using the parallel port, a proprietary card, or a SCSI interface.

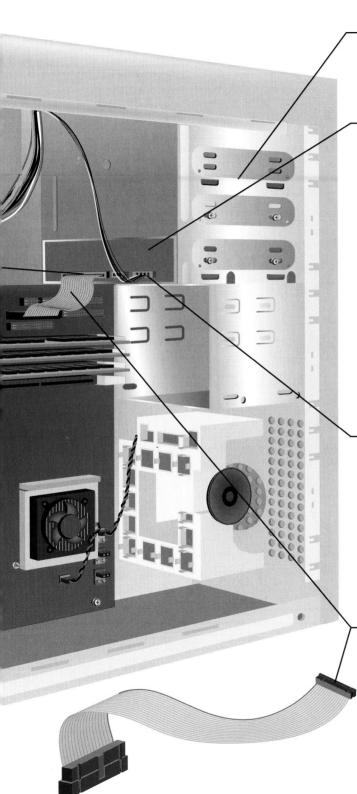

Drive bay
The tape drive, inside its sealed metal housing, fits into a drive bay on a computer. Drive bays come in three-inch and five-inch sizes, as do tape drives.

Tape drive
A tape drive is contained in a sealed metal housing. Electronics in the drive, such as read/write heads, allow it to copy data from a hard disk onto magnetic tapes placed inside the drive. These tapes can hold hundreds of megabytes, or even gigabytes, of data and can hold copies of entire hard disks. Tape backup software usually compresses data as it stores it, so you can hold much more data on a tape backup than you can on an equivalently sized hard drive. Entire hard drives can be copied onto one or multiple tapes.

The speed of the tape drive is dependent on the kind of controller they're connected to. A tape drive connected to a floppy drive controller transfers data at the same speed as a floppy drive (2.8 megabytes a minute), and an IDE/EIDE drive will go 20 to 33 megabytes per minute and beyond. If a tape drive comes with its own proprietary controller, it may work at higher speeds.

Power connector
The internal tape drive gets its power from the power supply. It connects to the power supply by a cable and connector that plugs into the tape drive. Most tape drives will connect with the larger 4-pin connector notched so that it will fit only one way.

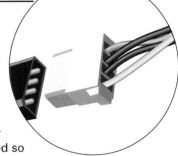

Ribbon cable
The controller sends and receives information to and from the tape drive via a ribbon cable. A connector at each end of the cable plugs into the tape drive and into the controller. In some cases, you'll use your existing hard drive IDE cable, in others you'll use your existing floppy cable, and in yet other cases you'll be given a cable to connect to the tape drive. There are also SCSI and external connections. Check your documentation to see which yours requires.

Before Installing a Tape Drive

Before you start to install your tape backup drive, you'll have to find out some things about your computer and prepare your PC for the installation. Here's what you should know and what you should do.

1 Determine the Type of Controller

Your tape drive connects to your PC via an IDE, SCSI, floppy drive, or proprietary controller. Some tape drives use a proprietary interface, which requires that you install a special card to which you'll attach your tape backup drive. For most purposes, an IDE interface will work fine. Some tape backups can also be installed as an external unit and can attach to the parallel port, USB port, or their own proprietary card.

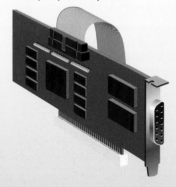

2 Check Your PC's Controller

Match the kind of tape drive and controller you want to buy to the controller you already have on your PC—and make sure that the controller can handle this new device. Check to see whether your existing controller has space to connect a tape drive. On some PCs, the controller is on the motherboard. On others, it's on a separate add-in card. If you can't fit another device onto the controller, consider buying a tape drive that connects through the parallel or USB port, or has its own card.

3 Verify You Have a Free Bay

Make sure that you have a free drive bay and that it can accommodate your tape backup drive. A three-inch tape backup drive can fit in both three- and five-inch size drive bays—to put it in the larger drive bay, you first have to install mounting rails. A five-inch tape backup unit, however, can't fit into a three-inch drive bay. If you don't have a drive bay free, you can install a parallel port tape backup drive, a USB unit, or an external drive that uses SCSI or its own card.

4 Find a Power Connector

Your tape backup drive needs to get electricity in order to work, which it gets from your power supply. Check to see that you have a spare power cable running from the power supply, that there's a free connector at the end of it, and that the cable and connector can reach to where you'll be putting in the drive. If you don't have a free power connector, you can buy a Y cable to split the power cable and gain an extra connector where you can plug in the drive.

5 Check the Ribbon Length

You attach the tape backup unit to your controller via the same ribbon cable that already runs from the controller to your hard disk or floppy disk. Make sure that this ribbon cable will reach from the controller to where you'll be installing your tape drive. In many cases, the ribbon cable will have several connectors on it, some of which may already be connected to existing devices such as your floppy drive or hard drive. Make sure there is a free connector.

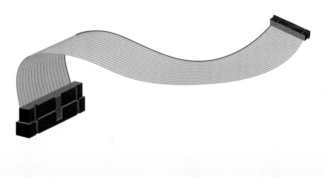

Watch Out!

- Make sure that you have a free drive bay—if not, install an external unit.
- If there's no room on your controller for the tape drive, install a parallel port, USB unit, or one that uses its own card as a proprietary controller.

How to Install a Tape Drive

After you've checked out your PC and prepared it for installing a tape backup drive, you're ready to install one. Open up the PC, slide the drive into a drive bay, attach the controller cable and power supply cable, and then turn on your computer and install drivers and backup software. Before doing anything, turn off your PC, remove the power cable and the case, and discharge static electricity or wear a wrist strap. Turn to Chapter 1, "What's Inside Your Computer," for more details.

1 Add a Proprietary Controller Card

Most tape drives connect via IDE or SCSI interfaces. However, if yours requires a proprietary card, install that, following the directions included with the tape drive. As with installing any other card, remove the backplate first, setting aside the screws so that you can use them to install the card. Next, carefully align the card in the slot and press down gently but firmly until the card is seated. Finally, when the card is securely seated, screw it into place.

2 Set the Jumpers

In some cases, you need to set jumpers on the tape drive so that it works properly with your PC. Check the tape drive's documentation for this. Turn to Chapter 1 for information on how to set jumpers.

3 Install the Tape Drive into the Bay

The tape drive should slide easily into the bay. After you slide the drive in, secure it by screwing it to the bay. When you screw the drive in, be careful not to overtighten so that you don't strip the screws.

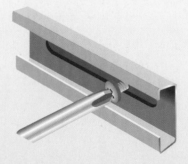

4 Attach the Ribbon Cables

Attach your tape drive to the PC by using the wide ribbon cables inside your PC. The ribbon originates on an IDE controller card on your PC or else on the motherboard itself. Locate a free connector. The ribbon cable has a stripe on one side, indicating it is the side of the cable for pin 1. Plug that into pin 1 on the tape drive; in some cases, the tape drive works off the floppy cable. If it does, check the documentation for where you need to plug the connector to the tape drive.

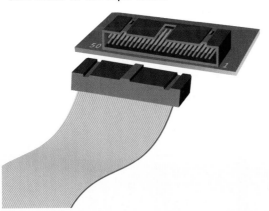

5 Attach the Power Cables

The tape drive gets its power from the power supply. A cable runs from the power supply, which you plug into the tape drive. The power supply cable has a connector on the end of it, which usually has four sockets encased in a small sheath of white plastic. Plug that into the connector on your tape drive. The tape drive should plug into the larger 4-pin connector, which is notched so that it will go in only one way. If there is no free connector, you can buy a Y splitter, which will give you an extra connector.

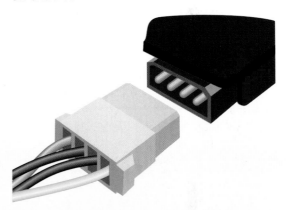

6 Install the Drivers

When you turn your computer back on, Windows usually won't recognize the tape drive. Often, you'll have to install special software that comes with the tape drive. In some cases, however, Windows might recognize that you've installed new hardware and will walk you through an installation wizard for installing drivers. For more information about installing drivers, turn to Chapter 1. After you've installed the drivers, install the backup software that came with the tape backup drive.

Watch Out!

- Try to match the size of your new tape drive to the size of your drive bay.
- If you don't have a free drive bay, consider installing a tape backup drive to your parallel port. These are easier to install than internal tape drives, but are much slower.
- Make sure that all the connections are tight before closing the case.
- When plugging the ribbon cable into your tape drive, make sure that the side with the stripe lines up with pin 1 on the tape drive.
- Make sure that when you connect the ribbon cable to the tape drive, the other connectors on the cable to your hard drive or CD don't come loose.

CHAPTER

Installing a Keyboard and Mouse

How a Keyboard and Mouse Work   130

How to Install a Mouse   132

How to Install a Keyboard   134

UPGRADING your keyboard and mouse or other pointing device is one of the easiest and least expensive ways to make your computing life more productive. Keyboards, such as the Microsoft Natural Keyboard, help minimize disorders related to typing such as carpal tunnel syndrome. And there are enhanced keyboards for Windows that have extra keys that give you fast access to features such as the Start menu or enable you to run specific programs. Similarly, a well-designed mouse makes it easier to point and click. And new mice, such as those with wheels on them, make it easier to scroll through programs and documents. If you have problems with a keyboard or mouse and can't fix it yourself, it's never worthwhile to try to get it repaired. Instead, buy a new one, and install it yourself, as detailed in this chapter. You also can install USB keyboards and mice.

How a Keyboard and Mouse Work

Keyboards and mice each plug into ports on your computer. There are several different kinds of ports for keyboards and mice, as you'll see in the following pages. Sometimes the ports for keyboards and mice look similar to one another. Make sure you plug them each into the proper ports. They are labeled with a tiny picture of a mouse and a keyboard, respectively.

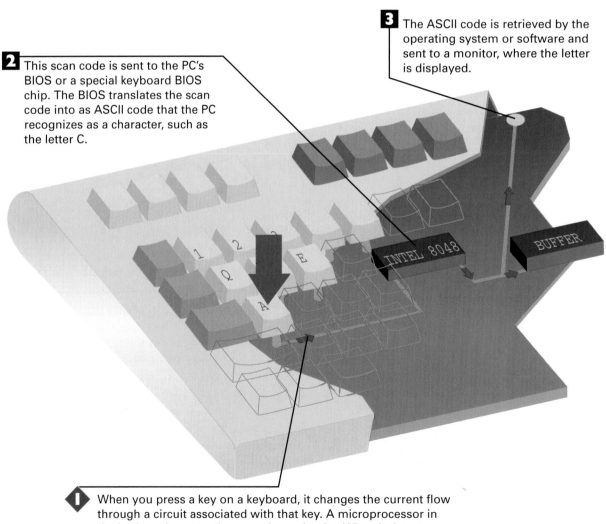

3 The ASCII code is retrieved by the operating system or software and sent to a monitor, where the letter is displayed.

2 This scan code is sent to the PC's BIOS or a special keyboard BIOS chip. The BIOS translates the scan code into as ASCII code that the PC recognizes as a character, such as the letter C.

INTEL 8048

BUFFER

1 When you press a key on a keyboard, it changes the current flow through a circuit associated with that key. A microprocessor in the keyboard constantly scans these circuits. When it detects a change in the current, it generates a scan code—a special code that indicates that a key has been pressed.

5 These rollers are each attached to wheels called encoders. As the rollers turn, they rotate the encoders. The rims of the encoders have many tiny metal contact points on them. The contact points touch contact bars and generate electric signals as the encoders move. The faster you move the mouse, the faster the encoders move, and more signals will be generated by the contact points and bars. Signals also are generated that indicate the direction of movement of the mouse.

6 The electrical signals are sent to the PC over the mouse's cable. Windows interprets these signals and moves your onscreen cursor accordingly.

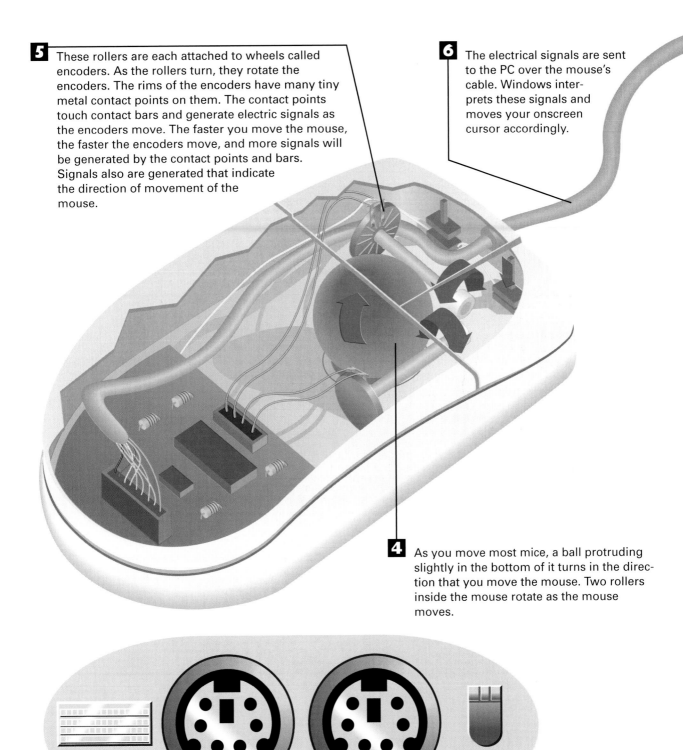

4 As you move most mice, a ball protruding slightly in the bottom of it turns in the direction that you move the mouse. Two rollers inside the mouse rotate as the mouse moves.

How to Install a Mouse

The main thing to keep in mind when installing a new mouse is the way it plugs into your PC. You can either connect it by plugging it into a PS/2 mouse port on your computer, or into a serial port. In most cases, you want to choose the mouse port. Some mice, such as those with wheels in them, require that you install special drivers. You do that after attaching your new mouse.

If you're considering an upgrade to a new mouse because the pointer doesn't seem to respond anymore, or responds erratically, first wipe the bottom of the mouse clean. You also can take out the little ball inside and clean that, as well as the contacts inside the mouse. Rubbing alcohol works well. Finally, use a new mouse pad. Often, grit and grime is the cause of this kind of problem, and you can save yourself some money by first cleaning the mouse.

▣ Determine the Type of Connector

You can plug a mouse into your PC in two different ways. You can plug it into a serial port or a PS/2 port. The connectors for each are pictured here. In general, it's a better idea to use a PS/2 port. When you use a PS/2 port, you won't use up a serial port, which is often used for other devices, such as modems. There's also less of a chance of software conflicts if you use a PS/2 mouse. However, if you don't have a PS/2 connector on your PC, you can use a serial port or a USB port.

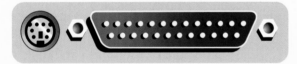

▢ Verify Port Size

There are two kinds of serial ports—a 9-pin serial port and a 25-pin serial port. Make sure that your mouse has the right connector for your PC. If it doesn't, you can buy an adapter that enables, for example, a 9-pin mouse to fit into a 25-pin serial port. To use it, plug your mouse into one end of the adapter. The other end plugs into your PC.

▣ Turn Off Your PC

Don't unplug the mouse until the PC is turned off. If you have a PS/2 mouse, you should be able to slide the connector right off. When you unplug the mouse, don't force it; it should slide off relatively easily. If you have a serial mouse, you have to unscrew it before you can slide it off. Sometimes you won't need a screwdriver for this. However, you might need a small flathead or Phillips screwdriver to unscrew it. After you unscrew the serial mouse, slide it off.

4 Plug In Your New Mouse

Be sure that you're plugging your mouse into the mouse connector and not the keyboard connector—they often look identical, but the keyboard connector has a picture of a keyboard, while a mouse connector has a picture of a mouse. Don't force the connector; that could damage it. For a serial mouse, tighten the screws either by hand or with a small flat-head or Phillips screwdriver. If your PC has two serial ports and you're plugging your mouse into a serial port, plug it into the same connector that your old mouse was plugged into.

5 Turn On Your PC

Your PC should automatically recognize the mouse when you turn it on. Some mice, however, can require special drivers—especially if you're upgrading from a normal mouse to a mouse with a wheel in the middle of it, such as the IntelliPoint mouse. In that case, install the mouse drivers after your PC turns on. See "Installing Hardware Drivers" in Chapter 1 for more information.

6 Customize How Your Mouse Works

Windows lets you adjust many of the mouse settings. You can adjust things such as the sensitivity, what the mouse cursor looks like, whether there should be animations, and similar features. Click the **Start** button, and then choose **Control Panel**. From the Control Panel, double-click **Mouse** and you are able to customize how your mouse works.

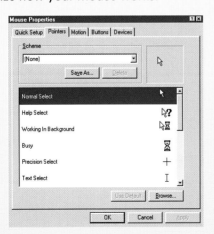

Watch Out!

- Match your mouse connector to the kind of connector on the back of your PC.
- Plug the mouse into the mouse connector, not the keyboard connector.
- Be sure the mouse is plugged in all the way before turning your PC back on.
- If your mouse requires special software, be sure to install its drivers after you turn your PC back on.

How to Install a Keyboard

Installing a keyboard is one of the simplest and most straightforward things you do when upgrading or enhancing a PC. As you see here, the main thing to look for is that you have the right kind of connector. If you have a damaged keyboard, don't bother to get it repaired. It's cheaper to buy a new one and install it yourself, unless you have a very expensive one, such as a wireless or ergonomic one.

1 Determine the Type of Connector

Keyboards have two main kinds of connectors—a larger 5-pin DIN keyboard connector and the smaller 6-pin mini DIN connector, also called the PS/2 connector. You can also install a USB keyboard. When you buy a new keyboard, you want to choose a connector of the same type that you already have; otherwise, it won't be able to be plugged into your PC.

2 Buy Another Keyboard

If you get a keyboard with a 5-pin DIN connector, but your PC accepts only a 6-pin PS/2 connection—or vice versa—you can still plug it in. You need a keyboard adapter. To use it, plug your keyboard into one end of the adapter. The other end plugs into your PC. If your keyboard cable isn't long enough, you can also buy an extension cable for it.

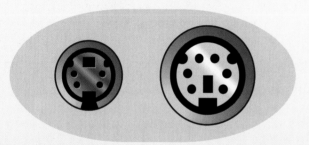

3 Unplug the Old Keyboard

Don't unplug the keyboard until the PC is turned off. When you unplug the keyboard, don't force it; it should slide off relatively easily.

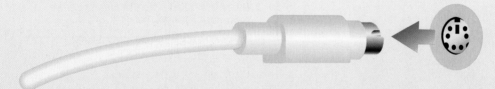

4 Plug In the New Keyboard

Be sure when you plug in the new keyboard that you align the pin connectors properly. Also, check to see that you're plugging it into the keyboard connector and not the mouse connector—they often look identical, but the keyboard connector has a small picture of a keyboard next to it, while the mouse connector has a small picture of a mouse. Don't force the connector into the plug—if it doesn't plug in easily, the pins probably aren't aligned. If you push, you could damage the connector.

5 Turn On Your Computer

When you turn it on, your computer should automatically recognize your new keyboard without any problems. However, if you haven't plugged it in properly, your keyboard might not boot up all the way. Many PCs beep twice to indicate when there's been a keyboard error, and often an error message also appears on your screen telling you there's been a problem with the keyboard. If this happens, turn off the computer, unplug the keyboard, and then plug it back in again. This should solve the problem.

6 Install Any Special Drivers

Some keyboards with extra features and capabilities might need to have drivers installed in order to make use of those features. If drivers are required, they come on a disk or CD with the keyboard. Install the drivers from the disk or CD to make full use of the keyboard's capabilities.

Watch Out!

- Match your keyboard connector to the kind of connector on the back of your PC.
- Be sure to turn off and unplug your computer before disconnecting the keyboard—otherwise, you could blow a small inline fuse on the motherboard.
- Plug the keyboard into the keyboard connector, not the mouse connector.
- Be sure the keyboard is plugged in all the way before turning your PC back on.
- Check to see there's nothing on the keyboard holding down a key when you turn your computer on. If there is, the computer might refuse to boot.

CHAPTER

Installing a Joystick or Other Gaming Devices

How a Joystick Works   **138**

How to Install a Joystick   **140**

IF you play games much, you'll want a joystick or other gaming device. A mouse and the keyboard simply don't offer the kinds of control that a joystick or other gaming device does.

Joysticks and other gaming devices enable you to more easily do things such as control the direction of your movement, especially in 3D and driving games. With a mouse or keyboard, it's awkward to control these kinds of games, but joysticks and other gaming devices make it easy to play the games with more natural movements. And gaming devices include a variety of programmable buttons that enable you to control features of games, such as accelerating or braking in driving games, or shooting weapons in action games.

Many new joysticks include a "force-feedback" feature, making for much more realistic game play. With force feedback, the joystick responds much as it would in real-life situations. For example, if you crash in the game, you'll feel the crash through a jolt in the joystick; or, if you're making a tight turn with a car at high speed, you'll feel the same kind of pressure on the joystick as you would on a car's steering wheel in the same situation.

It's quite easy to add a joystick. You connect it to your PC via a game port or a USB port, install software or drivers, and you're done. This chapter shows you how the devices work, as well as how to install them. You install other gaming devices in the same way as you install joysticks.

How a Joystick Works

Position sensors
Attached to the yoke are sensors that respond to the movements of the joystick in the X- and Y-axes. The sensors interpret the precise X-Y coordinates of each movement of the joystick and send signals describing the movement to the game card (or sound card, if the joystick is attached to a sound card, as many are). Software then interprets those signals and controls game play. In force-feedback joysticks, signals are sent back from the computer through software and the game or sound card—and these signals tell the joystick when to make a "jolt," to apply force to your hand, or similar motions.

Ports
The joystick attaches to a game port on a PC, which is often found on a sound card, although it can also be found on a separate game card. Joysticks can also attach to a USB port. In many cases, you can connect more than one joystick or gaming device to your PC through the use of a *Y-adapter*. Keep in mind, however, that in some instances you won't be able to use a Y-adapter to connect two gaming devices to your PC, because there may be incompatibilities among devices. Check the documentation to make sure.

Yoke
The joystick's handle is connected at its base to a yoke inside the joystick. This yoke enables the joystick to move freely in any direction.

X-Y coordinates
Your computer responds to the motion of your joystick by interpreting the position of the X-Y coordinates of the joystick handle. The joystick's X-axis controls the side-to-side motion in games; the Y-axis, shifted 90 degrees from the X-axis, controls forward and backward movements.

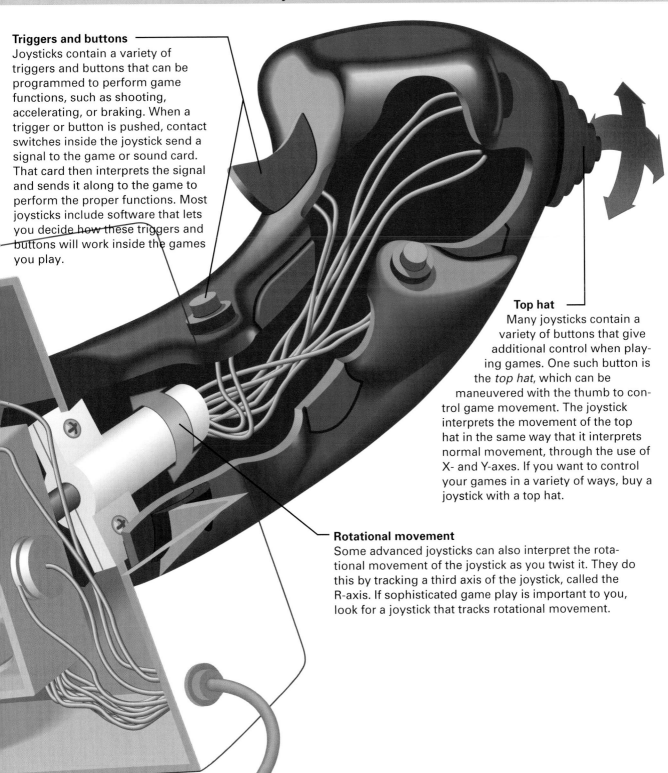

Triggers and buttons
Joysticks contain a variety of triggers and buttons that can be programmed to perform game functions, such as shooting, accelerating, or braking. When a trigger or button is pushed, contact switches inside the joystick send a signal to the game or sound card. That card then interprets the signal and sends it along to the game to perform the proper functions. Most joysticks include software that lets you decide how these triggers and buttons will work inside the games you play.

Top hat
Many joysticks contain a variety of buttons that give additional control when playing games. One such button is the *top hat*, which can be maneuvered with the thumb to control game movement. The joystick interprets the movement of the top hat in the same way that it interprets normal movement, through the use of X- and Y-axes. If you want to control your games in a variety of ways, buy a joystick with a top hat.

Rotational movement
Some advanced joysticks can also interpret the rotational movement of the joystick as you twist it. They do this by tracking a third axis of the joystick, called the R-axis. If sophisticated game play is important to you, look for a joystick that tracks rotational movement.

How to Install a Joystick

Whether you install a joystick or other gaming device, you follow the same steps: Plug in the device, run the installation software or add drivers, and then calibrate it.

1 Plug In the Joystick

The joystick plugs into the game port (sometimes called a MIDI port), which is usually found on the back of your PC. It's generally attached to your PC's sound card or a special gaming card. It will usually be a 15-pin female connector. Turn off your PC before plugging in the joystick. If you don't have a game port, install a sound card, which has one on it. Turn to Chapter 18, "Installing a Sound Card and Speakers," for information on how to install a sound card.

2 Attach a USB Joystick

If you are installing a USB joystick, attach the USB cable to your joystick and to the USB port on your computer. You don't have to turn off your PC before installing a USB joystick. If your USB ports are full with other devices, you can buy a USB hub that allows you to plug multiple USB devices into a single unit. For more information about USB devices, turn to Chapter 20, "Installing USB Devices."

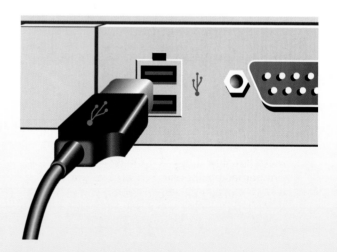

3 Install Manufacturer's Software

If the joystick comes with installation software, run it. Joysticks often come with installation software that sets up your joystick for you. If yours comes with installation software, run it now.

4 Install Windows Software

If no installation software is included, tell Windows to recognize your joystick by using the Add New Hardware feature. To do this, first go to the Windows Control Panel by clicking the **Start** button, choosing **Settings**, and then selecting **Control Panel**. Double-click **Add New Hardware**. A wizard launches that will guide you through installation. For some joysticks, you should instead use the "add" feature under Game Controllers in Control Panel. Check your documentation.

5 Insert Manufacturer's Disk

At some point, the wizard will ask whether you have a disk for your new joystick. If you have one, insert it at the right time, and then choose the device's .inf file from the disk. If no disks are supplied by the manufacturer, choose the type of joystick you have from the list supplied by the wizard. If your joystick isn't on the list, choose one from the list that will most closely match your joystick, which very often is CH Flightstick Pro.

6 Calibrate Your Joystick

For best gaming results, calibrate your joystick so that it responds in the best possible way. Check your joystick's documentation for details on how to do that. After you calibrate your joystick, you can program how it works for different games by choosing a "profile" for each game. Check your documentation to see how.

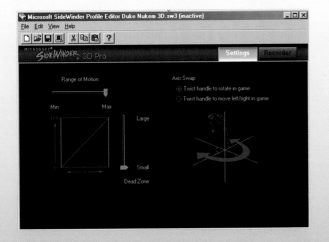

Watch Out!

- Before installing your joystick, check Windows' Device Manager to make sure that your game port is working properly.
- If your PC has more than one game port, connect the joystick to the game port on your sound card.
- Be sure that the connections you make are tight before using the joystick.
- After installing the joystick, check for updated drivers and other profile software from the manufacturer's Web site.

CHAPTER

Installing a Scanner

How a Scanner Works   144

How to Install a Parallel Port Scanner   146

How to Install a USB Scanner   148

How to Install a SCSI Scanner   150

THERE are several kinds of scanners that you can hook up to your PC, but the best kind is a flatbed scanner. Scanners enable you to take images and text from pictures, photographs, paper printouts, books, or other sources, and transfer them to your computer. To get the text and images into your computer, you first place the image source, such as paper, on a flatbed scanner, which then scans the image or text from the paper into your PC. This chapter shows you how to install a flatbed scanner; you can install other types of scanners, including handheld and page-fed scanners, the same way as you install flatbed scanners.

In general, scanners attach to a PC via the parallel port, a USB port, or via a SCSI connection. The SCSI connection transfers text and images to your PC from the scanner at the highest rate of speed, although it is also the most difficult to install. The easiest scanner to install is via the USB port, which transfers data faster than a parallel port scanner.

How a Scanner Works

Image
The process begins by placing an image face down on a glass window in the scanner. Beneath the glass window is a light source and a scanning mechanism—the scan head.

PC connection
The pixels are sent to the PC via one of a variety of physical connections. Some scanners are connected via the parallel port, others via a USB port, and still others via a SCSI connection. No matter what connection is used, the data is stored on the PC in a digital format.

Diodes
The scanner lens focuses the light onto devices called *diodes*. These diodes translate light into electrical current. As the strength of the light changes, so does the strength of the electrical current. When there is more light, the voltage is greater; when there's less light, the voltage is less.

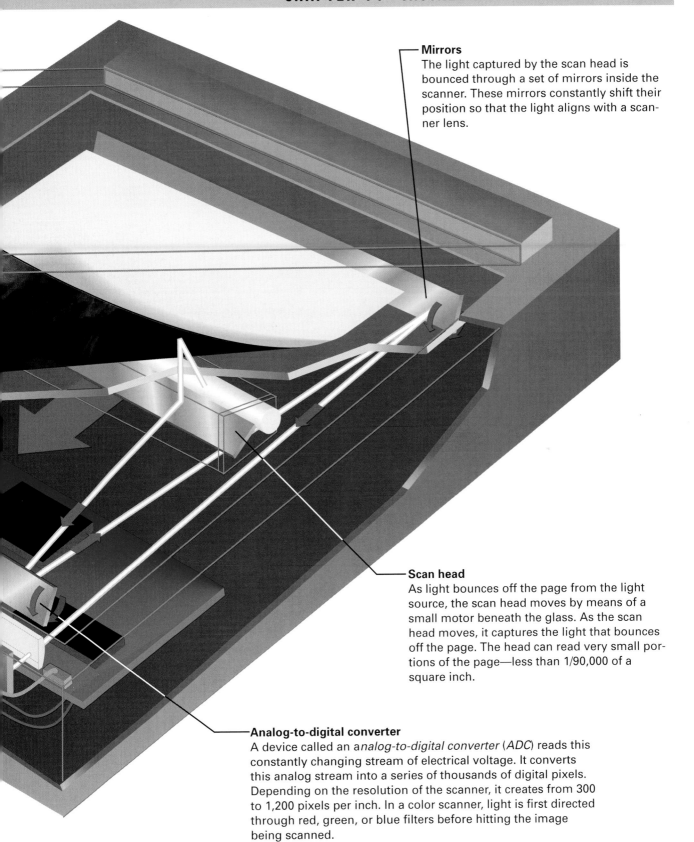

Mirrors
The light captured by the scan head is bounced through a set of mirrors inside the scanner. These mirrors constantly shift their position so that the light aligns with a scanner lens.

Scan head
As light bounces off the page from the light source, the scan head moves by means of a small motor beneath the glass. As the scan head moves, it captures the light that bounces off the page. The head can read very small portions of the page—less than 1/90,000 of a square inch.

Analog-to-digital converter
A device called an *analog-to-digital converter* (*ADC*) reads this constantly changing stream of electrical voltage. It converts this analog stream into a series of thousands of digital pixels. Depending on the resolution of the scanner, it creates from 300 to 1,200 pixels per inch. In a color scanner, light is first directed through red, green, or blue filters before hitting the image being scanned.

How to Install a Parallel Port Scanner

Parallel port scanners are easier to install than SCSI scanners, although they're also slower than SCSI scanners. Keep in mind when you install a parallel port scanner that you usually won't be able to use your printer and your scanner at the same time.

■ Place the Scanner on a Flat Surface

Before doing anything, turn off your PC. Next, put the scanner on a flat nearby surface, and make sure it's close enough to your PC so that its cable can reach your computer.

■ Attach the Parallel Cable

Unplug the printer's parallel cable from your PC and plug the scanner's parallel cable to your computer, into the port where the printer's cable was attached. When you plug the scanner's parallel cable to your PC, you plug its 25-pin female end into the PC. The other end of the cable plugs into the scanner's port. If you want to use your printer as well as your scanner, connect the printer to your scanner with cable, and then connect your scanner to your computer.

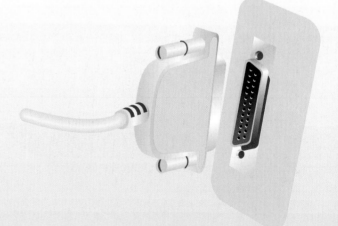

■ Turn On the Scanner

Plug the scanner's power cord into an outlet. When you plug it in, the scanner may turn on by itself. Some scanners need you to turn them on; others don't need to be turned on. If yours has an on/off switch, turn the switch on after you plug in the cord.

4 Turn On Your PC

When you turn on your computer, Windows will know new hardware has been added. If, when you turn on your PC, it doesn't automatically recognize that new hardware has been added, you can tell your computer that new hardware is present. To add the new hardware, first go to the Windows Control Panel by clicking the **Start** button, choosing **Settings**, and then selecting **Control Panel**. Double-click **Add New Hardware**. A wizard launches that will guide you through the installation process.

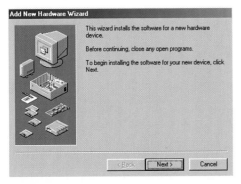

5 Insert the Driver Disk

At some point, the wizard will ask whether you have a disk for your new scanner. If you have one, insert it at the correct time, and then choose the device's INF file from the disk.

6 Calibrate the Scanner

Most scanners come with extra software you can use for scanning and using scanned images. Check the documentation to see whether yours does. If it does, install the software. For best scanning results, calibrate your scanner before you begin to use it. Check your scanner's documentation for details on how to do that.

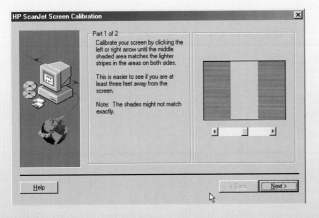

Watch Out!

- Before adding a parallel port scanner to a machine with an existing printer, you should go to the printer vendor's site and update to the latest drivers.

- Check the scanner's documentation to see whether the scanner requires an Enhanced (EPP, SPP, ECP) Parallel Port. If so, you may need to change this option under your CMOS.

How to Install a USB Scanner

DRIVERS

USB scanners are the newest type of scanners, and tend to be the easiest to install. Unlike parallel port scanners, you can also use them at the same time as your printer. They are, however, slower than SCSI scanners.

1 Place the Scanner on a Flat Surface

Before doing anything, turn off your PC. Next, put the scanner on a flat nearby surface, and make sure it's close enough to your PC so that its cable can reach your computer.

2 Connect the Scanner Cable

The scanner came with a USB cable. Attach it to your scanner. Look for the square end, and plug that into the proper port on the scanner.

3 Turn On the Scanner

When you plug the scanner into an outlet, it may turn on by itself. Some scanners need you to turn them on; others don't need to be turned on. If yours has an on/off switch, turn the switch on after you plug in the cord.

4 Install the Scanner's Software

Most scanners come with software you can use for scanning and using scanned images, and for setting up the scanner to work with your PC. If you have a USB scanner, install the software. In some instances, you won't need to first install your scanner software before installing the scanner—check the scanner's documentation to make sure.

5 Connect the USB Cable to the PC

Find the rectangular end of the USB cable, and plug it into the USB port on your computer. If your USB ports are full with other devices, you can buy a USB hub that enables you to plug multiple USB devices into a single unit. In some instances, you won't need to first install your scanner software before plugging in your USB cable. When you plug in the USB cable, it will automatically recognize you're adding new hardware. Check your system's documentation.

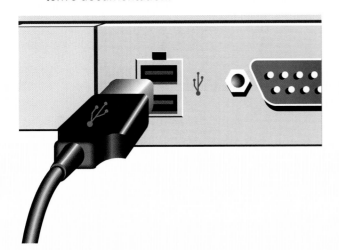

6 Calibrate the Scanner

When you restart your computer, it will recognize your scanner. If your scanner has more software beyond what you've already installed, it will prompt you to install that software now. You won't need to reboot your computer in all cases, because some scanners may not require that. Check your documentation. For best scanning results, calibrate your scanner before you begin to use it. Check your scanner's documentation for details on how to do that.

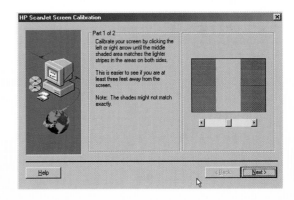

Watch Out!

■ If this is the first USB device you install, make sure your USB ports are enabled in your CMOS.

■ If you don't have a USB port on your PC, you can add one in. Turn to Chapter 20, "Installing USB Devices," to see how.

How to Install a SCSI Scanner

A SCSI scanner is the fastest scanner you can buy, although as with any SCSI device, it can be a bit problematic to install. If you already have a SCSI device or connection in your PC, though, it's easier than if you don't have the connection yet, because then you won't have to install a SCSI card as well.

You need a SCSI card in your computer to use a SCSI scanner. For information on how to install a SCSI card, turn to Chapter 9, "Installing a SCSI Drive."

1 Place the Scanner on a Flat Surface

Before doing anything, turn off your PC. Then, put the scanner on a nearby flat surface. Make sure that it's close enough to your PC so that its cable can reach your computer.

2 Plug In the SCSI Cable

Using a SCSI cable, connect your scanner to the SCSI port on your PC, or into the SCSI port of another SCSI device. When connecting the cable to the SCSI port, make sure that you don't mistakenly plug it into the parallel port. Sometimes a parallel port can look like a certain kind of SCSI connector. The parallel port is where your printer plugs into and is often labeled with a picture of a printer. Most SCSI connectors are 50-, 68-, or 72-pin connections.

3 Set the Scanner's SCSI ID Number

Every SCSI device must have a unique ID number. In scanners, you often set this from the back. If the scanner will be at the end of the SCSI daisy chain, plug a terminator into the scanner or use a dip switch. If this is the only external device that is going to be on your SCSI controller, and you have internal hard drives, you may have to disable the termination on your controller card in order for the scanner to work. Check your controller documentation on terminating external SCSI chains.

4 Turn On the Scanner

When you plug the scanner into an outlet, it may turn on by itself. Some scanners need you to turn them on; others don't need to be turned on. If yours has an on/off switch, turn the switch on after you plug in the cord.

5 Turn On Your PC

When you turn on your computer, Windows will know that new hardware has been added. If your PC doesn't recognize that new hardware has been added, add it yourself. Go to the **Control Panel** and double-click **Add New Hardware**. A wizard launches that will guide you through the installation process. At some point, the wizard will ask whether you have a disk for your new scanner. If you have one, insert it at the correct time, and then choose the device's INF file from the disk.

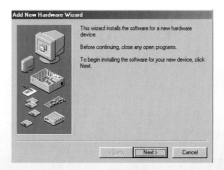

6 Calibrate the Scanner

Most scanners come with extra software you can use for scanning and using scanned images. Check the documentation to see whether yours does. If it does, install the software. For best scanning results, calibrate your scanner before you begin to use it. Check your scanner's documentation for details on how to do that.

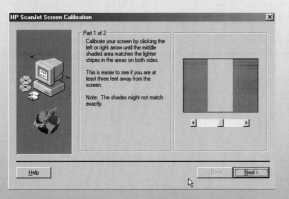

Watch Out!

- If you installed a SCSI controller with your scanner, when you turn on your computer, Windows will first have to install the SCSI controller before installing the scanner.

- If the SCSCI connection doesn't match your existing SCSI connector, buy a SCSI converter that will let you attach it.

CHAPTER

15

Installing a Digital Camera

How a Digital Camera Works   154

How to Install a Digital Camera   156

DIGITAL cameras are quickly replacing the more traditional kind. They enable you to preview pictures before taking them, and after you take the photos, no film is required—all you need is your computer. And if you take a photo you don't like, you don't waste any film—just delete it from your camera and try again.

After you take them, the pictures are stored in memory on the camera where you can view them on a small screen without using a computer. When you want to use the pictures, you attach the digital camera to your computer via a cable. You can then view the pictures in the camera, transfer them to your PC, and then manipulate them there or print them out on a color or black-and-white printer. A digital camera attaches to a PC via a serial cable or USB cable.

Your pictures are stored on a flash memory card in the camera. You can buy more than one card so that you can take more pictures, and also a card reader that connects to your PC. If you do that, you'll never have to connect the camera to your computer—you'll only need to put the card into the reader; then you'll be able to transfer pictures to your computer that way.

How a Digital Camera Works

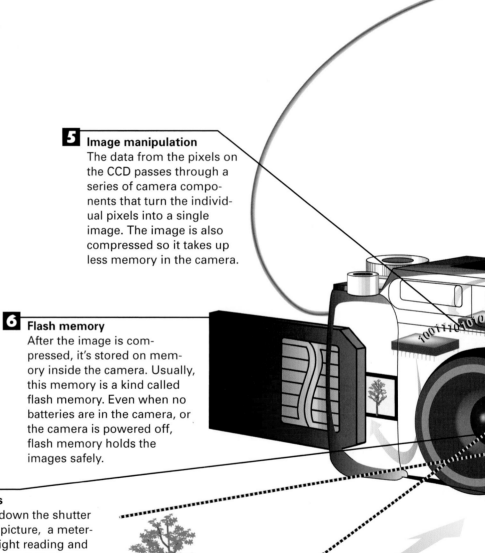

5 **Image manipulation**
The data from the pixels on the CCD passes through a series of camera components that turn the individual pixels into a single image. The image is also compressed so it takes up less memory in the camera.

6 **Flash memory**
After the image is compressed, it's stored on memory inside the camera. Usually, this memory is a kind called flash memory. Even when no batteries are in the camera, or the camera is powered off, flash memory holds the images safely.

1 **Shutter and lens**
When you hold down the shutter button to take a picture, a metering cell takes a light reading and determines how much light is required for the exposure. It then instructs the shutter to stay open for a specific amount of time. The lens focuses the image, as it does in a traditional camera.

7 **PC transfer**
To manipulate and print the pictures, you must transfer them to a computer. The digital camera attaches to the computer via a cable of some kind, often a USB or serial connection. Even after you transfer the pictures to your computer, they stay on the digital camera until you delete them either using the PC software or using the camera itself.

4 **Digital conversion**
After the exposure, each pixel's charge is converted into a digital number, corresponding to the amount of light that fell on that particular pixel.

2 **Image sensor**
Instead of hitting film, as in a traditional camera, the light hits an image sensor, called a charged-coupling device (CCD). The image sensor is a silicon chip about the size of a fingernail and contains a grid made up of millions of photosensitive pixels.

3 **Pixels**
Each site on the CCD captures a single pixel—either red, blue, or green. Where that color light falls on the pixel, it records the color; if the color doesn't fall on the pixel, it remains dark. Each pixel can record only a single specific color. So, if red light falls on a blue-recording pixel, for example, that pixel won't record any data. Each pixel retains a charge that corresponds to the brightness of the light falling on it. So, when a great deal of light falls on a pixel, it has a high charge, and if little light falls on it, it has a low charge.

How to Install a Digital Camera

Two major things must be done to install a digital camera. First, you must prepare the camera so it can be used on its own. Second, you must connect the camera to your PC and install software so the camera can transfer pictures to your PC. To prepare the camera, you must install batteries and a storage card, which holds the camera's pictures. Then, you connect the camera to your PC with a cable and install the camera software.

1 Install the Batteries

Open thebattery compartment and insert the batteries, taking care to line up the positive and negative terminals properly.

2 Insert the Memory Card

Most digital cameras require you to install a small memory card called flash memory or a smart card. This memory card is what holds your pictures. You can even buy additional memory cards and swap them to store more images. Insert the memory card into the camera. Some cameras also require that you format the memory card after you've installed it. Follow the camera's directions for how to format the card—each camera does it differently.

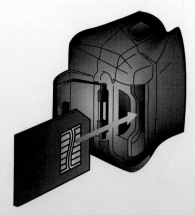

3 Turn On the Power

For many digital cameras, to turn on the power, all you need to do is slide open the lens protector on the front of the camera. If your memory card needs to be formatted, you'll usually get an error message telling you a problem exists with the card, so now is the time to format.

4 Connect the Camera to Your Computer

Some cameras connect via a USB cable, whereas others connect via a serial port. Either way, the cables will connect only one way, so don't force them. If you don't have a free USB port on your PC, you can buy a USB hub to give you four USB ports into which you can plug devices. If you don't have a USB port, you can install one in your computer. (To learn how to install USB hubs and ports, turn to Chapter 20, "Installing USB Devices.")

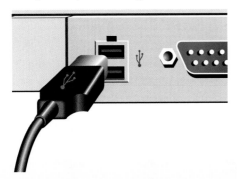

5 Run Software and Follow Installation Instructions

If you're connecting via a USB cable, your computer will recognize that you're adding a digital camera. The Add New Hardware Wizard will appear, or an installation routine will automatically start. Follow the onscreen directions for completing the installation. For serial connections, your computer might not recognize the camera, so you must install the software that came with your camera. Even if you install via USB, however, be sure you install the software for your camera after you follow the installation instructions. In either case, you might have to go through two installation routines: one to install drivers for the camera, and one to install software to work with the camera.

6 Take Pictures and Transfer Them

After you've installed the camera, unplug it and take pictures, following the camera's instructions. Then, use the camera software you installed to view the pictures on your camera and transfer them to your PC.

Watch Out!

- Be sure you install the correct type of memory card into your camera. 3.3V cards and 5V cards both exist, so match the proper card to your camera's specifications.

- Keep memory cards away from extreme heat and magnets—both can destroy data.

- Use only the type of batteries specified by the camera manufacturer. Some cameras can be damaged by overheating if you use manganese batteries.

- Never mix old and new batteries or different brands of batteries together.

CHAPTER

Installing and Upgrading a Graphics Card and Monitor

How a Graphics Card and Monitor Work   160

Before Installing a Graphics Card   162

How to Install a Graphics Card   164

How to Install a Monitor   166

How to Install a Second Monitor   168

How to Install a Flat Panel Monitor   170

ONE of the most important upgrades you can make to your computer is to add a new graphics card or monitor. You'll see the following improvements: a far richer and more detailed display on your computer; more of the screen displays, because you'll be able to run it at higher resolutions; and, particularly if you play games, you'll see a huge difference in the quality of how you run your software. The newest generation of graphics cards features 3D technology, which enables you to play the most realistic-looking three-dimensional games. In fact, without a 3D graphics card, there are many games you won't even be able to play. Many graphics and computer-aided design programs make use of 3D graphics cards as well.

This chapter shows you how to install a new graphics card and monitor, and also shows you how you can use two monitors on a single PC if you use Windows 98 or above.

How a Graphics Card and Monitor Work

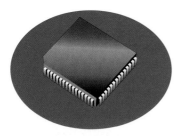

Embedded graphics chip

Some graphics processors aren't on a separate card, but instead are on a chip on the motherboard itself. If you want to upgrade a PC that has an embedded graphics processor, you first have to disable the graphics processor on the motherboard. Normally, this is done either via a jumper on the motherboard or by changing a BIOS setting. Check the documentation that came with your computer to see how to do it.

Graphics card

To display graphics on your PC, you need a graphics card. The card is attached to the motherboard via a slot. (In some cases, graphics capabilities are instead built directly into the motherboard via an embedded graphics chip.) There are many different kinds of cards with differing capabilities, such as 3D cards that accelerate the display of 3D graphics. As a way to speed up graphics processing, graphics cards have special graphics coprocessors that perform graphics tasks so that the main CPU doesn't have to. Graphics cards also have memory devoted solely to graphics. The more memory on a card, the higher the resolution and the greater the number of colors that can be displayed. Some new graphics cards require that you have an AGP slot on your computer, which increases your graphics processing even further.

Video port

The graphics card sends its signals to the monitor through a port on the back of the card. The monitor cable plugs into this port. It is normally a 15-pin female connector.

Monitor

The signals are sent to the monitor, where they're displayed. Monitors come in many different sizes, such as 15-inch, 17-inch, 19-inch, and 21-inch. If you want to use higher resolutions, you do best to use a large monitor. If you use high resolutions on a small monitor, it will be very hard to see anything.

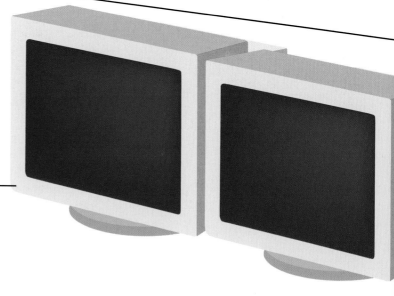

Two monitors

In Windows 98 and above, two monitors can be run off the same computer. In order to do that, you have to have two separate graphics cards, so that each monitor plugs into its own card. This works best if both graphics cards are the same make and model, although it's not required that they be.

Before Installing a Graphics Card

Before you install or upgrade a graphics card, there are a few basic steps you should take. You need to find out what card you now have, decide what card to buy, and make sure that whatever you buy works with your system and your monitor. Most newer 3D graphics cards also require that you have a Pentium running at 133Mhz or faster.

❶ Determine Graphics Card Type

Before you can decide what kind of graphics card to buy, you should know what you have now. To see the make of your graphics card, first right-click **My Computer** and choose **Properties**. Then, click **Device Manager**, click the **+** sign next to Display Adapters, and you see your graphics card. For more information about the card, right-click it and choose **Properties**. Also look for your system documentation; it has details about your graphics card.

❷ Determine Monitor Capabilities

When you buy a new graphics card, you want to be sure that it works properly with your monitor. Check your system documentation to see what kind of capabilities your monitor has. You especially want to know what the maximum resolution is and the maximum number of colors it can display, as well as its maximum refresh rate. To take full advantage of a new card, the monitor should be able to generate a 1,024×768 resolution at 16-bit or better color, and support a refresh rate of 70Hz or higher.

3 Determine the Type of Slot

You'll either be installing the new graphics card into the slot where you're going to take out your old graphics card, or you'll be putting it into an empty one. If you have a Pentium II PC, you might have an AGP slot with a graphics card in it. If you do, buy an AGP graphics card, because that's the fastest type. Otherwise, use a PCI slot, which is second only to AGP in terms of speed.

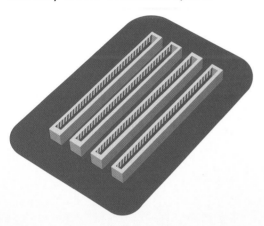

4 Decide What Card to Buy

Graphics cards can cost less than $100 or over $1,000. The more expensive cards are for those who do professional design or photo editing. The least expensive won't accelerate your PC for playing games. For most purposes, buy a card with 3D capabilities and with 8MB or more of RAM. The more RAM on the card, the higher the resolution and the more colors it will run. If you plan to play 3D games, get 16MB or 32MB. If you're going to install a flat panel monitor, you'll have to buy a digital graphics card.

5 Verify That the Card Matches

The card you buy has to be able to work in the slot that you're going to have free. And you want to match its capabilities to those of your monitor. Be sure that your card and monitor can both display at the resolution with the same number of colors—and that their maximum refresh rates match. Bring your monitor's specifications with you to the store so you can match it to your graphics card. If you're going to install a flat panel monitor, make sure the graphics card you buy will work with it.

6 Buy the Best You Can Afford

When buying a graphics card, it's best to buy more memory and capabilities than you need today. Will you be buying a larger monitor at some point? If so, you'll want to be sure that your card supports higher resolutions than you now use. And software—games in particular—continually needs more processor power and memory, so plan for tomorrow, not just today.

Watch Out!

- Be sure the graphics card you buy works with the slots you have on your PC.
- If you have a monitor that isn't capable of displaying high resolutions and many colors, consider buying a new monitor to take advantage of your new graphics card.
- Buy a card that will be capable of doing things you want to do in the future, not just today.
- In Pentium IIs, IIIs, and IVs, there are two types of AGP slots—AGP 2x and AGP 4x (which runs twice as fast as AGP 2x). Check the documentation for which yours is and buy the proper graphics card for it.

How to Install a Graphics Card

After you've decided what graphics card to install, you're ready to go. You'll have to open up your PC, take out your old graphics card, and then put in a new one.

1 Change Your Video Driver

Before installing a new video card, change the driver to a standard VGA driver. Right-click **My Computer**, choose **Properties**, click the **Device Manager** tab, click the **+** sign next to Display Adapters, and click your video card. Next, click the **Properties** button and then the **Driver** tab. Click **Update Driver**. When the screen appears asking, "What do you want Windows to do?" click the bottom button to display a list of all the drivers available on your computer. On the next screen that appears, choose **Show All Hardware**. Scroll to the top of the screen on the left and choose **Standard Display Types**. Then, from the right side, choose **Standard Display Adapter**. Reboot when prompted.

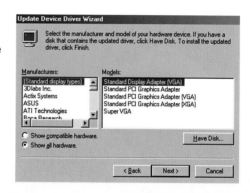

2 Take the Case off Your PC

Turn off your PC, remove the power cable and monitor cable, wear an antistatic wrist strap or ground yourself, and take the case off your PC. It's important to get rid of any static electricity by touching the power supply, because you don't want to harm any of your computer's internal components.

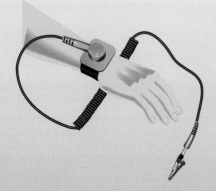

3 Remove Your Existing Card

Your graphics card is secured to the computer by a screw attaching it to the backplate. Using a Phillips screwdriver, remove the screw. After you remove the screw, remove the card. With one hand on each side of the card, pull it up firmly but carefully. If it won't budge, rock the back and then the front end to free it, and then pull it up.

4 Disable Embedded Graphics Chips

Some computers don't have graphics cards, but instead use a graphics chip embedded on the motherboard. If you have one like this, you have to disable the graphics chip before you can install a graphics card. You might have to disable it with DIP switches or jumpers, or it might be in the BIOS (in which case you'd have to disable the chip before you turn off your computer). Check your system documentation on how to do it.

5 Install the Graphics Card

Carefully position the card over the slot and push it down with even force. Press it down all the way. When the card is fully in the slot, screw it into the backplate using a Phillips screwdriver. If you're installing a board into a PCI slot, always install the graphics card in one of the first two slots. The slots are numbered on the motherboard.

6 Install Any Drivers

When you turn your computer back on, a dialog box should appear, walking you through installing drivers for your new graphics card. If Windows doesn't detect the card, go to the Windows **Control Panel** and double-click **Add New Hardware**. A wizard guides you through the installation process. If you have a disk from the manufacturer with drivers on it, insert it when prompted, and choose the driver from there. Restart Windows. If your graphics cards came with custom utilities and software, install them after you restart your computer.

Watch Out!

- If you turn your computer back on after installing a graphics card, no image appears on your screen, and you hear a beeping from the computer's speakers, you probably didn't seat the card properly in its slot. Open the case and reseat the card.

- When you put a graphics card into your PC, be sure that you press down all the way so that the connection into the slot is tight.

- Change your current video driver to standard VGA adapter before installing a new card.

- After installing the card, head to the manufacturer's Web site to download the newest drivers for your card—as video drives are updated all the time.

How to Install a Monitor

Installing a new monitor is one of the easiest ways to upgrade your PC. All you need to do is plug it in and install new drivers.

1 Unplug Your Old Monitor

Turn off your computer before installing a new monitor. And then, unplug your old monitor. You need to unplug its connection from your PC, and also unplug its power cord. In most instances, the power cord runs to an outlet, but in some cases, the power cord might plug into your PC.

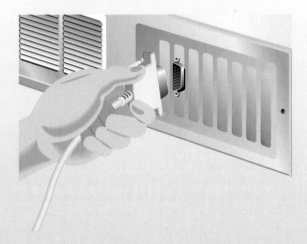

2 Plug In Your New Monitor's Cables

You need to plug cables into the PC's video port and into a power outlet. Plug your new monitor into the same video port where you unplugged your old monitor. Most monitors plug into a 15-hole port. Plug your monitor's power supply cable into an outlet. If your PC has a power supply cable, plug into it instead. Plug the power supply cable into your PC.

❸ Turn On Your Computer

When you turn your computer back on, it should detect your new hardware. Follow the directions for installing the drivers for your monitor. At some point the wizard asks whether you have a disk for your new monitor. If you have one, insert it at the right time, and then choose the driver from there. In many cases, you won't need to install drivers, because many monitors work with generic Windows plug-and-play monitor drivers.

❹ Troubleshoot Installation Problems

If Windows doesn't detect your monitor, you have to manually tell Windows to find it. Go to the **Control Panel** and double-click **Add New Hardware**. An installation wizard will launch. At some point the wizard asks whether you have a disk for your new monitor. If you have one, insert it at the correct time, and then choose the driver from there. If your monitor comes with special software or utilities, install them after you've installed the drivers.

Watch Out!

■ After you've installed your monitor, check the manufacturer's Web site to see whether newer drivers are available.

■ Your computer's capability to detect plug-and-play monitors may be disabled, To make sure it isn't, double-click the **Display** icon in Control Panel, click the **Settings** tab, click the **Advanced** button, click the **Monitor** tab, and make sure the check box is checked next to **Automatically detect plug-and-play monitors**.

How to Install a Second Monitor

If you have Windows 98 or better, you can take advantage of one of the more intriguing features of Windows—the ability to use two monitors simultaneously. Using two monitors gives you much more screen real estate, because you are able to work on both screens. Those who create graphics or use desktop publishing software will be most interested in installing two monitors. Here's how to do it.

▌ Install a Second Graphics Card

For Windows 98 or better to enable you to use two monitors, you need to have a second graphics card. First, install a graphics card and its drivers as outlined earlier in this chapter, while keeping your existing graphics card and monitor. Both graphics cards must be PCI or AGP style cards. It works best if both video cards are the same make, although it's not required.

▌ Plug In Your New Monitor's Cables

Attach your new monitor to the graphics card that you just installed. To do that, plug cables into the card's video port. Most monitors plug into a 15-hole port. After you do that, plug your monitor's power supply cable into an outlet. If your PC has the power supply cable, plug into it instead, and plug the power supply cable into your PC.

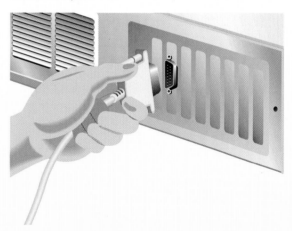

▌ Turn On Your Computer

When you turn your computer back on, a dialog box should appear, telling you that new hardware has been detected. Follow the directions for installing the drivers for your monitor. At some point the wizard asks whether you have a disk for your new monitor. If you have one, insert it at the correct time, and then choose the driver from there. In many cases, you won't need to install drivers, because many monitors work with generic Windows plug-and-play monitor drivers.

4 Troubleshoot Installation Problems

If Windows doesn't detect your monitor, you have to manually tell Windows to find it. Go to the **Control Panel** and double-click **Add New Hardware**. An installation wizard will launch. At some point the wizard asks whether you have a disk for your new monitor. If you have one, insert it at the correct time, and then choose the driver from there. If your monitor comes with special software or utilities, install them after you've installed the drivers.

5 Determine Your Primary Monitor

When you install a second monitor, you need to tell Windows which graphics card and monitor should be the primary one. To do this, right-click the **Desktop**, click **Properties**, and choose the **Settings** tab. Choose which display adapter you want to use as your primary adapter, and check off the box that says, "Extend my Windows desktop onto this monitor."

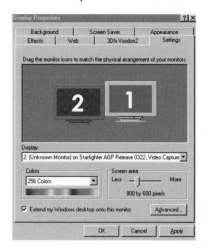

Watch Out!

- To use two monitors with Windows, you have to first install a second graphics card.
- After you've installed your second monitor, check the manufacturer's Web site to see whether there are newer drivers available.
- When installing a second monitor to use in Windows, the video cards for both monitors must be AGP or PCI.
- Your computer's capability to detect plug-and-play monitors may be disabled, To make sure it isn't, double-click the **Display** icon in Control Panel, click the **Settings** tab, click the **Advanced** button, click the **Monitor** tab, and make sure the check box is checked next to **Automatically detect plug-and-play monitors**.

How to Install a Flat Panel Monitor

Many people feel that flat panel monitors offer richer colors and a more pleasurable computing experience than traditional monitors. They're more expensive, but many people believe they're worth the extra cost. The most difficult part of installing a flat panel monitor is making sure that it works with your computer's graphics card. Many flat panel monitors are digital and require a special digital graphics card in order to work. Analog flat panel monitors generally don't require a special graphics card. Check before buying. If you require a special card, you'll have to install it before installing the monitor.

1 Match a Card to Your Monitor

Flat panel digital monitors require digital graphics cards in order to work. Additionally, not all digital flat panel monitors work with all digital graphics cards, so be sure that the card and monitor will work together. Often, it's a good idea to buy the card and the monitor together as a package, to ensure they work together. If you're buying an analog flat panel monitor, you probably won't have to buy a new graphics card.

2 Unplug Your Old Monitor

Turn off your computer before installing the monitor. Then, unplug your old monitor. You need to unplug its connection from your PC, and also unplug its power cord. In most instances, the power cord runs to an outlet, but in some cases, the power cord might plug into your PC.

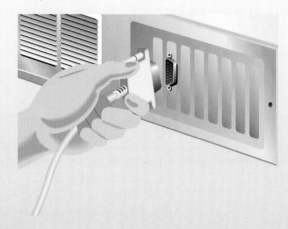

3 Install the Digital Graphics Card

Install a digital graphics card as you would any other graphics card, according to the instructions earlier in this chapter.

4 Plug In Your New Monitor's Cables

You need to plug cables from your monitor into your digital graphics card's video port and into a power outlet. The plug on your graphics card and the cable from your new flat panel monitor might look different from those of your previous graphics card and monitor. To get power to the monitor, you'll have to plug its power cord to its power pack, and its power pack to a wall outlet.

5 Turn On Your Computer

When you turn your computer back on, it should detect your new hardware. Follow the directions for installing the drivers for your video card, and for your monitor. At some point the wizard asks whether you have a disk for your new card and monitor. If you have one, insert it at the correct time, and then choose the driver from there.

6 Troubleshoot Installation Problems

If Windows doesn't detect your monitor, you have to manually tell Windows to find it. Go to the **Control Panel** and double-click **Add New Hardware**. An installation wizard will launch. At some point the wizard asks whether you have a disk for your new monitor. If you have one, insert it at the correct time, and then choose the driver from there. If your monitor comes with special software or utilities, install them after you've installed the drivers.

Watch Out!

■ After you've installed your monitor, check the manufacturer's Web site to see whether newer drivers are available.

■ Your computer's capability to detect plug-and-play monitors may be disabled, To make sure it isn't, double-click the **Display** icon in Control Panel, click the **Settings** tab, click the **Advanced** button, click the **Monitor** tab, and make sure the check box is checked next to **Automatically detect plug-and-play monitors**.

CHAPTER

Installing a NetCam

How NetCams Work   174

How to Install a NetCam   176

ONE of the more amazing devices you can add to your computer is a NetCam—a small video camera that can send video to your PC, and that often sells for about $100, or even less. One example of such a camera is the popular HomeConnect line of cameras from 3Com. You can use NetCams for many things. One of the more popular uses is for videoconferencing, in which you can not only talk to other people over the Internet, but also see video of them. And they can see you and hear you.

NetCams can be used for more than videoconferencing, though. You also can use them to send live pictures to a Web site. In addition, you can capture videos into a computer file that you can view and listen to and that you can send to others. As you'll see in this chapter, it's surprisingly easy to install a NetCam. NetCams attach to your PC via a USB port or an add-in card. If you buy a NetCam that attaches via an add-in card, you first must install the card. For USB, you install via the USB port on your PC.

How NetCams Work

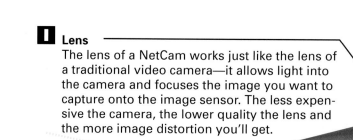

1 Lens
The lens of a NetCam works just like the lens of a traditional video camera—it allows light into the camera and focuses the image you want to capture onto the image sensor. The less expensive the camera, the lower quality the lens and the more image distortion you'll get.

5 NetCam card
Other NetCams attach to your PC using an add-in card on the motherboard. In these cases, the video processing unit sends the data to the card, which sends the video stream to the PC. In general, NetCams that attach this way offer higher frame rates than USB NetCams, because data can be transferred at a higher speed from the motherboard than by using a USB port.

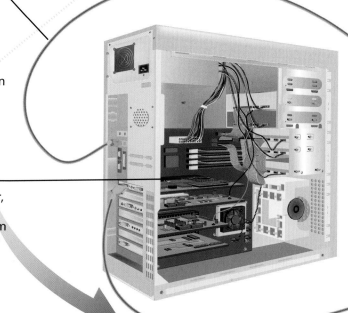

6 Video driver
The video stream is sent to a video driver, the PC's graphics unit. In some cases, the video driver manipulates the video stream so that it displays better on a PC. In other cases, though, it simply passes the video stream to a piece of the video.

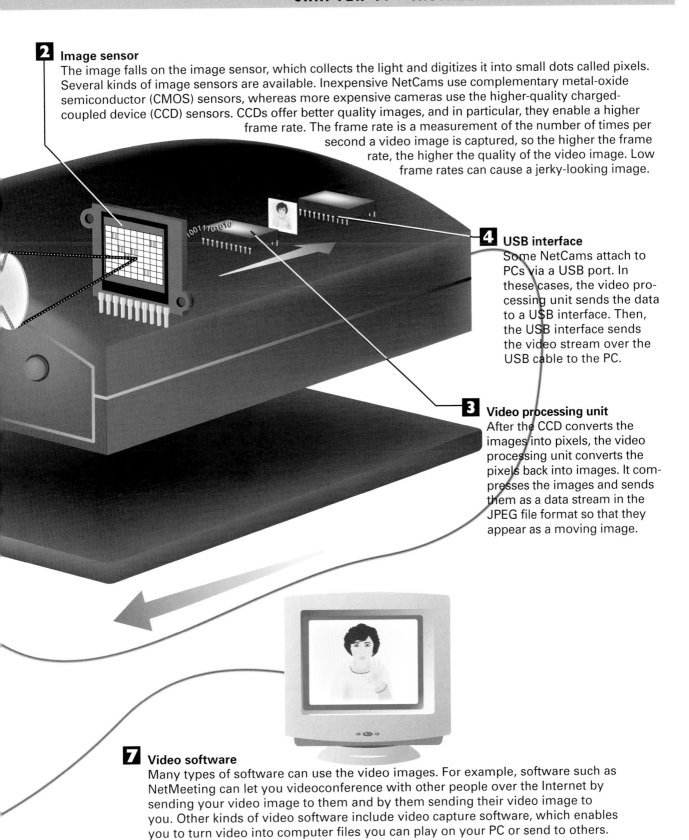

2 **Image sensor**
The image falls on the image sensor, which collects the light and digitizes it into small dots called pixels. Several kinds of image sensors are available. Inexpensive NetCams use complementary metal-oxide semiconductor (CMOS) sensors, whereas more expensive cameras use the higher-quality charged-coupled device (CCD) sensors. CCDs offer better quality images, and in particular, they enable a higher frame rate. The frame rate is a measurement of the number of times per second a video image is captured, so the higher the frame rate, the higher the quality of the video image. Low frame rates can cause a jerky-looking image.

4 **USB interface**
Some NetCams attach to PCs via a USB port. In these cases, the video processing unit sends the data to a USB interface. Then, the USB interface sends the video stream over the USB cable to the PC.

3 **Video processing unit**
After the CCD converts the images into pixels, the video processing unit converts the pixels back into images. It compresses the images and sends them as a data stream in the JPEG file format so that they appear as a moving image.

7 **Video software**
Many types of software can use the video images. For example, software such as NetMeeting can let you videoconference with other people over the Internet by sending your video image to them and by them sending their video image to you. Other kinds of video software include video capture software, which enables you to turn video into computer files you can play on your PC or send to others.

How to Install a NetCam

NetCams can do many things for you: let you videoconference with other people, enable you to put live images on your own Web site, and let you capture video and then send that video to friends and family. To work, NetCams must connect to your PC in some way. Some NetCams attach via a USB port, whereas others connect via a special card you insert in your computer. NetCams that attach via special cards usually can display crisper-looking video than NetCams that attach via a USB port. In this task, you learn how to install a NetCam that requires you to first install a card. As with installing any card in your computer, first turn off your computer, ensure that you have no static discharge, and then remove the case. For information on how to do that, turn to Chapter 1, Task 1, "How to Open the Case." To learn how to install a USB device, see Chapter 20, "Installing USB Devices."

1 Find a Free Slot

After you remove your computer's case, look on the motherboard and locate an empty slot. To fit the card into place, you must remove the small metal flap protecting the slot. The flap is held in place by a small screw. Remove the screw (it's usually held in place by a Phillips screw) and then remove the flap. Put the screw in a safe place—you're going to need it to secure the card you're inserting.

2 Install the Card

Align the card in the free slot, making sure the connectors on the card line up properly with the slot into which you're inserting the card. Then, using two hands, apply gentle, even pressure to push the card down into the slot. After the card is in place, press down firmly to ensure that it's all the way into the slot. To make sure the card won't come loose, screw it into place. Use the same screw you removed from the metal flap, and screw the card into the same place where the metal flap was screwed in.

3 Connect the NetCam to the Card

Using the cable that came with the NetCam, attach one end to the card you just installed and the other end to your NetCam. Many NetCams come with built-in microphones so you can talk to others while you see them. To use the microphone, you might need to connect a cable from the NetCam to a port on your sound card. Check your documentation to see whether that is required. If you have a USB-connected NetCam, you generally won't need to install the extra sound cable.

4 Turn On Your Computer

Turn your computer back on. When you do, Windows will detect that you've installed a NetCam and an Add New Hardware Wizard will appear. Follow the directions for installation, including adding the manufacturer's disk if you're prompted. If the Add New Hardware Wizard doesn't launch, run it manually by clicking the **Start** button, choosing **Settings**, selecting **Control Panel**, and then double-clicking **Add New Hardware**.

5 Install the Software

To use your NetCam, you must install the software that came with it. Depending on your brand of NetCam, it might have several pieces of software—for example, to enable videoconferencing and videocapture. You're not limited to the software that came with the NetCam; you can use many other types of software, such as NetMeeting, Microsoft's free videoconferencing software.

6 Focus the NetCam

Run the software and test and focus the NetCam. Some, but not all, NetCams come with a lens that can focus, so use it until you get a sharp image. If your NetCam doesn't come with a lens, try moving the camera closer to or farther away from the image you want to display, until the image is as sharp as possible.

Watch Out!

- Be sure the NetCam network card is seated firmly—if it isn't, your NetCam won't work.
- Don't press too hard when inserting the card or you could damage the card or the motherboard.
- Go to the NetCam manufacturer's site and download the latest drivers and software.
- If can see video but not hear sound after you install your NetCam, make sure you have properly connected your NetCam to your sound card.

CHAPTER

Installing a Sound Card and Speakers

How a Sound Card Works   180

How to Remove an Existing Sound Card   182

How to Install a Sound Card   184

How to Install Speakers and a Microphone   186

TO play music and listen to voices, hear game sound effects, hear system sounds, and hear other kinds of sounds on your PC, you need a sound card. A sound card plugs into your motherboard on an empty slot, connects to your CD-ROM drive via an audio cable, and plays sounds through speakers that you plug into the back of the sound card.

These days, almost any program you run includes sounds, and so any properly equipped PC should include a sound card. If you already have an older sound card, you might want to upgrade it to improve the quality of the sound it can play, particularly sounds that are an integral part of games, entertainment programs, or other multimedia software. And if you don't have a sound card, you'll want to install one to take advantage of new software.

A sound card by itself won't let you listen to sounds and music. To hear them, you also need to buy a set of speakers and hook them up to your sound card.

This chapter shows you how to take out your old sound card, if you already have one, how to install a new one, and how to hook up speakers and a microphone.

How a Sound Card Works

Sound card

A sound card plugs into an empty slot on a PC. All communications between the PC and sound card take place through the connections between the sound card and the motherboard on the slot. The card converts the digital signals used by computers to analog signals that are used by speakers. Some sound cards might be embedded on your motherboard and will not use a slot in your PC. If you have an embedded sound card, you need to check your motherboard's documentation on how to disable the onboard sound card before you install a new one. This is normally done via a jumper on the motherboard.

Electromagnet

The weak electrical current is amplified by an amplifier. This stronger current is sent to power an electromagnet inside a speaker. This electromagnet makes speaker cones vibrate, and these vibrations are what create sound.

TIMPANI
E#=011010
C = 0110011
A = 01010101
TRUMPET
C = 0111111
D = 000101
A = 10111110

D=00010101

LOOK UP TRUM

1010111101001

DAC

DAC chip

The DSP takes the file and decompresses the data in it. After it decompresses the data, it transfers the data to a digital-to-analog converter (DAC) chip. The DAC chip converts the digital data to an analog electrical current that constantly changes.

MIDI sound

Most sound cards also can play musical instrument digital interface (MIDI) sound. MIDI is a special computer music format that has been developed to conserve disk space. MIDI technology doesn't record the actual sounds. Instead, it saves a set of instructions describing how music sounds on electronic versions of musical instruments. These MIDI instructions are sent to the DSP. The DSP is able to interpret the instructions and know which instruments should play the music and how it should be played.

MIDI FILE

Wavetable synthesis

Some sound cards use *wavetable synthesis* to reproduce music. In this technology, sound samples from musical instruments are stored on a sound card ROM chip. The more memory on a sound card, the more sounds it can play, and it will have more realistic and vivid sound. To play the sound, the DSP looks in the ROM's table. If the sound is there, the sound card plays it. If, though, the sound is supposed to be a clarinet's B-flat, but the ROM has only a sample of a B note for the clarinet, the DSP processes the B note sound sample and lowers it to a B-flat pitch.

DSP chip

When the sound card needs to play a recorded sound, as found on a WAV file, the CPU fetches the WAV file containing the compressed digital information from the hard drive or CD-ROM, and sends that file to a chip called a Digital Signal Processor (DSP) on the sound card.

ROM

DIGITAL SIGNAL PROCESSOR

CPU

WAV FILE

MIDI FILE

How to Remove an Existing Sound Card

If you already have an existing sound card in your system, you want to remove it before you install a new sound card. Here's how to remove your existing sound card.

1 Remove the Existing Sound Card

Before installing a new sound card, it's a good idea to uninstall drivers and other software for your existing card. Remove the software by going to the Control Panel, choosing **Add/Remove program**, and uninstalling any drivers or software that came with the sound card. To make sure that everything has been removed, right-click the **My Computer** icon in Windows, choose **Properties**, and then choose the **Device Manager** tab. Click **Sound Video and Game Controllers** and choose your existing sound card. Click **Remove** and follow the instructions. Also, remove any special software installed specifically for the sound card, because that software won't work with your new card.

2 Detach Devices

If you look on the back of your sound card—what faces outside your computer—you see several connectors and plugs. A variety of devices might be connected to the sound card, such as speakers, headphones, a microphone, a joystick, or other gaming devices. Unplug all these devices after first turning off your PC.

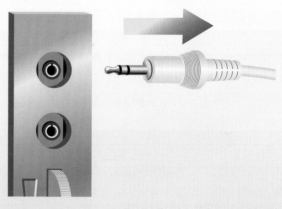

3 Disconnect Cables

Cables and devices might be attached internally to your sound card. Disconnect the CD or DVD audio cable. Note all the various connections so that when you put in a new sound card, you make those same connections again. There are two types of CD audio cables. Be sure your new sound card either comes with a audio cable that fits your CD or that your existing cable fits into the new sound card.

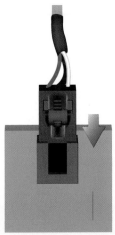

4 Remove the Backplate

The sound card is secured to your system by a screw connecting it to the backplate. Remove that screw, probably with a Phillips screwdriver.

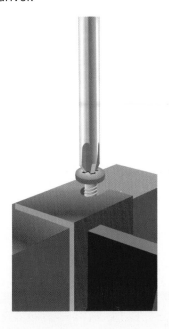

5 Lift Out the Sound Card

Now that everything is disconnected from the sound card, you can lift it free from the system. Hold the card by its top edge with two hands and lift straight up. If the card doesn't move, pull up one edge slightly first, and then lift up the other.

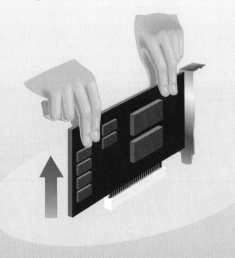

6 Double-Check Software

You want to be absolutely sure that all the old software and drivers for the old sound card are gone from your system. After you remove the sound card, reboot your computer and run the **Add/Remove Wizard** from the Control Panel. In most cases, the wizard won't find any software associated with the card, but if it does, tell it to remove the software.

Watch Out!

- Keep the screw from your old sound card; you'll use it when you install the new one.

How to Install a Sound Card

If you don't yet have a sound card in your PC, you have to start off by opening your PC's case, then putting the card into an empty slot, and then installing drivers and other software for making the card work with your PC. You first have to open the case. Turn to Chapter 1, "What's Inside Your Computer," for more information. If you already have a sound card, turn to the illustration on the preceding page, explaining how to take out an existing sound card.

1 Set the Jumpers or Switches

If you buy a plug-and-play sound card, you shouldn't have to worry about setting jumpers and switches. Otherwise, you might need to set jumpers and switches to set it to specific IRQ and DMA settings. Check your sound card documentation to see what you should set the switches to.

2 Insert the Sound Card

Locate an empty slot. Remove the backplate and set the screw aside. Insert the sound card by first putting it into the connector, and then pressing down evenly until the sound card is all the way in. Be sure the card is in tight, but don't press too hard.

3 Screw the Card into the Backplate

To be sure that the sound card doesn't come loose, you need to screw it into the backplate. Using a Phillips screwdriver, screw in the sound card, but be careful not to overtighten so that you don't strip the screw.

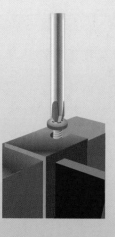

4 Connect the CD Audio Cable

For the sound card to work with the CD drive, you need to attach the card to the CD-ROM drive. Locate the CD audio cable running from the CD-ROM drive, and attach it to the sound card. Connecting this audio cable is what enables you to listen to audio CDs on your computer. You may also have to connect an audio cable to your DVD drive or DVD decoder card.

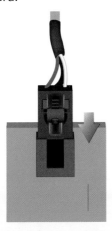

5 Turn On Your PC

After you turn your PC back on, it should automatically recognize that you've installed a new piece of hardware. An Add New Hardware Wizard dialog box appears. Follow the directions for installing your sound card.

6 Run Add New Hardware Wizard

If Windows doesn't recognize that you've added a sound card, run the Add New Hardware Wizard. First go to the Control Panel by clicking the **Start** button, and then choose **Control Panel** from Settings. Double-click **Add New Hardware**. You have the option of using drivers supplied with your sound card, or using the ones supplied by Windows. Use the ones supplied by the manufacturer, and insert the manufacturer's disk. There might be other applications on the manufacturer's disk, so install those, too.

Watch Out!

■ When you put in the sound card, be sure that it is seated tightly into the slot, to ensure that the card will work.

■ To play music CDs with your CD drive and sound card, you need a software CD player installed. You can use the one included with Windows.

■ Sound card drives are updated all the time, so after you install and configure your sound card and it's working correctly, go to the manufacturer's site and download the latest driver update for your sound card.

How to Install Speakers and a Microphone

After you have your sound card installed, you need a set of speakers. You might also want to plug in a microphone, as well. There are many different kinds of speakers with many different kinds of connections. Depicted is the most common setup, but check your documentation to see whether you need to do anything different.

1 Connect the Main Speaker Plug

Typically, in a set of speakers, there is a main speaker plug that goes from one of the speakers to the sound card. When you plug the speaker into the sound card, be sure that you're plugging it into the speaker plug and not the microphone plug. There should be a small picture or label telling you which is the speaker plug and which is the microphone plug. There also might be a plug for headphones, so don't plug the speaker into those, either. Some sound cards have two speaker plugs and a microphone plug.

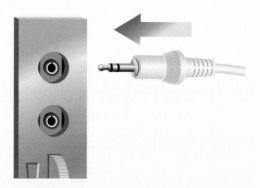

2 Install a Subwoofer

Subwoofers provide the deep bass sound of a sound system. They work best when located next to the base of a wall. If you have a subwoofer, connect a speaker wire from the main speaker to the subwoofer. Be sure that you connect the proper wire to the subwoofer—not one designed to plug into the secondary, satellite speaker. In some instances, the subwoofer has connections to both speakers. Check your documentation.

3 Connect a Wire to the "Satellite"

After you've hooked up the main speaker to the sound card, you need to connect a wire from the main speaker to the secondary "satellite" speaker so that it can receive sound.

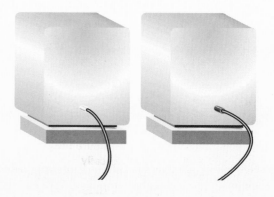

4 Plug In the Speaker's Power Cord

Most speakers need to receive external power, so plug in the speaker's power cord. If you have a subwoofer, you might need to plug that in as well.

5 Turn On the Speakers

After everything is plugged in, turn on the speakers. They're now ready to use with your sound card. The switch for the speakers also might be found on the subwoofer. Often, speakers come with a volume control, so you can regulate the loudness.

6 Plug In a Microphone

Sound cards come with a microphone jack. This enables you to record your voice and sounds. Plug the microphone into the microphone jack, being sure that you don't plug it into the headphone or speaker jack.

Watch Out!

- When hooking up speakers, be careful to put the speaker plug into the proper connector on the back of the sound card—not into the microphone jack.

- If you are having trouble recording with your microphone, check your sound card documentation to see how you enable "full duplex" operation.

- If you can hear sound but not music or vice versa from data disks, check your DMA settings for a conflict. If you cannot hear music or audio CDs, check to be sure the CD-ROM audio cable has been connected properly.

CHAPTER

Installing an MP3 Player

How an MP3 Player Works   190

How to Install an MP3 Player   192

MP3 players are small, portable devices that can play music recorded in a variety of digital formats, notably in the MP3 format. Although the devices are typically called MP3 players, they often can play music recorded in other formats, such as the Windows Media format (WMA).

Music must be transferred from a PC to an MP3 player—the MP3 player has no other way to get music into it. In fact, the PC controls not just placing files in the MP3 player, but also deleting files from it as well.

You get music to place in an MP3 player in several ways. Digital music can be downloaded from the Internet, or you can insert an audio CD into your computer and convert that music into the MP3 format (or another music format). This is called *ripping* music from a CD. Software that is typically called Jukebox software—such as Real JukeBox—can be used to rip music in this way, and it also can be used to transfer music files to an MP3 player and delete files from the player.

The music is commonly stored in flash memory on the MP3 player, although other kinds of storage are available as well. MP3 players usually come with 32MB, 64MB, and sometimes more memory and can be expanded by adding flash memory cards to a special slot in the MP3 player. For example, the newest version of the popular Rio MP3 player lets you add 340MB of memory via its "backpack" memory feature.

The first MP3 players connected to the computer via the serial port, but newer players connect via the high-speed USB port. This means it takes far less time to transfer music from the PC to the MP3 player than it used to. Some players even let you connect via both the USB and serial ports.

How an MP3 Player Works

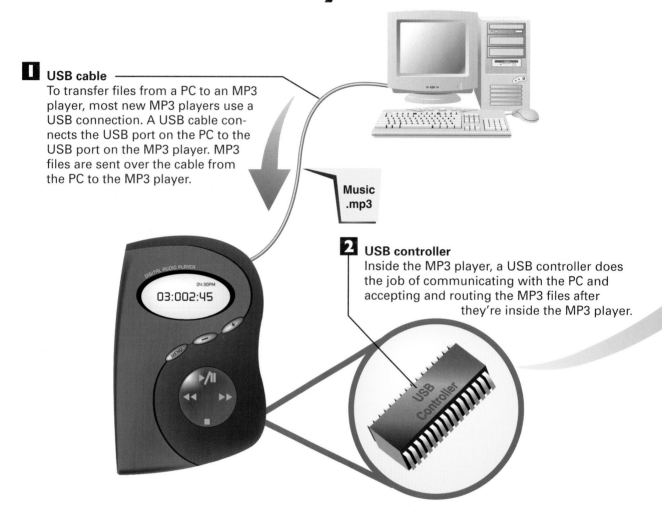

1 **USB cable**

To transfer files from a PC to an MP3 player, most new MP3 players use a USB connection. A USB cable connects the USB port on the PC to the USB port on the MP3 player. MP3 files are sent over the cable from the PC to the MP3 player.

Music .mp3

2 **USB controller**

Inside the MP3 player, a USB controller does the job of communicating with the PC and accepting and routing the MP3 files after they're inside the MP3 player.

USB Controller

6 Headphone jack

The DAC converter then sends the music to the headphone jack and into the headphone, which plays the music.

3 ARM processor

Many MP3 players, such as the Rio series of MP3 players, use a special processor called an ARM processor. This ARM processor is the brains of the MP3 player, and like a computer's microprocessor, it handles the device's central tasks. When MP3 files are received by the USB controller, they're sent to the ARM processor.

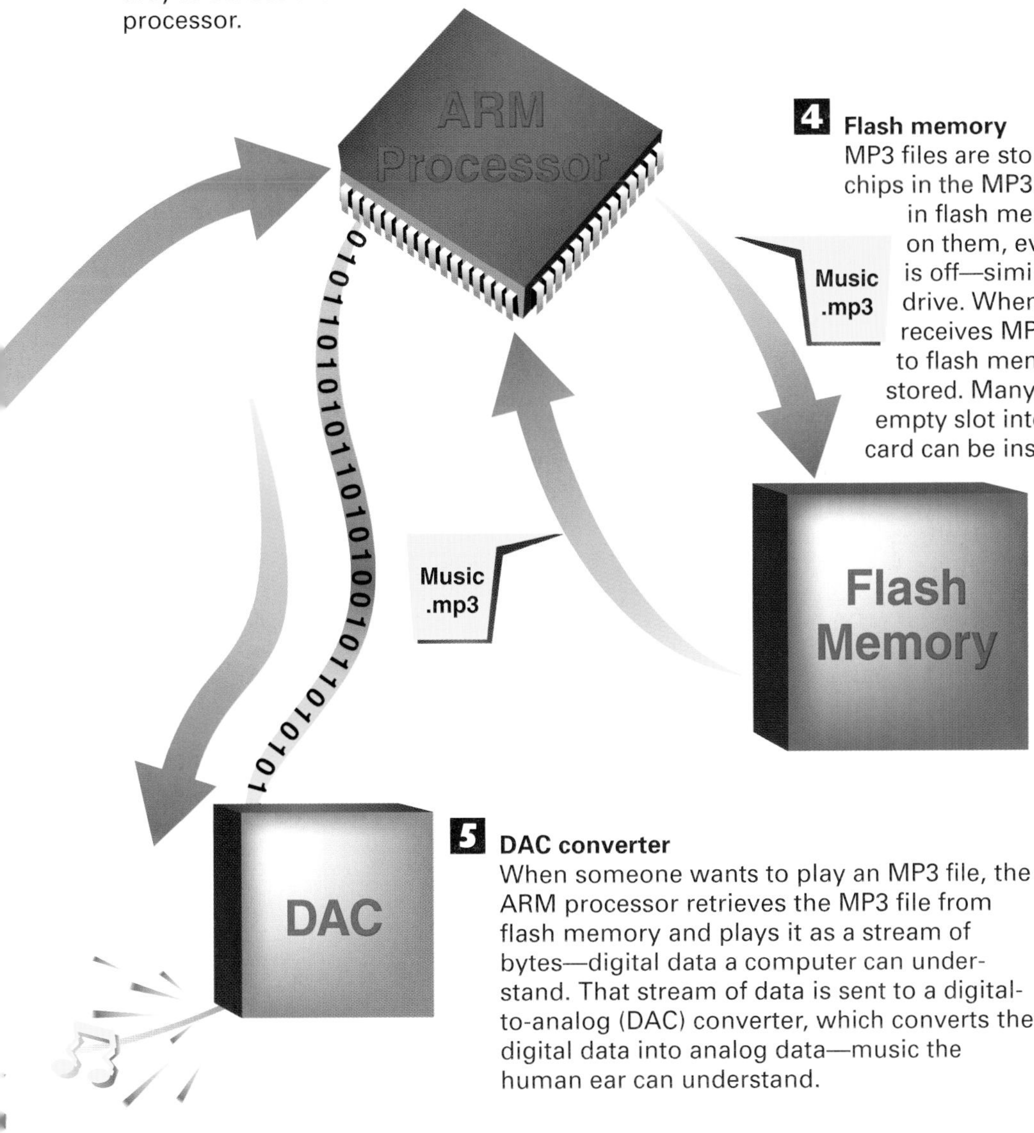

ARM Processor

4 Flash memory

MP3 files are stored in flash memory chips in the MP3 player. Anything stored in flash memory chips stays stored on them, even when the MP3 player is off—similar to a computer's hard drive. When the ARM processor receives MP3 files, it sends the files to flash memory, where they're stored. Many MP3 players have an empty slot into which a flash memory card can be installed, as a way to increase the amount of music that can be stored and played from the MP3 player. (Some MP3 players have hard disks to hold music rather than flash memory.)

Music .mp3

Music .mp3

Flash Memory

5 DAC converter

When someone wants to play an MP3 file, the ARM processor retrieves the MP3 file from flash memory and plays it as a stream of bytes—digital data a computer can understand. That stream of data is sent to a digital-to-analog (DAC) converter, which converts the digital data into analog data—music the human ear can understand.

DAC

How to Install an MP3 Player

Installing an MP3 player is easy. Whereas older players sometimes required you to connect them to your computer via a serial port to copy MP3 files to them, the newer ones all connect via a USB port. To install the player, you install software, connect the USB cables, and then install drivers. After the player is installed, you transfer files to the player via the USB port and delete files from the player that way, as well.

1 Install the Software

You transfer files to your MP3 player and delete files from the player by using software you install on your PC. Before connecting the MP3 player, install the software that came with the MP3 player. You also can use JukeBox software to do this, such as Real JukeBox or MusicMatch JukeBox. Both are available for free from download sites on the Internet.

2 Turn On the MP3 Player

Look for the switch—sometimes it's a very small one. And remember to first install a battery. MP3 players typically run on batteries—usually AA batteries. They often need only one.

3 Connect the MP3 USB Cable

The MP3 player came with a special USB cable designed specifically for it. One end is small and designed to fit into a special port on the MP3 player. Find the port and plug in the cable.

4 Connect the USB Cable to the PC

The other end of the USB cable is rectangular and designed to plug into a PC. The USB cable connects only one way, so don't force it. If you don't have a free USB port on your PC, you can buy a USB hub that will give you four USB ports into which you can plug devices. If you don't have a USB port, you can install one in your computer. (To learn how to install USB hubs and ports, turn to Chapter 20, "Installing USB Devices.")

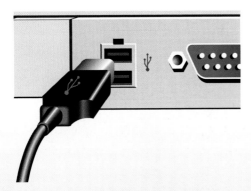

5 Follow Any Installation Instructions

When you plug in the USB cables, your computer will recognize that you're adding an MP3 player. The Add New Hardware Wizard will appear, or an installation routine will automatically start. Follow the onscreen directions for completing the installation.

6 Run the JukeBox Software

Now that your MP3 player is installed, you should transfer MP3 files to it so you can listen to them. To transfer the MP3 files, when your MP3 player is connected to your PC, run the JukeBox software that came with the player—or use other JukeBox software such as Real JukeBox—and transfer music files to the MP3 player. JukeBox software also can be used to convert music from audio CDs into MP3 files.

Watch Out!

- Use only the USB cable that comes with your MP3 player—off-the-shelf USB cables typically won't fit into your MP3 player.

- If you notice that MP3 files "skip" or are in some other way distorted, it might be that the CDs from which you're recording have small scratches or dirt on their undersides. Wipe the bottom sides of CDs with a soft cloth before converting them—that may solve the problem.

- Some of the MP3 files you can get from the Internet might violate copyright laws because the recording artists haven't agreed to have those files posted online.

CHAPTER

20

Installing USB Devices

How the Universal Serial Bus Works   **196**

How to Install USB Devices   **198**

How to Install a USB Hub   **200**

How to Install a USB Card   **202**

PERHAPS the best news in the last several years for those who want to expand and upgrade their computers is the advent of the Universal Serial Bus, more commonly known as USB. USB provides the easiest way yet to attach devices such as scanners, joysticks, keyboards, mice, modems, removable drives, MP3 players, digital cameras, and more to your computer.

With USB, you don't need to remove your PC's case in order to install anything—you only need to plug the device into the USB port. In fact, in general, you won't even need to turn off your computer, because USB devices are "hot swappable," which means that they can be installed without turning off your computer.

Another big plus of USB is that you can daisy-chain up to 127 devices to your computer using its USB. Sometimes, devices let you plug other USB devices into them. For example, if you install a scanner, it might have a second USB port, into which you can plug another USB device—you won't have to plug that device into your computer's USB port; instead, you plug it into the extra port on another USB device. However, not all USB devices have these extra ports, and a solution to the problem is to buy a USB "hub"—a device that you plug into your computer's USB port, and in turn, into which you can plug several USB devices. This is how you can connect up to 127 devices to your USB port, by using many hubs.

If you've bought a computer in the last several years, the great odds are that it comes with one or two USB ports. However, if your computer didn't come with a USB port, you can install a USB card if you use Windows 98 or above. You can then plug USB devices into that card.

Note that there are two speeds of USB—the older USB 1.1, which allows devices to communicate with your PC at 12 megabits per second, and the newer USB 2.0 standard, which allows devices to communicate at 40 times the speed—480 megabits per second. Many computers use the 1.1 standard, because the USB 2.0 standard only started being used in 2001.

In this chapter, you see how you can install USB devices into your computer. And if you don't have a USB port, you see how you can install a USB card so you can take advantage of USB technology. Finally, you'll learn how to install a USB hub, to make it easy to daisy-chain many USB devices.

How the Universal Serial Bus Works

Daisy-chained devices
The Universal Serial Bus (USB) enables up to 127 devices to be attached in daisy-chain fashion to your computer via the USB port. A USB controller in your PC is the brains of USB. If you don't have a USB port and controller, you can add them by installing a USB card on your PC, but only if you have Windows 98 or above.

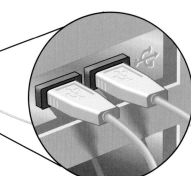

USB ports
Computers have either two or more USB ports. Whether you have one port or two, however, up to 127 devices can be daisy-chained via USB to a computer. Plugs from USB devices attach to USB ports—in this way, USB devices can be connected to your computer without your having to open the case. USB ports are marked with the special symbol you can see in this illustration.

USB hubs
The way you can connect up to 127 devices to your USB port is by using USB hubs. A hub attaches to a USB port, or to another USB hub. These hubs have USB ports on them, enabling numerous USB devices to be plugged into them.

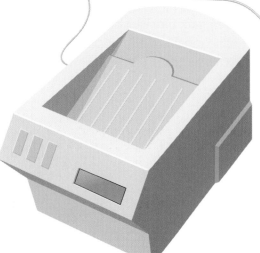

Power

D+

D-

Ground

USB cables
Inside USB cables are four wires. Two of these wires are used to provide electricity to the USB devices attached to your computer. One of those wires provides the electricity, whereas the other is a ground. (Some USB devices, such as scanners, require more electricity than the USB cables can provide, and so also still need to be plugged into a power outlet.) The other two wires, D+ and D-, are used for transmitting data and commands.

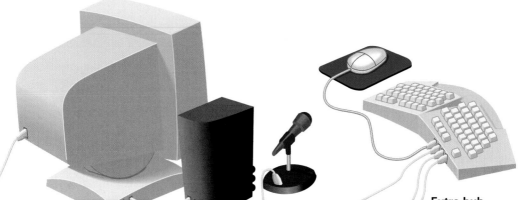

USB device as a hub
Some USB devices include extra USB ports so that they can function like a hub. In this way, for example, a monitor could have USB speakers, a microphone, and a keyboard plugged into it.

Extra hub
Devices and hubs can be daisy-chained, enabling many devices to be attached to one another. As you can see pictured here, a keyboard that has been plugged into a monitor can in turn have a mouse, a digitizing pen, and other devices plugged into it.

Automatic configuration
After you install a new USB device, the USB controller communicates with the device, in essence asking it to identify itself. This helps the controller decide whether the device is a high-speed device such as a monitor, scanner, or printer and so can communicate at 12 megabits a second, or whether it's a slower device, such as a keyboard or mouse that transfers data at 1.5 megabits per second. In the newer USB 2.0 standard, devices can communicate at 480 megabits per second. (By way of comparison, a serial port communicates at 100 kilobits a second while a parallel port communicates at about 1.5 megabits per second.) The USB controller also assigns the device an identification number.

Data transfer priorities
The USB controller assigns three different levels of priorities to devices attached to it, in this order:

Highest priority This is assigned to an Isochronous or real-time device such as a video camera or a sound device. In these kinds of devices, the data is not allowed to be interrupted.

Medium priority This is assigned to devices such as keyboards, mice, and joysticks, in which the device doesn't always need to use USB to communicate with the computer, because it's not constantly in use. However, when it is used, the data needs to be transferred immediately.

Lowest priority This is assigned to devices such as printers, scanners, and digital cameras in which a great deal of data needs to be sent all at once, but in which it won't be a problem if the data is delayed slightly in being transferred.

How to Install USB Devices

The newest way to connect devices such as scanners, digital cameras, and many other computer peripherals to your computer is via the Universal Serial Bus (USB) port. When you use a USB port, you don't need to take the case off your PC, and you don't need to try to share a parallel port with a printer. Instead, you connect the device to the USB port, run installation software, and you're ready to go. Almost all USB devices are "hot swappable," meaning you can connect and disconnect them while your machine is running; digital cameras and joysticks are good examples of this. Here's how to install a USB device. For more information on how to install specific devices, turn to the proper chapter.

▌1▐ Make Sure You Have a USB Port

You are able to install a USB device only if you have a USB port on your PC. Look for one or two rectangular ports on the front, side, or rear of your PC, with the USB symbol next to them.

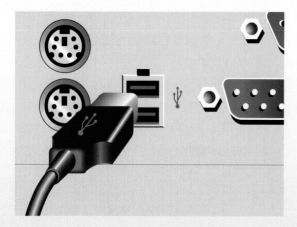

▌2▐ Check Device Manager Settings

Most versions of Windows support USB, although Windows 95 support is erratic. To be sure that your computer properly supports USB, you should check the Device Manager and look for the USB setting. To do that, right-click the **My Compute**r icon, and choose **Properties**. Then, click the **Device Manager** tab, and scroll down. You should see a USB controller entry, and it shouldn't be expanded to show any exclamation points next to any of the entries within it.

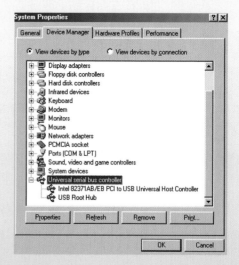

▌3▐ Install Device Software

Some devices, such as scanners, require that you install special software in order for them to work. If your device requires special software, install it now.

4 Turn On the Device

First, connect the device's power cable. Some devices need to be plugged into a wall outlet. If the device you're installing needs to be plugged in, plug it in and turn it on.

5 Connect the USB Cable

The device comes with a USB cable. The cable has a rectangular end and a square end. Plug the square end into the device, and the rectangular end into the computer. The USB cable connects only one way, so don't force it. If you don't have a free USB port on your PC, you can buy a USB hub that will give you extra USB ports that you can plug devices into. And if you don't have a USB port, you can install one in your computer.

6 Restart Your Computer

After you restart your computer, Windows recognizes that you've added new hardware and an Add New Hardware Wizard launches. Follow the directions for installing your new hardware. If you have a disk from the manufacturer, insert it when asked to, so that Windows will use the manufacturer's drivers. You also can install some USB devices when the computer is still running. In that case, wait a few seconds after you install it, and the Add New Hardware Wizard appears. (Note that some USB devices don't require that you restart your computer when you install them.)

Watch Out!

- Check the Device Manager to be sure that your system properly recognizes your USB port.
- Check your CMOS to be sure that USB is enabled in it.
- Be sure that all the USB connectors are tight.
- Use the manufacturer's disk when the Add New Hardware Wizard asks whether you have a disk from the manufacturer.

How to Install a USB Hub

In theory, USB allows you to daisy-chain up to 127 devices off a single USB. But there's a problem with doing that—most PCs come with only one or two USB ports, and most USB devices don't have any extra ports into which you can attach other USB devices. So, in practice, it appears that you can attach only one or two USB devices to your PC at one time. The way around the problem is to buy a USB hub. These inexpensive devices plug into your USB port and give you four or more USB ports into which you can plug other devices. And you can daisy-chain USB hubs by plugging them into one another, so they're an easy way to connect as many USB devices as you need.

1 Attach the AC Adapter

Most USB hubs come with an AC adapter so that they can receive electricity from a power outlet. Although a hub can instead get its electricity from your computer, some USB devices are power-hungry, so you should use the AC adapter, especially when first installing the hub. Plug the AC adapter into the hub, and then plug the adapter into a power outlet.

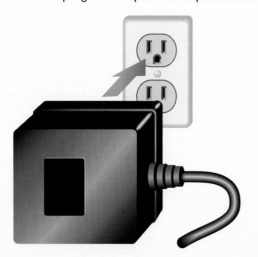

2 Connect the USB Cable to Your PC

The hub comes with a USB cable. The cable has a rectangular plug and a square plug. (The rectangular plug is called the USB-A connector, whereas the square plug is called the USB-B connector.) Plug the rectangular end (the USB-A connector) into the matching USB port on your computer. The USB cable connects only one way, so don't force it.

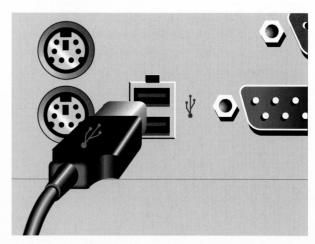

3 Connect the USB Cable to the Hub

Connect the square plug on the USB cable to the matching port on your USB hub. (This port will be the USB-B connector type.) Usually, the port on the hub will be set away from the other USB ports, all of which are the rectangular, USB-A connector type. Sometimes this port will be called the root port. The USB cable connects only one way, so don't force it.

4 Connect the USB Devices to the Hub

Following the instructions in the previous task, connect USB devices to your hub in the same way as you would connect them to your PC. Remember that the rectangular plug in each case connects to the USB hub, whereas the square plug connects to the USB device.

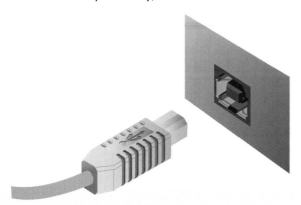

5 Try Out the Devices

Try using each of the devices, to be sure they work. If one or more doesn't work, the problem is probably that you didn't put in the connectors properly, so be sure the connectors are seated firmly in their ports.

6 Test the Devices Without AC Power

If you want to run the hub without AC power, unplug the AC adapter and then test each device in turn. If they all work properly, you will be able to run the hub without the external AC power. However, if you have problems running any of them, you'll need to use the AC power. Also, some hubs require AC power, so check the documentation before trying to run the hub without external power.

Watch Out!

- Some USB devices, such as some USB CD-RW drives, require that you connect directly to your computer, not to a hub. Read the documentation for your devices to see whether they can be connected to a hub.

- Double-check that you connect your PC to the hub via the hub's root port; otherwise, the hub won't work.

How to Install a USB Card

If you don't have USB ports on your computer, you might be able to get USB by installing a USB card, which gives you two USB ports and all the capabilities of USB as if it were built into your system. In order to install a card, you need Windows 98 or above and a free PCI slot—without either of them, you won't be able to install one. As with installing other cards, the first step is to take the cover off your PC, being careful to ground yourself and discharge any static electricity before touching anything inside your computer. See Chapter 1, "What's Inside Your Computer," for more details.

1 Find an Empty PCI Slot

USB boards work only when installed in PCI slots, so you have to be sure you have one free. It has to be version 2.1 or better for the PCI standard. Check your system documentation to be sure your slot adheres to those standards.

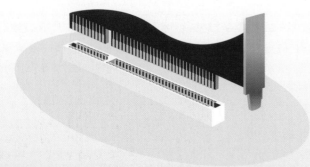

2 Remove the Slot's Backplate

In order to install the card, you have to remove the slot's backplate so that you can fit the card in. Unscrew the screw holding the backplate to the slot, and be sure to keep the screw in a safe place, because you'll be using it to secure the USB card.

3 Install the Card into the Slot

Align the card with the slot, and then gently push the card all the way in until it's firmly seated. After it's solidly in place, screw in the card using the screw from the backplate.

4 Install the USB Drivers

After you've installed the card, turn your computer back on. Windows detects the new hardware and launches the Add New Hardware Wizard. Follow the instructions for adding new hardware. Have your Windows or manufacturer's disk handy, because the drivers will be on either of those disks.

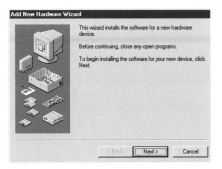

5 Be Sure USB Is Enabled

To see whether USB is now enabled on your computer, check the Device Manager. Right-click **My Computer**, select **Properties**, click the **Device Manager** tab, and scroll down until you see the Universal Serial Bus Controller listing. Click the **+** sign and be sure the new controller is listed, such as "Opti 82C861 PCI to USB Open Host Controller." There should be no yellow "!" or "?" marks or a red "X" anywhere.

6 Install and Test a USB Device

You're now ready to install a USB device. There are two ports on the back of the card that you've installed, and they are accessible from the back of your computer. Install the device or devices as outlined earlier in the chapter. It should now work properly. If not, you might need to update your BIOS, or try installing the card into a different slot.

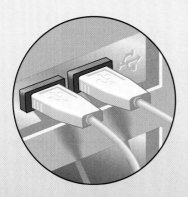

Watch Out!

- If the USB doesn't work, it might be because your BIOS doesn't support it. Upgrade your BIOS to be sure. Turn to Chapter 2, "Installing a New Motherboard or CPU," for information on how to upgrade a BIOS.

- Install a USB card only if you have Windows 98 or above. Although some versions of Windows 95 support USB, even those versions can be problematic.

- If Windows doesn't recognize USB, try installing the card into a different slot.

Installing a Modem

How a Modem Works   206

How to Install an Internal Modem   208

How to Install an External Modem   210

Testing and Troubleshooting
Your New Modem   212

How to Install a Cable or DSL Modem   214

TO communicate with the world, you need a modem. Modems enable your computer to send and receive information from other computers. In doing so, modems enable you to do things such as hook up to the Internet, browse the World Wide Web, and send and receive email. Modems also include fax capabilities so you can send and receive faxes.

Traditional modems come in two types—internal modems and external modems. *Internal* modems are less expensive but more difficult to install. Generally, it's worth the extra money to buy an external modem.

When buying a new modem, be sure to buy the fastest one possible. The fastest modem and slowest modem don't differ greatly in cost. Look for a V.90 56K modem—that ensures it will be compatible with other high-speed modems.

Installing an external modem is a simple matter of connecting it to your serial port, plugging a phone line into it, and installing drivers. An internal modem is a little more difficult to install because you first must open your computer's case and insert the modem into an open slot on the motherboard.

In addition to traditional modems that use phone lines, you also can get a high-speed connection to the Internet with a cable or DSL modem. These aren't true modems, and they work differently from traditional modems. But they enable you to connect to the Internet at very high speeds—significantly faster than modems that use regular telephone lines.

How a Modem Works

External modem
An external modem plugs into a serial port or USB port on the computer. It gets its power from an AC adapter that plugs into an electrical outlet. Your modem will attach to either a 25-pin or 9-pin serial port. Adapters/gender changers are available if your modem cable does not match the PC connection.

Serial port
Data is sent to and received from the computer via the serial port or USB port, through the modem, and then onto the phone lines.

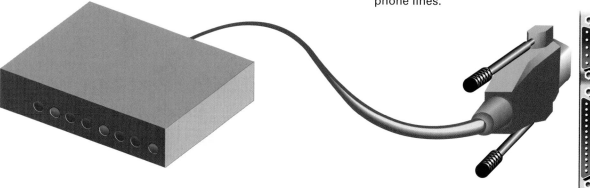

Data
Your computer works with digital data—binary bits of information that are either on or off. The telephone system, on the other hand, works with analog information—streams of continuous electric current that vary in frequency and strength. When you send information from your modem to another modem, such as on the Internet, the digital data in your computer must be changed to analog information so it can be sent via the telephone system. The computer sends digital information to the modem, which changes it—modulates it—into analog signals.

Modem
The analog signals travel over the phone system and are received by another modem, where they are changed by the receiving modem—demodulated—from analog data back to digital data and then sent into the computer via the serial port. This modulating and demodulating of data is what gives the modem its name: MOdulating/DEModulating.

Phone line
The phone line plugs into the jack on the back of the modem and connects the modem to the phone system. You can connect the modem directly to the phone system without a telephone by connecting the line directly to the line jack.

Phone jack
The phone jack is a second connector on the back of the modem. By plugging a telephone into this jack and then plugging the line jack into the phone jack on your wall, you are able to use your telephone when you're not using your modem.

Internal modem
An internal modem is installed in an empty slot on a computer's motherboard. It has its own serial port, so it need not be connected to an existing one on the PC. It draws its power from the motherboard.

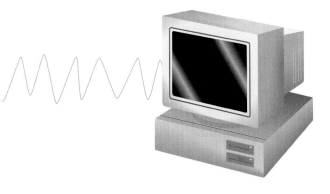

How to Install an Internal Modem

If both of your serial ports are in use, such as by mice and other devices, you must install an internal modem. If you have an older computer and want to install a high-speed modem, you might need to install an internal modem as well. That's because you need a special serial port, called a 16550 UART, if you want to send and receive data at high speeds, and many older computers don't have that kind of port. Internal modems include that high-speed serial port already built in.

1 Find Free COM Ports

To communicate with the outside world, your computer uses a communications port, which is also called a serial port or COM port. You won't be able to configure your internal modem to use a COM port that's already in use. To find out which COM ports are in use in your computer, in Windows, right-click the **My Computer** icon and choose **Properties**. Choose the **Device Manager** tab and click the **+** sign next to the Ports item. You then will see a list of the COM ports that are in use.

2 Find a Free Slot

You'll be plugging your modem into a free slot. You can either use the slot your existing internal modem uses. Or, if you don't yet have an internal modem, you can plug it into an empty slot. If you don't yet have an internal modem, find a free slot; then, remove the bracket in front of it. If you already have an internal modem, remove it and use that slot.

3 Set the Jumpers

Some internal modems require you to set jumpers to configure them for certain COM ports or other hardware configurations, such as IRQ. Set them now. Sometimes you can set the jumpers to Plug and Play (PnP) mode, which enables Windows to set up your modem for you.

4 Install the Modem in the Slot

The modem should slide into the free slot fairly easily. Press down gently but firmly. You might have to use two hands. After you are sure the modem is plugged all the way in, screw the modem into the spot where the bracket used to be, using the screw you previously removed.

5 Connect the Phone Cord

If you're dedicating a phone line to your modem, plug one end of the phone cord into the phone jack, and the other end into the modem's connector. If your modem is going to share a phone line with your telephone, you have to use two jacks on the modem. One jack is labeled phone and the other is labeled line or telco. Attach a phone cord from the phone jack on the back of the modem to the telephone, and a phone cord from the line jack on the back of the modem to the wall jack. Then, close the case and turn on your PC.

6 Install the Modem Drivers

After you turn on your computer, Windows should launch an installation wizard. If it doesn't, go to the **Control Panel**, double-click the **Modems** icon, and then double-click the **Add** button. Windows will probably detect your model of modem and which port you're using. If it doesn't, add them manually. When prompted for a driver, use the driver disk or CD that came with the modem. In some cases, you must run an installation program from the CD to install the drivers.

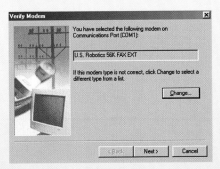

Watch Out!

- Be sure the modem is properly seated in its slot before closing the case.
- Check the manufacturer's Web site to see whether newer drivers are available—or whether a "patch" is available that you can download to your modem's BIOS to make it work better.
- Verify that the phone jack you're connecting to has a dial tone; otherwise, your modem won't work.

How to Install an External Modem

External modems are more expensive than internal modems, but are easier to install. They also have the added benefit of having lights that blink, telling you what's happening during your communications session, as well as easy access to control how loud the modem speaker is. Additionally, resetting the modem is easy in the case that something goes wrong—you just flick a switch. Here's what you need to know about installing an external modem.

1 Plug In Your Modem

Look on the back of your computer and find a free serial port. Most PCs have two serial ports, which are usually 9-pin male connectors. However, in some instances, one might be a 9-pin connector and the other a 25-pin connector. After turning off your computer, plug one end of a serial cable into your modem and the other into a free serial port on the back of your computer.

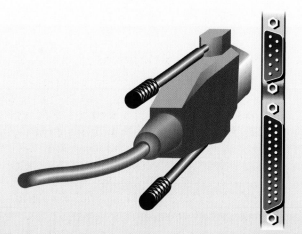

2 Connect the Power Cord

Your modem comes with an AC adapter, which might have a large transformer at the end where it plugs into a wall outlet. Plug one end of the adapter into your modem and the other into the wall outlet or power strip.

▋ Plug In the Phone Cord

If you're dedicating a phone line to your modem, plug one end of the phone line into the phone jack and the other end into the connector on the back of the modem. If your modem is going to share a phone line with your telephone, use two jacks on the back of the modem. One should be labeled phone/telco and the other should be labeled line. Attach a phone cord from the phone jack on the back of the modem to the telephone and a phone cord from the line jack on the back of the modem to the wall jack.

▋ Turn On Your Modem

You now can turn on your modem by using its power switch. When you turn it on, an LED or light indicator should turn on. Next, turn on your computer.

▋ Install the Modem Drivers

After you turn on your computer, Windows should launch an installation Wizard. If it doesn't, go to the **Control Panel**, double-click the **Modems** icon, and then double-click the **Add** button. As you're walked through the setup process, tell your computer the make and model of your modem and which COM port to use. Windows will probably detect your model of modem and which port you're using, but if it doesn't, add them manually.

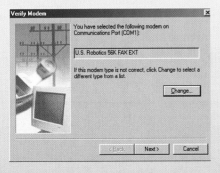

▋ Install Extra Software

During installation, you might be asked whether you have modem driver software on disk or whether to use a driver from Windows. It's always best to use the driver software supplied with your modem, so insert that disk into your computer and tell the Installation Wizard to use the software from that disk. In some cases, you must run an installation program from the CD to install the drivers.

Watch Out!

- Check the manufacturer's Web site to see whether newer drivers are available—or whether a "patch" is available to download to your modem's BIOS to improve its performance.
- Verify that the phone jack you're connecting to has a dial tone; otherwise, your modem won't work.

Testing and Troubleshooting Your New Modem

Computer communication via modem is notoriously finicky. Many things can go wrong—COM port conflicts can occur, as can problems with the phone line and many other kinds of problems. Here's how to test out and troubleshoot your new modem.

1 Use Windows Diagnostics

Windows has diagnostic software for detecting modem problems. Click the **Start** button, and then choose **Settings** from the Control Panel. Double-click the **Modem** icon. Next, click the **Diagnostics** tab, and then click your modem. Click the **More Info** button. If a problem with your modem setup does exist, you get an error or a "port already open" message.

2 Try Connecting to the Internet

Dial in as normal. If you've never connected before, use HyperTerminal, which is built into Windows, to test your modem. In Windows 98, click the **Start** button, and then choose **Programs**, **Accessories**, **Communications**, and then **HyperTerminal**. You'll see several icons, including one for MCI Mail. Double-click the icon to dial in. If your PC dials your modem and you make a connection, it's working properly. If not, check out the following troubleshooting tips.

3 Check for a COM Port Conflict

To check whether a conflict exists, first right-click **My Computer** and choose **Properties**. Next, choose the **Device Manager** tab. Click the **+** sign next to the Ports item and other items, such as the mouse and CD drive. A yellow circle with an exclamation point or a red "X" means a conflict exists. If so, change the COM port setting of your modem by double-clicking the **Modems** icon in the Control Panel, selecting your modem, clicking the **Port** drop-down control, and choosing a different COM port.

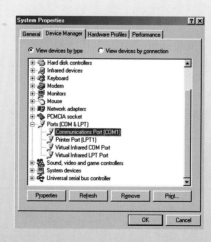

4 Check the Phone Cords and Line

Double-check that the phone cords are plugged in properly; in their respective jacks; and secured into the modem, telephone, and wall jack. Also try making a phone call using the phone line you're using to ensure that the problem isn't with the line itself rather than with your modem.

5 Reseat the Internal Modem

Open the case, making sure to first turn off all power, take out the power cord, and discharge any static electricity. Check that the modem is seated securely in the slot. If the connection isn't tight, the modem won't work.

6 Check the External Plug

An external modem has to get electricity from the wall outlet to work. Make sure everything is plugged in and that the modem is turned on. If it's not plugged in or turned on, it will not work. You'd be surprised at how often this is the cause of a modem problem. If your modem is plugged in and turned on, you should see lights lit up on it.

Watch Out!

- If HyperTerminal isn't installed, you can add it by using the Add/Remove programs feature in the Windows Setup section of the Control Panel.

How to Install a Cable or DSL Modem

Cable modems and DSL modems both connect at high speeds to the Internet. Although they're called modems, they don't actually work like modems—they use a different technology. Both need to be connected to your PC via a network card, so you first must install a network card before installing either of these modems. In this task, I give instructions for installing a cable modem, but installing a DSL modem is similar. Check with your DSL provider for precise details on how to do it.

1 Install a Network Card

Your computer connects to a cable or DSL modem via a network card (often called a *NIC*), so before you can install a cable or DSL modem, you first must install the card. Turn to Chapter 24, "Installing a Home Network," Task 1, "How to Install a Network Card," to learn how to install one.

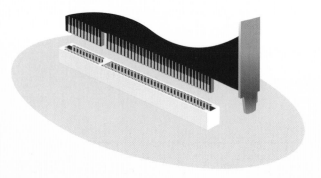

2 Find the Card's MAC Address

Every network card has a specific number that identifies it to the network and Internet. The number is called a *MAC address* or an *adapter address*. To find your card's MAC address, click the **Start** menu, click **Run**, type in `WINIPCFG`, and press **Enter**. (In Windows NT/2000, open a command-prompt window and type `Ipconfig/all` and press **Enter**.) Click the down arrow until you see your network card listed. The MAC address is the long number listed next to Adapter Address. It will read something like this: 00-20-B4-E0-3C-4D.

3 Connect the Modem to Your Cable System

Connect the coaxial cable to the coaxial port on your cable modem. The cable company first must come out to run cable to a spot near your computer.

4 Connect the Modem to Your NIC

Use Ethernet cabling to connect your modem
to your network card. Ethernet cabling is typically thicker than telephone wire but has a
connector that looks and works much like
phone wire—you connect it the same way
you plug a telephone into a telephone jack.
Connect the other end of the cable to your
network card (NIC). Both ends of Ethernet
cabling are the same, so it doesn't matter
which end you plug into the modem and
network card.

5 Turn On the Cable Modem

Find the on/off switch and turn it on.

6 Call Your Cable Company

To start using your cable modem, you need to
call your cable company and give them your
network card's MAC address. After you call
and give them the information, you should be
able to begin using the Internet at high speed
with your cable modem.

Watch Out!

- Be sure you use Ethernet cable and not a
  phone cord when connecting your cable
  modem to your network card.
- When finding your MAC address, be sure
  to scroll down to the name of your network card—if you give the PPP adapter
  address, for example, your cable modem
  won't work.
- You must have something called TCP/IP
  installed and configured properly, and the
  IP address field must be set to **Obtain IP
  Address Automatically**. Check your system documentation or network card documentation, or with your cable company
  to learn how to do it properly.

CHAPTER

22

Installing a Printer

How a Printer Works   218

How to Install a New Printer   220

PRINTERS change as quickly as do computers these days. Laser printers, once the exclusive province of the office because they were so expensive, have dropped in price enough so that they're affordable for the home. And some color inkjet printers now sell for little more than $100, although if you want higher-quality color and faster speed, you have to pay more than that—often in the $200 to $500 range. But even in that range, it's cheaper than ever to buy a new printer.

When buying a new printer, you want to get as high a resolution as possible, measured in dots per inch. And you also would like to get the fastest printer you can afford, measured in pages printed per minute. If you're buying an inkjet printer, you notice that black-and-white pages print faster than color pages, so when buying, take into account which kinds of pages you expect to print more, and buy according to that.

After you buy a printer, you'll find it's easy to install. You need the proper printer cable—and in almost all cases, a cable won't come with the printer, so if you don't have one, buy it when you buy the printer. In addition to a printer cable, you need a printer driver. In most cases, this driver is on a CD or floppy disk provided by the manufacturer, but if it's not, you can use the drivers built into Windows.

Printers are becoming increasingly popular, as well. For more information on installing USB hardware, turn to Chapter 20, "Installing USB Devices."

How a Printer Works

Processor
A processor inside the printer receives the instructions on what needs to be printed. The processor controls the printer mechanism and instructs the printer on what to do.

Parallel port
Using the printer driver, your PC sends the data to be printed through its parallel port. (Some printers attach to your PC through a USB connection, and in that instance, the data would be sent through the USB port.)

Print head
Different kinds of printers, such as laser printers and inkjet printers, use different technologies to do their actual printing. An inkjet printer, for example, uses a print cartridge that moves sideways across a piece of paper, which fires colored ink through tiny nozzles onto paper.

Printer cable
The data travels over a special printer cable (also called a parallel cable or a Centronics cable), and then into a port on the printer. If the printer is a USB printer, it instead travels over the USB cable.

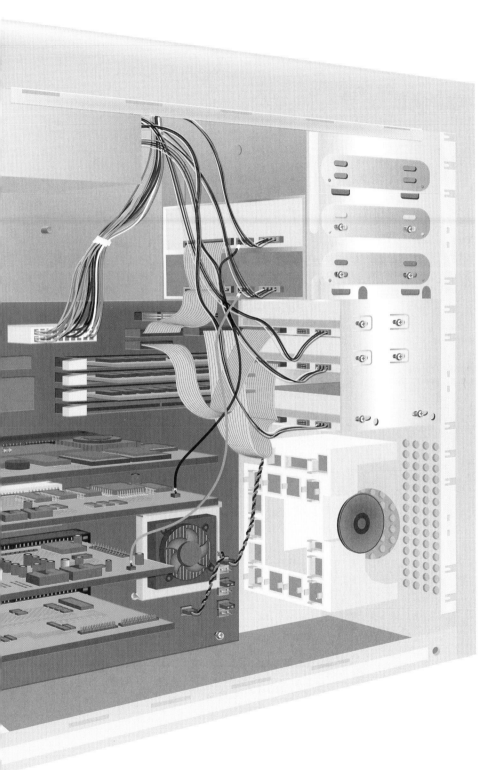

Page description language

When your PC is ready to print something, it needs to tell the printer how to print it, so it must include information about fonts, where to print text, how to print pictures, and so on. It does this by using the printer's page description language. The most common page description language is PCL, used by Hewlett-Packard printers. PostScript is a common page description language as well.

Printer driver

In order to translate what's on your PC into the printer description language, your PC needs to use a piece of software called a printer driver. This driver takes the information from your file and formats it in such a way that the printer can understand it, using the printer's page description language. Each printer has its own unique printer driver.

How to Install a New Printer

Installing a printer is a simple matter of buying the right cable, making sure you plug it into the proper ports on your PC and printer, and installing the right driver. Be sure, when you buy your new printer, that you buy a cable as well, because many printers are sold without cables.

1 Get the Correct Printer Cable

A printer attaches to a PC via the PC's parallel port (also called a Centronics port), a female 25-pin connection. Your printer also has a 25-pin female connection, which might instead be a long serrated slot. Your printer cable should match the printer and PC ports.

If your printer has extra features such as bidirectional printing, enhanced parallel port (EPP), or extended capability port (ECP), buy a cable that has IEEE 1284 printed on it. You often can use CMOS to set your parallel port to use ECP or EPP.

2 Plug In the Cable

After turning off your printer and computer, take off the computer's power cable. Next, plug the printer cable into the proper port on your PC. Some PCs have 25-pin female serial ports, as well as 25-pin parallel ports, so be sure to plug the cable into the parallel port.

The parallel port on your computer is a female connection. After you plug each cable in, secure the cable. Sometimes you do this by tightening tiny screws, and other times by simply snapping wire connectors on each side of the connector.

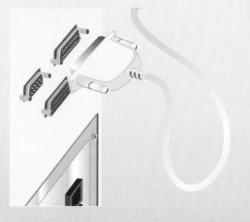

❸ Install the Ink Toner or Cartridge

The printer you've bought might or might not already have an ink cartridge (for inkjet printers) or toner cartridge (for laser printers) in it. Usually, they don't. Follow the manufacturer's instructions for installing the cartridges. Inkjet printers might require more than one cartridge—they might require two or even three. Check your printer documentation to be sure you get the right cartridges.

❹ Install the Printer Drivers

In Windows, select **My Computer** from the Desktop, and then select **Printers**. Double-click the **Add Printer** icon to launch an Add Printer Wizard. You'll be asked for the model of your printer, and also for the location of your printer driver, if you have one. Type in its location on your floppy disk or CD-ROM drive. If you don't have a disk, use the Windows drivers. In some cases, to install a printer driver, you have to run the setup program from the printer-supplied CD in order to install the driver.

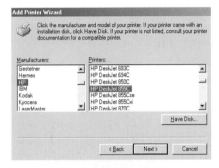

❺ Print Out a Test Sheet of Paper

To be sure your printer is working properly, print out a test sheet of paper. The Installation Wizard asks you whether you want to do this, so be sure to answer Yes. After it prints out, you'll be asked whether it printed properly. Allow enough time for the printer to print the test page before answering Yes or No. You also can print out a test page by going through the **Control Panel**, choosing the **Printers** folder, right-clicking the correct printer, and choosing **Print Test Page** from the General tab.

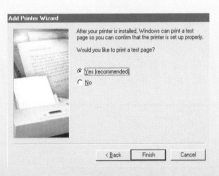

Watch Out!

■ Be sure that you buy the proper printer cable—if you have a bidirectional printer, be sure the cable has IEEE 1284 printed on it.

■ Plug the printer cable into the parallel port on your computer. Some serial ports might look like parallel ports because they have a 25-pin connection like a parallel port.

■ If a printer driver didn't come with your printer, check the manufacturer's Web site or else use a driver that comes in Windows.

C H A P T E R

23

Upgrading Notebook Computers

How a Notebook Computer Works   224

How to Install PCMCIA Cards   226

How to Install a Docking Station   228

AT first blush, it might appear difficult to upgrade a notebook computer (sometimes called a laptop computer, as well). Notebook computers are self-contained units that have most of their capabilities, such as graphics adapters, built right into their internal motherboard. Unlike desktop PCs, they mainly use nonstandard components, so that you can't mix and match components—for example, batteries often work with only one kind of notebook. The same holds true for hard disks, CD-ROM drives, DVD drives, and other peripherals—you can't mix and match them.

However, there are simple ways that you can expand and upgrade your existing notebook. One of the easiest is to install what are called PCMCIA cards—credit-card–size devices that plug into PCMCIA ports on your notebook, usually on the notebook's side. You can buy PCMCIA modems, network cards, and even hard disks, and they're all easy to install, as you see later in this chapter.

Another simple way to expand and upgrade your notebook is to buy a docking station. A docking station is a unit that you plug your notebook into, and that expands the capability of your notebook. You can plug a monitor, keyboard, mouse, printer, modem, and other peripherals into the docking station. You'll be able to use docking stations built only for the specific make and model of your notebook computer, though, so keep that in mind when buying one.

How a Notebook Computer Works

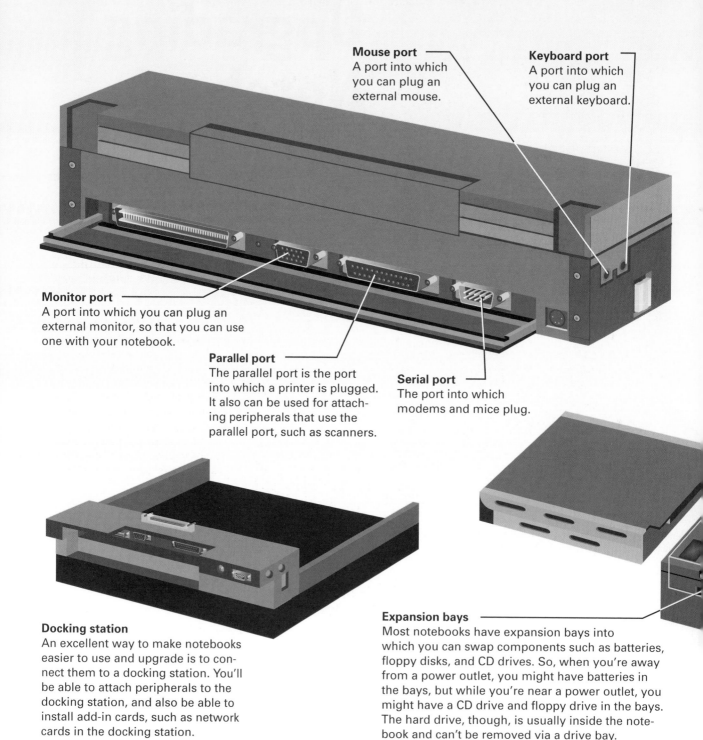

Mouse port
A port into which you can plug an external mouse.

Keyboard port
A port into which you can plug an external keyboard.

Monitor port
A port into which you can plug an external monitor, so that you can use one with your notebook.

Parallel port
The parallel port is the port into which a printer is plugged. It also can be used for attaching peripherals that use the parallel port, such as scanners.

Serial port
The port into which modems and mice plug.

Docking station
An excellent way to make notebooks easier to use and upgrade is to connect them to a docking station. You'll be able to attach peripherals to the docking station, and also be able to install add-in cards, such as network cards in the docking station.

Expansion bays
Most notebooks have expansion bays into which you can swap components such as batteries, floppy disks, and CD drives. So, when you're away from a power outlet, you might have batteries in the bays, but while you're near a power outlet, you might have a CD drive and floppy drive in the bays. The hard drive, though, is usually inside the notebook and can't be removed via a drive bay.

PCMCIA slots

PCMCIA slots are the slots into which PCMCIA cards attach to the notebook. There are three types of PCMCIA slots, corresponding to the types of PCMCIA cards. A Type I slot can accommodate a single Type I card. A Type II slot can accommodate one Type II card, or two Type I cards. A Type III slot can accommodate one Type III card, or a Type I and a Type II card.

PCMCIA cards

One way to upgrade the capabilities of a notebook is to install PCMCIA cards. PCMCIA cards are credit-card–size devices that are put into special PCMCIA slots in the side of the notebook. Modems, network cards, and many other add-ins are available on PCMCIA cards. There are three types of PCMCIA cards. Type I cards are up to 3.3 millimeters thick. They are mainly used for adding memory to a computer. Type II cards are up to 5.5 millimeters thick, and are commonly used for modems and network cards. Type III cards can be up to 10.5 millimeters thick and can be used for hard disks, as well as other devices.

Release latch

You usually install components in drive bays simply by slipping them into the drive bay. When you slip them in, a latch usually locks into place. To remove the component, you usually press on the latch and slide the component out.

How to Install PCMCIA Cards

A notebook computer isn't as expandable as a desktop PC because there are no expansion slots. That doesn't mean, however, that you can't add capabilities to it. The main way you upgrade a notebook is via PCMCIA cards—credit-card–size pieces of electronics that you slide into PCMCIA slots built into the notebook. You can buy PCMCIA modems, network cards, and other peripherals for your notebook. Here's how to do it.

1 Determine the Type of Slot

If you have an older notebook, it might have a Type I PCMCIA slot or slots. If that's the case, you won't be able to use newer Type II or Type III PCMCIA cards in it. So be sure that your PCMCIA card works with your computer.

2 Verify You Have a Free Slot

Notebooks commonly have one or two PCMCIA slots. Be sure that you have one free and that it can accept a PCMCIA card. In some instances, a PCMCIA card takes up more than one slot. And Type II or III cards might take up two slots, so if you have only one slot free, it might not be able to accept a Type III PCMCIA card.

3 Turn Off Your Notebook

You shouldn't install a PCMCIA card in your notebook if it's turned on or plugged in. So, turn it off, and also unplug the power cord.

4 Slide In the PCMCIA Card

Look for the end of the card with the connector on it. That's the end that you put into the slot. The card should slide in easily. Be careful to align it properly so that you don't bend the notebook's internal connector pins. Be sure that the top of the card faces upward—many cards mark the top. When it's aligned properly, push until it's seated firmly in the slot.

5 Turn On the Notebook

Now it's time to get the PCMCIA card to work with your computer. Plug the notebook in or else be sure that it has charged batteries in it. Then, turn the computer on.

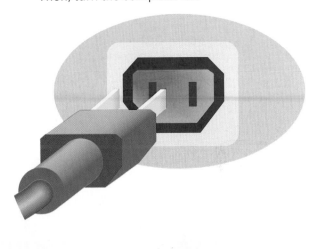

6 Install the Drivers

After you turn your computer on, it should recognize that you've added new hardware, and launch an Add New Hardware Wizard. Follow the steps for adding the hardware, and use the drivers supplied with the card. If your computer doesn't recognize the card, add it manually. From the **Control Panel**, double-click **Add New Hardware**. The Add New Hardware Wizard will then launch. Some notebooks come with PCMCIA management software, which pops up when you first install the card.

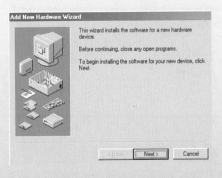

Watch Out!

- Be sure that you have free PCMCIA slots, and that they're of the right type for the PCMCIA card you plan to install.

- When sliding in the card, be sure that it's aligned properly, and don't push too hard or you'll damage the internal connector pins.

- After you've installed the card, go to the manufacturer's Web site and check if there are any new drivers available for the card. If there are, download and install them.

- If Windows doesn't recognize the PCMCIA card, check to see whether there is PCMCIA installation software on your notebook, and run that.

How to Install a Docking Station

Perhaps the best way to make a notebook easier to use, and to upgrade its capabilities, is to get a docking station for it. A docking station has connectors for a monitor, keyboard, mouse, printer, speakers, and other peripherals. You plug your notebook into the docking station, and then plug a keyboard, mouse, and other peripherals into the docking station, so that you can use them with the notebook. Many docking stations also let you install an add-in card, such as a network card, that will then work with your notebook. Not all docking stations and notebooks work the same way.

■ Buy the Right Station

The only docking station that works with your notebook is one designed specifically for it, often available only from the notebook manufacturer. So, be sure that when you buy a docking station, it matches your make and model of notebook.

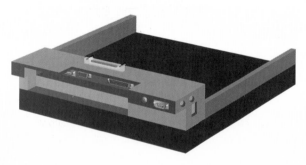

■ Turn Off Your Notebook

After you turn off your notebook, unplug any peripherals attached to it, including the power cord. Close the display panel. You need the back of the notebook free in order to attach it to the docking station. And many notebooks can't be attached to the docking station while the notebook's power is on and while the display panel is open.

3 Locate the Docking Station

There is a connector on the back of your notebook that plugs into the docking station. On many notebooks, a panel protects the connector. Slide that door open to expose the connector. There also might be panels that protect the notebook's serial, parallel, and monitor ports. Slide those closed to protect them.

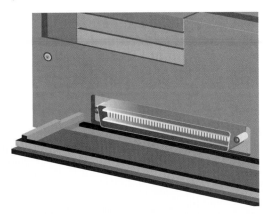

4 Connect the Docking Station

On many notebooks and docking stations, there is a set of guide pins on the docking station that line up with holes on connectors on each side of the connector on the back of the notebook. Align those guide pins first, and then gently push the computer into the docking station until it's secure. On many docking stations, you hear a click when the computer is connected.

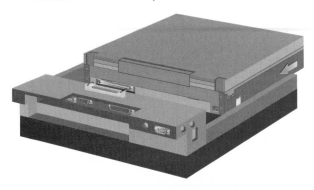

5 Turn On the Notebook

Plug in the docking station's power cord, attach your peripherals, and turn the notebook on. Your peripherals should all work automatically. If, however, you get an Add New Hardware Wizard, follow the instructions for adding the hardware. After you've installed the docking station, if you install any cards into it, you'll install them the same way as you would in a desktop computer, except that you'll install them in the docking station instead of in an empty slot on the motherboard.

Watch Out!

- Never lift the notebook and the docking station when they are connected to one another—you might damage both of them.

- Be sure that the docking station you buy is specifically built for the manufacturer and model of your notebook.

- Turn off your computer and close its display panel before installing it into the docking station, unless its documentation specifically tells you otherwise.

CHAPTER

Installing a Home Network

How Home Networks Work   232

How to Install a Network Card   234

How to Install the Network   236

THESE days, many homes have not just one computer in them, but two, three, and sometimes even more. The problem with having multiple computers in a home is that they can't communicate with one another or share devices such as printers. An even bigger problem is that the computers can't share a high-speed Internet connection, such as a cable modem or DSL modem, because those devices allow only one computer to plug into them.

A home network can solve the problem. It can enable several computers to share a single high-speed Internet connection, as well as enable them to share devices such as printers. Many types of home networks can be set up, but the most common and most useful one—especially for sharing a high-speed Internet connection—is one that uses a hub/router all the computers plug into. To set up a home network, as you'll see in this chapter, you must install network cards in each computer, and then connect the computers to a hub/router using special cabling called Ethernet cable.

How Home Networks Work

You can install many types of home networks. Some enable you to network PCs using your home telephone lines, whereas others allow you to network them wirelessly. But the most common kind of network, pictured here, is one that uses a hub/router and network cards.

Internet

Cable modem

7 Firewall

When a network is connected to the Internet via a high-speed connection such as a cable modem or DSL modem, it's vulnerable to hackers. To keep hackers out, a firewall is used. The firewall stops any unauthorized access to the network or any computers on the network. A firewall can be software or a combination of hardware and software.

4 TCP/IP address sharing

A network hub/router can enable several computers to share an Internet connection, such as a high-speed cable modem or DSL modem. One way it does this is by allowing several computers to share a TCP/IP address, sometimes called an Internet address. To the rest of the Internet, every computer on the network looks as if it has the same Internet address—which is why the computers can all share the connection. But inside the network, the hub/router gives each computer a different internal address.

Firewall

Alert Power AA CD   RD SD OH TX COLL 1 2 3 4

Hub/router

1 Network hub/router

The heart of a home network is the network hub/router—a device that connects PCs with one another and lets them communicate and share resources, such as a high-speed connection to the Internet via DSL or cable modem. The hub physically connects all the PCs to one another, whereas the router connects the network to the Internet. Although hubs and routers can be sold separately, for many home networks, they are both contained in the same device.

5 Printer sharing

One reason for setting up a home network is to enable several computers to share a single printer. The printer is attached to a single PC. Other PCs on the network can send a request to use the printer. The request goes through the hub/router and is then routed to the PC attached to the printer. The printer then prints out what was requested, just as if the local PC were printing it.

2 Network card

To be on a network, a computer needs a network card (sometimes called a NIC for "network interface card"). The computer sends and receives requests for data and other services through the network card.

Network card

Ethernet cable

3 Ethernet cable

Connecting the computers to the hub is special Ethernet cable, made up of a kind of shielded wiring that enables computers to communicate with each other over high speeds.

Ethernet cable

6 File sharing

A network enables computers to share files with one another—allowing PCs to access files from other computers on the network as if they were on its own hard disk. The request goes through the hub/router and is then routed to the PC whose files the first computer wants to share. The first computer can then access those files just as if they were on its own hard disk.

cable

Music .mp3

How to Install a Network Card

For you to be able to set up a home network, each of the computers you want to connect must have a network card installed in it. You connect the network cards to your home network hub/router with an Ethernet cable. Before you can do that, though, you first must install a network card in each computer. (Note: If you already have a network card in one of your computers that is attached to your DSL or cable modem, you won't have to put in a new network card—just use the one that is already there.) You can buy a variety of network cards and cabling for a home network. The most reliable and highest speed are Ethernet cards and cables, so that's what you'll learn to install in this task. As with installing any card in your computer, first turn off your computer, be sure you have no static discharge, and then remove the case. For information on how to do that, turn to Chapter 1, Task 1, "How to Open the Case."

① Buy the Right Card

You should buy network cards that will work properly with the network you're going to install. Buy a PCI network card instead of an ISA network card because PCI cards are much easier to set up. Also, the most common network cards—and network hub/routers—are sold in 10-megabit and 100-megabit speeds. Match the speed of the card you buy to the hub/router you buy.

② Find a Free Slot

After you remove your computer's case, look on the motherboard and locate an empty slot. To fit the card into place, you must remove the small metal flap protecting the slot. The flap is held in place by a small screw (usually a Phillips screw). Remove the screw and remove the flap. Put the screw in a safe place—you'll need it to secure the card you're inserting.

❸ Install the Card

Align the card in the free slot, making sure the connectors on the card line up properly with the slot into which you are inserting the card. Then, using two hands, apply gentle, even pressure to push the card down into the slot. After the card is in place, press down firmly to ensure that it's all the way in the slot.

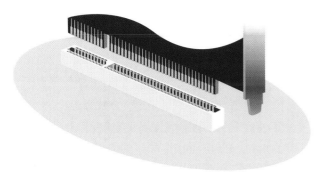

❹ Screw the Card in Place

To ensure that the card won't come loose, screw it into place. Use the same screw you removed from the metal flap, and screw the card into the same place where the metal flap was screwed in.

❺ Turn On Your Computer

Turn your computer back on. When you do, Windows will detect that you've installed a network card and an Add New Hardware Wizard will appear. Follow the directions for installation, including adding the manufacturer's disk if you're prompted. If the Add New Hardware Wizard doesn't launch, run it manually by clicking the **Start** button, choosing **Settings**, selecting **Control Panel**, and double-clicking **Add New Hardware**. If Windows doesn't recognize the card, follow the installation instructions that came with your network card.

❻ Check the Card Configuration

To ensure that your network card has been installed properly, check the Device Manager. Right-click **My Computer**, choose **Properties**, and click the **Device Manager** tab. Scroll down until you see **Network Adapters** and make sure no yellow ! or red X is next to your network card.

Watch Out!

- Be sure the network card is seated firmly—if it isn't, you won't be able to connect your PC to your home network.
- Don't press too hard when inserting the network card or you could damage the card or motherboard.
- Go to the network card manufacturer's Web site and download the latest drivers for the card.

How to Install the Network

As I explained earlier in the chapter, you can install many types of home networks, but the best one for most homes that plan to use a network for sharing a cable modem or DSL modem is one that uses a combination hub and router. (The router and hub aren't separate from each other, but they could be; in addition, both perform separate tasks.) Each PC can then connect to the Internet through a cable modem or DSL modem by way of the hub/router. The router and hub aren't separate from one another—they look like one device. First, you must set up the hub/router and connect PCs to it; after the network is running, you connect it to a cable modem or DSL modem. In this chapter, I'll show you how to connect using a cable modem. Connecting via a DSL is similar, but not identical, so check with your DSL provider about how to connect a home network to a DSL modem.

▌1▐ Plan Your Network

Before installing any hardware, decide where you want to place the hub/router and measure the distance between each computer and the hub/router. Make sure you have enough cable to reach between them. If your computers will be in different rooms, determine how you will run cable between the rooms. Try to keep your hub/router close to your cable modem or DSL modem so they can be easily connected.

▌2▐ Turn Off Your Computers

Power off any of the computers you plan to connect to your home network.

▌3▐ Turn On the Hub/Router's Power

Connect the hub/router to a power outlet, and then find the on/off switch for the hub/router and turn it on.

4 Connect the PCs to the Hub/Router

For each computer you plan to network, plug an Ethernet cable into the port on the hub/router, and then connect the other end of each cable to the network card on each computer.

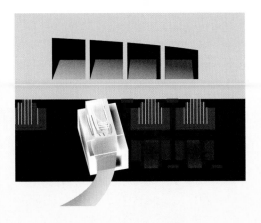

5 Power On Your PCs

Turn on the power for each of the PCs you've connected to the network. To ensure that all the connections are working, look at the lights on the hub/router and on the network cards on the PCs. If all are properly connected, a green light should be visible on each device. If they don't all have green lights, a problem might exist, so check the cables and connections.

6 Run the Home Networking Wizard

You now need to configure each of your computers so that it works on the network. If you have Windows Millennium Edition (also called Windows Me), a Home Networking Wizard can be run, which automatically sets up your PCs for networking. To run it, double-click **My Network Places** on the desktop, double-click the **Home Networking Wizard** icon, and follow the directions onscreen. If you have a version of Windows other than Me, check your hub/router's documentation or Windows documentation for help setting up the network.

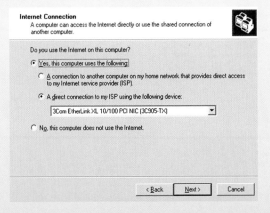

7 Explore Your Network

You should now be able to connect to other computers on your home network. In Windows 95 and 98, double-click the **Network Neighborhood** on the desktop, and you'll see other computers connected to the network. In Windows Me, double-click **My Network Places** on the desktop, double-click **Entire Network**, and double-click the workgroup icon to see the computers.

How to Install the Network *(continued)*

8 Troubleshoot Any Problems

If all your PCs don't show up on the network, check that the cables are all securely connected and that the hub/router is plugged in and its power is turned on. If that doesn't help, turn off the hub/router and PCs and make sure the network cards you installed are seated tightly.

9 Connect Your Cable Modem or DSL Modem

At this point, your network is installed and the computers can connect to each other, but they aren't connected to the Internet. You're ready to connect your network to your cable modem. First, make sure your cable modem is turned on and plugged in. Next, look for a port on the hub/router called the **Cascade Port**, **Uplink Port**, or **WAN Port** and connect the Ethernet cable to the port. Then, connect the other end of the Ethernet cable to your cable modem. If a switch labeled "Cascade" is near the port, make sure it is set to the Cascade position.

⑩ Configure TCP/IP Properly

Your computers need what is called an IP address to use the Internet. To get that address, you need to configure something called TCP/IP. On each PC, right-click the **Network Neighborhood** icon and choose **Properties**. Then, scroll through the list and find your network card. When you find it, highlight it, click **Properties**, and then click the **IP Address** tab. Make sure the **Obtain an IP address automatically** button is selected. Also, ensure the hub/router you bought is configured to assign IP addresses to each of the computers on the network—it's commonly called DHCP. Each hub/router does it differently, so check your documentation to see how to configure yours.

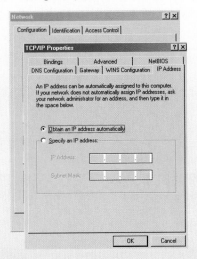

⑪ Verify You Can Use the Internet

Each of the computers on the network should now be capable of accessing the Internet. However, cable companies have varying rules and ways of allowing home networks to access the Internet. If you have a problem getting connected to the Internet, first check that TCP/IP is installed properly, as outlined in the previous step. Then, check with your cable company for help troubleshooting the problem.

⑫ Install a Firewall

When you connect your network to the Internet, you potentially open it up to hackers. To protect your network and computers, install a firewall on your hub/router. Your hub/router should come with firewall software. Read the documentation to learn how to install it.

Watch Out!

- Be sure to use Ethernet cable and not phone line cable when putting together your network. If you use telephone line, the network won't work.

- Check with your cable company or DSL provider before installing a home network in which several PCs will share an Internet connection. Some companies have restrictions or technical information you need before you can install such a network.

- When you first turn on your hub/router and PCs attached to it, wait a few minutes before using Network Neighborhood or My Network Places. It can take a while after the computers boot up for them all to talk to one another.

- If you want to allow PCs to share printers and other devices such as scanners, you must designate them as shared devices. Check your hub/router's documentation or Windows documentation to see how to do this. However, you should not use file sharing and printer sharing if you're connecting your network to the Internet because hackers could then possibly hack into your computers.

CHAPTER

25

Performing Computer Maintenance

Computer Maintenance You Should Perform   242

What to Check for When
You Run into Problems   244

WHEN it comes to taking care of your computer, the old adage, "An ounce of prevention is worth a pound of cure," couldn't be more true. The best way to help ensure that you won't need to needlessly repair your PC is to perform basic computer maintenance—doing things such as scanning your hard disk for errors, using antivirus software, and cleaning out the inside of your PC.

In this chapter, we look at the basic computer maintenance you should perform regularly—everything from backing up your hard disk, to creating a Windows "rescue" disk, to making sure that you always have the latest drivers for your hardware, to how to blow dust out of the inside of your computer. If you regularly follow this advice, your computer will be more likely to keep running at tip-top shape.

And we also look at basic troubleshooting tips, should something go wrong with your PC. Before calling in a technician, or deciding to replace a computer part, there are a variety of steps you can take that can save you time and money. Doing basic things such as checking whether your add-in boards are properly secured, whether the cables are all tight, and even whether everything is plugged in, means less hours of computing frustration—and less money spent on needless repairs.

Computer Maintenance You Should Perform

The best way to be sure that nothing goes wrong with your computer is to perform computer maintenance on your software and hard disk regularly. Take the following steps and you'll help make sure that you'll fix problems with your computer—before they happen.

◻ Scan Your Hard Disk for Errors

As you use your computer, you can get disk "errors," which can result in the loss of data, programs not running, and even worse. To be sure that you clean up any disk errors, run the ScanDisk program in Windows. It searches your hard disk for errors, and fixes them if it finds any. To use it, click the **Start** menu, choose **Programs**, and then **Accessories**. From the Accessories menu, choose **System Tools**, and then choose **ScanDisk**.

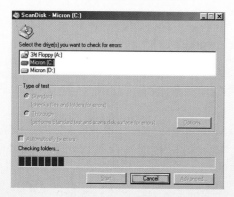

◻ Defragment Your Hard Drive

As you use your hard disk, the files and programs on it become fragmented and spread out over your entire hard disk. So your hard disk has to work harder in order to fetch them. This slows down your hard disk and makes your computer work less effectively. Most versions of Windows have defragmentation software built into them. To use it, click the **Start** menu, choose **Programs**, and then **Accessories**. From the Accessories menu, choose **System Tools**, and then **Disk Defragmenter**.

◻ Create a Windows Startup Disk

A Windows Startup disk lets you start up your computer from its floppy drive, if something goes wrong with your computer or hard disk and it won't start. To create a Windows Startup disk, choose **Settings** from the Start menu, and then choose **Control Panel**. After Control Panel opens, double-click **Add/Remove Programs**. From the window that appears, click the **Startup Disk** tab and follow the instructions for creating a Startup disk. Use a blank floppy disk or one with data you don't mind losing.

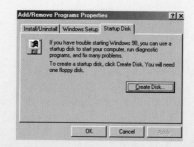

❹ Run Antivirus Software

You can get a computer virus from anywhere—the Internet, via email, from your company's network, or even from software you buy in a store. To be sure that your computer doesn't get infected, buy and run antivirus software, such as Norton's AntiVirus. Most antivirus software has an "auto-protect" feature in which the antivirus runs all the time, constantly checking your system to make sure it doesn't have a virus. To be safe, use the auto-protect feature. In addition, regularly scan your computer for viruses.

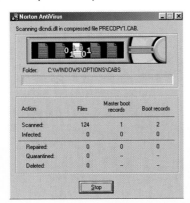

❺ Back Up Your Hard Disk

To be sure that you don't lose any vital information, back up your hard disk to a tape drive, a removable drive, floppy disks, your company's network, or even to the Internet. Windows includes backup software. To use it, click the **Start** menu, choose **Programs**, and then **Accessories**. From the Accessories menu, choose **System Tools**, and then **Backup**. You also can buy special backup software that has more features than the backup software built into Windows.

❻ Check the Web Sites

Drivers are required for hardware such as printers, modems, graphics cards, and other devices to work with Windows. Sometimes the drivers have small bugs in them, or become outdated. To be sure that you don't run into hardware problems, it's a good idea to regularly check manufacturer's Web sites to see whether they have new versions of drivers that you can download and install. Video and sound drivers are often updated every three to six months.

Watch Out!

- Don't let too much time go between scanning your disk for errors—that way you won't run into trouble.

- Every month, check the Web site of the company that makes your antivirus software to see whether they have new "virus definitions." And before running antivirus software for the first time, get the newest virus definitions.

- Defragment your hard disk regularly so that it doesn't slow down dramatically.

- Regularly check Web sites for the latest updated video and sound drivers—outdated drivers are among the most common causes of computer problems.

What to Check for When You Run into Problems

Computers are such complex pieces of equipment that there are literally thousands of unique problems that can occur—and it often can be almost impossible to track down the source of the problem. Here, however, are things you should do when you run into a problem on your PC.

1 Restart Your Computer

Problems might occur for unexplained reasons, and then never happen again. Often the simplest way to fix them is to restart your computer. Shut the computer down by clicking the **Start** menu and choosing **Shut Down**. If that doesn't work, try pressing **Ctrl+Alt+Delete** twice. If neither of those works, try pressing the **Reset** switch on your computer. If that doesn't work, or if your computer doesn't have a reset switch, press the **Power** button to turn it off, and then press it again to turn it back on.

2 Ensure Everything Is Plugged In

You'd be surprised how frequently the cause of a computing problem is simply that not all the hardware has been plugged in and turned on. As technical support personnel will tell you, many printer "problems" are caused by the printer not being plugged in.

3 Check Your Cables and Connections

Often, the cause of the problem is loose cables, switches, or connections. Check external connections and cables to see that they're tight. If that doesn't solve the problem, check the internal connections, such as between controller cards and cables, or drives and cables, to make sure they're tight. Pay particular attention to all the connections of your power supply cable. If those connections become loose, your computer won't turn on.

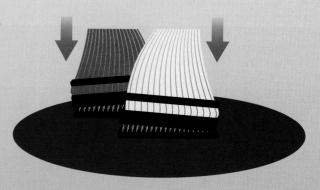

4 Use the Windows Device Manager

The Windows Device Manager checks your hardware to see whether everything is working properly, so it's a good place to troubleshoot problems. To get to it, right-click **My Computer** and choose **Properties**. Then, click the **Device Manager** tab. If Windows detects problems with a device, you'll see an exclamation mark next to it.

5 Look for Signs of Overheating

Turn off your PC and let it cool down for an hour. Then, turn it back on again. If the problem goes away, but then returns after your PC has been on for a while, the problem might be caused by overheating. If your microprocessor chip has a cooling fan, make sure it's connected and working. Check any other fans inside your case as well. Use canned air to blow away dust—dust can lead to overheating.

6 Reseat Add-In Boards and Chips

It's possible that the problem was caused by an add-in card that was loose. You won't be able to tell that they're loose by looking at them, so you'll have to reseat each of them. Make sure each is firmly seated into the slot on the motherboard. Also check the chips on your motherboard, such as the CPU, to see whether they've come loose. Reseat each of them to make sure that they're firmly in position. And make sure your RAM is connected tightly as well.

Watch Out!

- If you have a PC with many drives, add-in cards, and other devices, your power supply might not provide enough electricity to power them. Consider buying a new power supply.

- A common cause of PC problems is programs running in the background that you might not know about. To see what is being loaded at your computer's startup, click **Start**, **Run**, then type `msconfig` and click **OK**. In the box that appears, click the **Startup** tab and you'll see all the programs that run at startup. Uncheck any and reboot, and the program won't run. That might solve your problem. If not, you can have the program run at startup by checking its box.

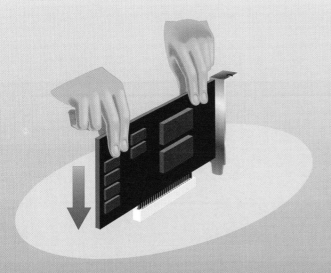

Glossary

3D card A graphics card, used primarily for games, which enables realistic 3D motion.

A

Adapter card *See* Expansion card.

Add-in card *See* Expansion card.

AGP (Accelerated Graphics Port) A bus specification that enables 3D graphics to display quickly on a computer.

Antivirus software Software that checks a computer for viruses and eradicates them if it finds them.

Audio cable A cable that runs between a CD-ROM drive and a sound card and that enables the sound card to play audio CDs.

B

Backplate A metal plate attached to the motherboard and case, which helps secure add-in cards to the motherboard.

Baud Baud was the prevalent measure for data transmission speed until it was replaced by a more accurate term: bps (bits per second).

Bidirectional parallel port A parallel port that enables data to flow in two directions between the PC and printer.

BIOS (Basic Input/Output System) The system that performs all the basic functions of your computer, such as sending information from your keyboard to your PC. The system BIOS is contained on the BIOS chip.

BIOS chip A chip that contains a system's BIOS.

Bootup screen The first screen you see when you start your computer.

C

Cable modem A device that enables your computer to access the Internet at high speed via the cable TV system. Although it's called a modem, it uses different technology from modems that use traditional telephone lines.

Cache memory Random access memory (RAM) that a computer microprocessor can access more quickly than it can access regular RAM.

CD-R drive A CD-ROM drive that lets you write data one time to special CDs.

CD-ROM drive A device that can run CD-ROMs.

CD-RW drive A CD-ROM drive that lets you write data many times to special CDs.

Centronics port *See* Parallel port.

Chip puller A tool for removing chips from your PC.

CMOS battery A small battery that provides power to the CMOS chip.

CMOS chip A chip that contains a record of the hardware installed on your PC. The CMOS battery supplies it with power so the data remains stored even when the computer is turned off.

CMOS setup screen A screen that enables you to change your CMOS settings.

COM port   *See* Serial port.

Controller   A device found on an add-in card or on the motherboard that connects the motherboard to a hard drive.

Controller card   An add-in card that has a controller on it. *See also* Controller.

CPU (Central Processing Unit)   The main processor on a PC, such as a Pentium chip.

D

Daisy-chain   A configuration in which devices are connected one to another.

Defragmenter   Software that makes a hard disk run more quickly by *defragmenting* it—placing all related pieces of files next to one another so they can be called into memory more quickly.

Device driver   A file that controls a particular type of device that is attached to your computer and that is required for the device to run. Device drivers exist for printers, displays, CD-ROM readers, disk drives, and so on.

Device Manager   A troubleshooting utility in Windows that shows information about the devices attached to your PC, such as hard drives, monitors, and video cards.

DHCP (Dynamic Host Configuration Protocol)   A computer protocol that assigns a different IP address to a computer each time it connects to the Internet. When you set up a home network to share a high-speed Internet connection, such as a cable modem, you often need to also set up DHCP.

Digital camera   A camera that records and stores photographic images in digital format, which can be sent to a computer.

DIMM (Dual Inline Memory Module)   A kind of RAM used in newer PCs. It attaches to the motherboard via a series of pins.

DIN connector   A connector that connects a keyboard to a computer.

DIP (Dual Inline Package)   A kind of RAM used in older computers.

DIP switch   A switch on an add-in card or on the motherboard that is used to configure a computer or peripherals.

Display adapter   *See* Graphics card.

Docking station   A piece of hardware you attach to a laptop that enables the laptop to use expansion cards and devices such as external monitors and keyboards.

Drive bay   A bay inside a PC into which you install devices such as hard disks, floppy disks, and CD-ROM drives.

Driver   A piece of software used to enable a peripheral, such as a printer or video card, to work with your PC.

DSL modem   A device that enables your computer to access the Internet at high speed via special DSL lines. Although it's called a modem, it uses different technology from modems that use traditional telephone lines.

DVD decoder card   An add-in card that helps play DVDs.

DVD drive   A drive that can run DVD discs or play DVD movies.

E

EDO RAM (Extended Data Output RAM)   A type of random access memory.

Enhanced parallel port   A parallel port that enables data to flow in two directions between the PC and printer.

Enhanced parallel port cable   A cable you must use if you want to take advantage of the enhanced parallel port. The numbers and IEEE 1284 are printed on the side of an enhanced parallel port cable.

EPP/ECP (Enhanced Parallel Port/Enhanced Capability Port)   A kind of parallel port that enables data to flow in two directions between the PC and peripherals. It also enables higher data transfer rates than the original parallel port. EPP is for nonprinter peripherals; ECP is for printers and scanners. *See also* Enhanced parallel port and Enhanced parallel port cable.

Expansion card   Also called adapters or add-in cards, these plug into the motherboard on expansion slots and expand how your PC can be used. Video cards, disk controllers, and graphics cards are just a few of the expansion cards you can add to a PC.

Expansion slot   A slot on the motherboard into which expansion cards can be plugged.

F

FAT and FAT32 (File Allocation Table) A table an operating system maintains on a hard disk that provides a map of the clusters (the basic unit of logical storage on a hard disk), detailing where files have been stored.

Firewall   A hardware and software combination that protects a computer from being attacked by hackers on the Internet. Using a personal firewall is a good idea when setting up a home network connected to the Internet—it can keep it from getting attacked.

Flash memory   A kind of memory that can be easily updated by running a patch or piece of software. BIOS chips often contain flash memory, and so easily can be updated by running software. Flash memory is also called flash RAM.

Floppy drive   A drive that stores information on removable disks that hold 1.44MB of data.

Format   To prepare a disk, such as a hard disk, so it can be used by a computer.

G

Game port   A port into which you plug a joystick or other gaming device.

Graphics accelerator   A graphics card, chip, or chipset that speeds up the displaying of graphics on a PC.

Graphics card   An add-in card that gives your computer the capability to display graphics and video on your monitor.

H

Hard drive   Where your data and programs are stored. They stay on the hard disk even when you turn off your computer.

Hardware driver   *See* Driver.

I

IDE (Integrated Drive Electronics)   A standard that details the way in which a computer's motherboard communicates with storage devices, such as hard disks.

IDE/EIDE hard drive   A hard drive that connects to the motherboard via an IDE/EIDE controller card.

Indicator light   The light or lights on the front of the PC that show the computer is turned on, or that the hard disk or CD-ROM drive is being used.

Ink cartridge   A cartridge for inkjet printers.

IP address   A set of numbers, such as 150.2.123.134, that identifies each computer connected to the Internet. To use many Internet services, each computer must have a unique IP address.

J–L

Joystick   A device for playing games, which plugs into the game port.

Jumper   A small set of pins that is set in a particular way on the motherboard or add-in card to configure devices to work with a PC.

Keyboard port   A port into which the keyboard is plugged.

LAN (local area network)   A network of computers connected together so they can share files and printers and also share a high-speed Internet connection, such as a cable modem. This enables them all to access the Internet from one connection.

M

Mac address   A number that identifies a network card. Each network card has a unique Mac address so that it's the only one in the world with that address. When you install a cable modem, you must tell your cable provider your network card's Mac address; otherwise, you won't be able to connect to the Internet.

Memory bank   A series of slots or sockets on the motherboard that holds RAM.

Memory socket   A socket on the motherboard into which RAM is installed.

Microprocessor   *See* CPU.

Modem   Short for *modulator/demodulator*. A device for connecting a computer to other computers or the Internet. Modems can be located outside the computer (called an external modem), or inside the computer (called an internal modem).

Motherboard   The main part of the PC—a very large board into which the CPU, add-in cards, chips, RAM, and many other devices are plugged.

Mounting rails   Rails inside a drive bay to which hard drives and other storage devices are attached.

Mounting screws   Screws that secure a drive into a drive bay.

Mouse port   A port into which the mouse is plugged.

MP3 file   A computer file ending in the extension .mp3 that when run plays music.

MP3 player   A small portable device that can play MP3 files.

N–O

Nanosecond   The speed at which RAM is rated. The lower the nanosecond rating, the faster the memory. So, for example, a 60-nanosecond chip is faster than an 80-nanosecond chip.

NetCam   A small, inexpensive video camera that attaches to your computer and lets other people see videos of you live over the Internet.

Network card (NIC)   An add-in card that enables a computer to be connected to a network or to the cable system or DSL line to get a high-speed Internet connection.

Network hub   A device to which PCs are connected that enables them to communicate with one another and enables each PC to gain access to the Internet, through the hub.

Nonparity RAM chips   RAM chips that do not perform error checking to see whether any other memory chips are not functioning properly. This is a newer type of memory used in 486 PCs and Pentiums.

Operating system   Software that handles all the major operations of a computer.

P–Q

Parallel port   A port into which the printer is plugged. It also can be used for scanners and other external devices.

Parity RAM chips   RAM chips that perform error checking to see whether any other memory chips are not functioning properly. This is generally an older type of memory. Usually, 486 PCs and Pentiums use memory that is nonparity. Parity RAM chips have nine chips on them, instead of the eight found on nonparity memory.

Partition   A separate portion of a hard drive. It can also be used as a verb: You divide a hard drive into sections by partitioning it.

PCMCIA card   A credit-card–size add-in card that plugs into a laptop computer and gives it extra functionality. Modems and network cards are common PCMCIA cards.

PCMCIA slot   A slot into which a PCMCIA card is plugged.

Peripheral   A general term that refers to any device, such as a printer, modem, scanner, or others, that isn't required for the basic functioning of a computer but that can be used to enhance the way it works, or that gives it extra functionality.

Phone jack   A connector into which you plug a telephone wire so you can connect your modem to the telephone system.

Pickup tool   A tool for picking up small objects that have fallen into your computer.

Port   A connection on your computer into which you plug a cable, connector, or device.

Power cable   A cable that connects the power supply and provides power to devices in the PC, such as hard drives and floppy drives.

Power supply   A device inside your PC that provides power to your PC by converting the current from your wall outlet to the type of power that can be used by your PC and all its components.

R

RAM (Random Access Memory)   Memory where programs are run and data is stored while the data is being manipulated. When you turn off your computer, any information in RAM is lost.

RAM cache   Memory that sits between your CPU and your main RAM. Information is shuttled here from the main RAM so that it's available more quickly to the CPU.

RAMBUS   A type of high-speed RAM used in the fastest and most expensive computers.

Removable drive   A device that stores data permanently like a hard drive or a floppy drive does, but on removable disks. These disks commonly hold several hundred megabytes or more of data.

Reset button   A button that turns off your computer and then automatically turns it back on.

Ribbon cable   A wide ribbonlike cable that connects a drive to a disk controller.

RIMM (RDRAM Inline Memory Module)   A form of high-speed memory used by the newest, most powerful computers.

ROM (Real Only Memory)   Memory that can be read but can't be changed.

ROM BIOS chip   A chip that holds the code necessary for starting up your computer and for basic functions of receiving and sending data to and from hardware devices, such as the keyboard and disk drives.

S

SCSI (Small Computer Systems Interface) A hardware interface for connecting hard disks, scanners, CD-ROM drives, and other devices to a PC.

SDRAM (Synchronous Dynamic Random Access Memory) A generic name for various kinds of DRAM that are synchronized with the clock speed for which the microprocessor is optimized.

Serial port A port into which modems and other devices are plugged.

SIMMs (Single Inline Memory Modules) A kind of RAM used in newer PCs. They attach to the motherboard via a series of pins.

Socket 7 The descriptive term for the way certain Intel Pentium microprocessors plug into a computer motherboard so they make contact with the motherboard's built-in wires or data bus.

Sound card An add-in card that enables your computer to play music and sounds.

T

Tape drive A drive that enables data to be copied to a tape. The tape can hold hundreds of megabytes of data and is commonly used to back up data and hard disks.

TCP/IP (Transmission Control Protocol/Internet Protocol) The basic communication language or protocol of the Internet. It also can be used as a communications protocol in the private networks called intranets and in extranets.

Terminator A device attached to a device on the end of a SCSI daisy-chain that lets the chain know the device is the first or last device in the chain.

Toner cartridge An ink cartridge for laser printers.

U

UART (Universal Asynchronous Receiver/Transmitter) The chip that controls a computer's serial port and controls the interface to serial devices such as modems.

Universal Serial Bus (USB) A standard that enables devices to be easily connected to a PC without having to open the case.

Uplink port A port on a network hub that connects the hub to a cable modem or another external device for accessing the Internet.

USB hub A device that enables many USB devices to connect to a computer at the same time.

USB port A port that uses the USB standard and that enables USB devices to easily connect to a PC.

V–X

Video port A port on the back of a graphics card to which the monitor is connected.

Virus A destructive program that can wreak havoc on a PC.

WebCam *See* NetCam.

Y–Z

Y2K bug The incapability of certain computers or computer functions to work when the year 2000 occurred.

Zip drive A removable drive that can hold 100MB or more of data.

Index

Symbols

3D graphics cards, 159. *See also* graphics cards
how it operates, 160
16550 UART serial ports, 208

A

AC adapters, 200
AC power supplies, 52
accessing
CMOS, 31
CMOS settings, 36
system information, 20
Accessories menu commands
Communications, 212
System Tools, 21, 243
adapter address, 214
adapters (keyboard), 134
ADC (analog-to-digital converters), 145
Add button, 209
Add New Hardware command (Control Panel menu), 147, 171
Add New Hardware Wizard, 185
adding
additional floppy drives, 79
hard drives, 57-60, 66
hardware, scanners, 147
memory, 48-49
addresses
adapter, 214
MAC, 214
AGP slots, 163
analog-to-digital converters (ADC), 145
scanners, 145
ARM processor, 191
attaching audio cables, 87
ATX form factor, 30
audio cables, 83
attaching, 87
automatic configuration, USB, 197
avoiding electric shock, 55

B

backing up
hard drives, 26, 62, 104, 243
installing motherboards, 31
Backup command (System Tools menu), 243
Basic Input/Output System (BIOS) chip, 21-24
upgrading, 21
batteries
CMOS, 14, 36
failure, 36
installing, 156
motherboard, 24
removing, 37
replacing, 36-37
bays
drive, 9, 15
drives
locating, 105
tape drives, 123
expansion, 224
free, 84
locating, 124
BIOS, 21
flash, 24
upgrading, 38
installing, 38
settings, 105
upgrading, 27, 38-39
BIOS (Basic Input/Output System) chip, 21-24
upgrading, 21
BIOS settings, checking before installing hard drives, 62
bootable floppy disks, 84
creating, 105
booting from floppy disks, 70
buttons, 139
Add, 209
More Info, 212

C

cables
audio, 83
attaching, 87

CD audio, connecting to sound cards, 185
connecting, 35
controller, connecting, 109
data
connecting, 86, 98
connecting to hard drives, 69
decoder, DVD drives, 93
disconnecting, 68
disconnecting from sound card, 183
Ethernet, 233
installing, 214-215
LED, connecting, 35
modem, connecting, 238
monitor, plugging in, 166
parallel, connecting, 146
power
attaching, 127
connecting, 35
floppy drives, 77
power supply, 119
printer, 218-220
ribbon, 63, 83
attaching, 127
DVD drives, 93
floppy drives, 75-76
IDE hard drive, 58
length, checking, 85, 125
tape drives, 123
SCSI, 103
connecting, 150
sound card, connecting, 96
speaker, connecting, 98
TV-out, connecting, 98
unplugging, 33
USB, 190, 196
connecting, 199
connecting to hubs, 201
connecting to PCs, 149, 200
connecting to scanners, 148
calibrating scanners
parallel port, 147
SCSI, 151
USB, 149

cameras, digital, 153
    connecting to computers, 157
    digital conversion, 155
    flash memory, 154
    how it operates, 154
    image manipulation, 154
    image sensor, 155
    installing, 156-157
    lens, 154
    PC transfer, 155
    pixels, 155
    shutter, 154
capabilities, monitors, 162
cards
    connecting NetCam to, 177
    controller, 102
        SCSI, 106-107
    graphics, 159
        how it operates, 160
        installing, 164-165
    NetCam, 174
    network, 233-234
        installing, 214, 234-235
    removing, 32
    sound, checking for, 85
    USB. *See* USB cards
cases
    opening, 12-15
    removing, 13
    screws, 13
        removing, 13
CCD (charged-coupling
    device), 155
CD audio cable, connecting to
    sound cards, 185
CD drives, 81-83
    controllers
        connecting, 85
        determining, 85
    data cables, connecting, 86
    how they operate, 83
    installing, 86-87
        precautions, 84-85
    replacing, 88-89
    speed, 81
CD-ROM, 8
CD-ROM drives, 25
central processing unit. *See*
    CPU
changing CMOS settings, 69
charged-coupling device
    (CCD), 155

checking
    BIOS settings before installing
        hard drives, 62
    drive bay before installing
        hard drives, 63
    modem system settings, 212
    phone cords, 213
    phone jacks, 213
    phone lines, 213
checking for overheating, 245
chip puller, 7
chips
    BIOS, 21
        upgrading, 21
    CMOS, 14
    DAC, 180
    DSP, 181
    embedded graphics, 160
    ROM BIOS, 14
choosing motherboards, 30
cleaning the mouse, 132
CMOS (Complementary Metal-
    Oxide Semiconductor), 20, 24
    accessing, 31
CMOS battery, 14, 36
CMOS chip, 14
CMOS screen, 21
    BIOS settings, 105
CMOS settings
    accessing, 36
    changing, 69
    restoring, 37
COM port, 208. *See also*
    communications ports; serial
    ports
commands
    Accessories menu
        Communications, 212
        System Tools, 21, 243
    Communications menu,
        HyperTerminal, 212
    Control Panel menu, Add
        New Hardware, 147, 171
    My Computer icon context
        menu, Properties, 198
    Programs menu, Accessories,
        21, 212
    System Tools menu
        Backup, 243
        System Information, 21
communicating devices, 24

Communications menu
    commands, HyperTerminal, 212
communications port, 208. *See
    also* COM port; serial ports
Complementary Metal-Oxide
    Semiconductor. *See* CMOS
computer maintenance, 242-243
configuration, memory, 47
connecting
    cable modems, 238
    cables, 35
        data, 98
        LED, 35
        power, 35
        sound card, 96
        speaker, 98
        TV-out, 98
    cameras to computers, 157
    CD audio cable to sound
        cards, 185
    CD drive controllers, 85
    connectors, 35
    data cables to hard drives, 69
    decoder cards, 98
    DSL modems, 238
    Internet, 212
    modems to cable systems, 214
modems to NIC, 215
    modems to serial ports, 210
    MP3 USB cable, 192
    NetCam to cards, 177
    parallel cables, 146
    parallel ports to
        motherboard, 24
    PCs to hub/router, 237
    phone cords to modems,
        209-211
    power cables, 109
    power cords to modems, 210
    power supply, Zip drives, 117
    serial ports to motherboard, 24
    USB cables, 150, 199
        to hubs, 201
        to PCs, 149, 193, 200
        to scanners, 148
    USB devices to hubs, 201
    Zip drives, motherboard, 119
connections, scanners, 144
connectors
    connecting, 35
    determining type, 132-134
    power, 83

free, 84
  tape drives, 123-125
removable drives, 114
removing, 32
unplugging, 33
Control Panel menu commands,
  Add New Hardware, 147, 171
controller cables,
  connecting, 109
controller cards, 102
  installing, 64-65
  proprietary, installing, 126
  SCSI, 106
    installing, 106-107
controllers, 83
  connecting, 85
  determining, 85
  DVD drives, 93-95
  floppy drives, 75
  IDE hard drive, 59
  tape drives, 122-124
types of, determining, 85
conversion, digital, 155
converter, DAC, 191
cookie, removable drives, 114
cooling, CPU, 28
cords, power, 12
CPU (central processing unit),
  14. *See also* microprocessors
  cooling, 28-29
  installing, 28-29, 34
  LIF socket, removing from, 28
  socket types, 27
  specifications, 31
  speed, determining, 26
  testing, 29
  type, determining, 26
  type 1 slot, removing from, 29
  upgrading, 26-27
CPU cooling units, 28-29. *See
  also* heat sinks
CPU socket, 25
current, electromagnetic, 180

D

DAC chips, 180
DAC converter, 191
daisy chain, 103
daisy-chained devices, 196
data cables
  connecting, 98
    CD drives, 86
  connecting to hard drives, 69

data transfer, USB, 197
DC power supplies, 52
decoder cables, DVD drives, 93
decoder cards
  connecting, 98
  DVD drives, 92
determining
  CD drive controllers, 85
  controllers, DVD drives, 95
  CPU socket type, 27
  CPU speed, 26
  monitor capabilities, 162
  need for parity chips, 46
  primary graphics card, 169
  primary monitor, 169
  SCSI ID numbers, 110
  type of
    connector, 132-134
    CPU, 26
    graphics card, 162
    PCMCIA slot, 226
    slot, 163
Device Manager, 245
  enabling USB, 203
Device Manager tab, 198, 245
device software, installing, 198
devices
  communicating, 24
  disconnecting from sound
    cards, 182
  removing, 32
  SCSI
    installing, 104. *See also*
      SCSI devices, installing
    terminating
      (internal/external), 111
  storage, 25. *See also* CD-ROM
    drives; floppy drives; hard
    drives
  USB
    connecting to hubs, 201
    installing, 198-199, 203
Diagnostics tab, 212
digital cameras, 153
  batteries, 156
  connecting to computers, 157
  digital conversion, 155
  flash memory, 154
  how it operates, 154
  image manipulation, 154
  image sensor, 155
  installing, 156-157

lens, 154
PC transfer, 155
pixels, 155
shutter, 154
digital conversion, 155
Digital Versatile Discs. *See*
  DVDs
DIMMs (dual inline memory
  modules), 25, 45
  installing, 49
  parity chips, 45-46
  removing, 49
diodes, 144
  scanners, 144
DIP switches, 16
DIPs (dual inline packages), 44
disconnecting
  cables, 68
  cables from sound cards, 183
  devices from sound cards, 182
disks
  drivers, 19
  floppy, bootable, 84, 105
  hard
    backing up, 26
    formatting, 109
  Zip removable drives, 114
docking stations, 224
  installing, 228
drive, hard, setting jumpers, 67
drive bays, 9, 15
  checking before installing
    hard drive, 63
  locating, 105
  tape drives, 123
drive speed, 81
drive switches, setting, 86-88
driver disks, 19
drivers
  installing
    graphics cards, 165
    keyboard, 135
    modems, 209-211
    installing, 209-211
    monitors, 167, 171
    mouse, 133
    printer, 219
    software, 87-89, 99
    tape drives, 127
    USB, 203
  updating, 243

drives
  CD, 81-83
    controllers, 85
    data cables, connecting, 86
    how they operate, 83
    installing, 84-87. *See also*
      CD drives, installing
    replacing, 88-89
    speed, 81
  CD-ROM, 25
  DVD, 93
    controllers, 95
    installing, 94-96. *See also*
      DVD drives, installing
  external tape drives, 122
  floppy, 8, 15, 25
    adding additional, 79
    controller, 75
    installing, 73, 78-79
    mounting screws, 75-77
    power cables, removing, 77
    power supply, 74
    read/write heads, 75
    removing, 76-77
    ribbon cables, 75-76
    testing, 79
  hard, 25
    adding, 57-60, 66
    backing up, 104
    connecting data cables
      to, 69
    formatting, 70-71
    freeing space, 60
    IDE, 58-59
    installing, 68
    partitioning, 70
    precautions before
      installing, 62. *See also*
      hard drives, precautions
      before installing
    purchasing, 61
    replacing, 57-61, 68-69
    SCSI, 108. *See also* SCSI
      hard drives
    slow, 60
  master, 97
  primary, 97
  removable, 15, 113. *See also*
    Zip drives
    connectors, 114
    cookie, 114
    metal shield, 115
    read/write heads, 115
    zip disks, 114

SCSI
  installing, multiple,
    110-111
  terminating, 108
secondary, 97
slave, 97
tape
  controller, 122-124
  drive bays, 123
  drivers, installing, 127
  external drives, 122
  free bays, 124
  how it operates, 123
  installing, 124-126. *See
    also* tape drives,
    installing
  installing drivers, 127
  power cables, 127
  power connectors, 123-125
  ribbon cables, 123-127
Zip, 113
  connecting power supply
    to, 117
  connecting to
    motherboards, 119
  installation software, 119
DSL modems
  connecting, 238
  installing, 214-215
DSP chips, 181
dual inline memory modules.
  See DIMMs
dual inline packages. *See* DIPs
DVD drives, 8, 93
  controllers, 93-95
  decoder cables, 93
  decoder cards, 92
  graphics cards, 92
  installing, 96
    precautions, 94-95
  power connectors, 93
  ribbon cables, 93
DVDs (Digital Versatile
  Discs), 91

E

ECC (error correcting code
  memory), 45
ECP (extended capabilities
  port), 147
EISA slot, 163
electric shock, avoiding, 55
electricity, static, 12

electromagnetic current, 180
embedded graphics chip, 160
enabling USB, 203
enhanced parallel port (EPP),
  147. *See also* ECP; SPP
EPP (enhanced parallel port),
  147. *See also* ECP; SPP
error correcting code memory
  (ECC), 45
Ethernet cable, 233
expansion bays, 224
expansion boards, 16
  DIP switches, 16
  jumpers, 16
expansion cards, jumpers, 17
expansion slots, 15
external drives, tape drives, 122
external modems, 205-206
  installing, 210-211
external SCSI devices,
  terminating, 111

F

failure, batteries, 36
fans, 11, 52
file sharing, 233
firewall, 232
  installing, 239
flash BIOS, 24
  upgrading, 38
flash memory, 154, 191
flash upgrades, BIOS, 38
flat panel monitors, 170
  installing, 170
flatbed scanners, 143
flathead screwdrivers, 6
floppy disks
  bootable, 84
    creating, 105
  booting from, 70
floppy drives, 8, 15, 25
  adding additional, 79
  controller, 75
  installing, 73, 78-79
  mounting screws, 75
    removing screws, 77
  power cables, removing
    cables, 77
  power supply, 74
  read/write heads, 75
  removing, 76-77
  ribbon cables, 75
    removing cables, 76
  testing, 79

focusing, NetCam, 177
force-feedback feature (joysticks), 137
form factors, 30
ATX, 30
formatting hard drives, 70-71, 109
free drive bays, 84
locating, 105
tape drives, 124
free power connectors, 84
free slots, 105
freeing hard drive space, 60

G

game port, 10
General tab, Print Test Page, 221
graphics cards, 159
compatibility with monitors, verifying, 163
determining type of slot, 162-163
drivers, installing, 165
DVD drives, 92
how it operates, 160
installing, 162-165
multiple, installing, 168
primary, determining, 169
purchasing, 163
grounding wrist strap, 7

H

handheld scanners, 143
hard disks
backing up, 26, 243
formatting, 109
PCMCIA, 223
hard drives, 25
adding, 57, 60, 66
backing up, 104
installing motherboards, 31
connecting data cables to, 69
formatting, 70-71
freeing space, 60
IDE, 59
controller, 59
power connections, 59
ribbon cable, 58
installing, 68
jumpers, setting, 67
partitioning, 70

precautions before installing, 62
backing up data, 62
checking BIOS settings, 62
checking drive bay, 63
ribbon cables, 63
purchasing, 61
replacing, 57-61, 68-69
SCSI, installing, 108-109
slow, 60
hardware
drivers, installing, 18
scanners, adding, 147
troubleshooting, 245
heat sinks, 29. *See also* CPU cooling units
Home Networking Wizard, 237
home networks, 231
Ethernet cable, 233
file sharing, 233
firewall, 232
how they operate, 232
installing, 236-239
network cards, 233-235
network hub/router, 232
planning, 236
printer sharing, 232
TCP/IP address sharing, 232
troubleshooting, 238
hot swappable, 195-198
hubs, 195
network, 232
USB, 149, 196
HyperTerminal, 212
HyperTerminal command (Communications menu), 212

I

icons
MCI Mail, 212
Modems, 209
ID numbers, SCSI, 110
IDE hard drive, 59
controller, 59
power connections, 59
ribbon cable, 58
image sensors, 155, 175
images, scanners, 144
indicator lights, 9
ink cartridges, installing, 221
inserting
modems into slots, 209
sound cards, 184

installation problems, monitors, 171
multiple, 169
installation software, Zip drives, 119
installing
batteries, 156
BIOS, 38
cables, 214-215
controller cards, 64-65
CPU, 28-29, 34
device software, 198
digital cameras, 156-157
DIMMs, 49
docking stations, 228
drivers
graphics cards, 165
modems, 209-211
monitors, 167-171
mouse, 133
software, 99
tape drives, 127
USB, 203
drives
CD, 84-87. *See also* CD drives, installing
floppy, 78-79
tape, 124-126. *See also* tape drives, installing
DSL modems, 214-215
DVD drives, 96
precautions, 94-95
firewall, 239
floppy drives, 73
graphics cards, 162-165
multiple, 168
hard drives, 68
hardware, drivers, 18
home networks, 236-239
ink cartridges, 221
joysticks, 140
manufacturer's disk, 141
keyboard drivers, 135
keyboards, 130-134
microphones, 186-187
modem drivers, 209
modems
external, 210-211
internal, 208-209
monitors, 166, 170
flat panel, 170
multiple, 168-169

motherboards, 30-31, 34-35
  backing up hard drives, 31
mouse, 130-132
MP3 players, 192-193
MP3 software, 192
NetCam software, 177
netcams, 176-177
network cards, 214, 234-235
PCMCIA cards, 226-227
power supplies, 54
printers, 220
proprietary controller
  cards, 126
RAM, 34
RIMMs, 49
scanners, 143
    parallel port, 146-147
    SCSI, 150-151
    USB, 148-149
SCSI controller cards,
  106-107
SCSI devices, precautions,
  104-105
SCSI hard drives, 108-109
    multiple, 110-111
SDRAM, 49
SIMMs, 48
software, USB scanners, 148
software drivers, 87-89
sound cards, 184-185
speakers, 186-187
subwoofers, 186
tape drives, 124-125
toner cartridges, 221
USB cards, 202
    PCI slot, 202
USB devices, 198-199, 203
USB hubs, 200-201
insufficient disk space
  messages, 60
interfaces, USB, 175
internal modems, 205-207
  advantages, 210
  installing, 208-209
internal SCSI devices,
  terminating, 111
internal Zip drives, installing,
  118-119
Internet, connecting to, 212
IP Address tab, 239
ISA slot, 163
isochronous, 197

J

jacks
  line, 211
  modems, 11
  phone, 211
joysticks, 137
  buttons, 139
  force-feedback feature, 137
  how they operate, 138-139
  installing, 140
    manufacturer's disk, 141
  ports, 138
  position sensors, 138
  rotational movements, 139
  top hat, 139
  triggers, 139
  X-Y coordinates, 138
  yoke, 138
JukeBox software, 189
  running, 193
jumpers, 16-17
  setting
    hard drive, 67
    modems, 208
    tape drives, 126

K

keyboard ports, 10, 224
keyboards
  adapters, 134
  determining type of
    connector, 134
  drivers, installing, 135
  installing, 130, 134
  plugging in, 135
  unplugging, 134

L

laptop computers. *See* notebook
  computers
LED cables, connecting, 35
LED indicators, 53
lens, 154, 174
LIF (low-insertion force)
  sockets, 27
    removing CPU from, 28
lights, indicator, 9
line jacks, 211
locating
  adapter address, 214
  MAC address, 214
  memory sockets, 48
low-insertion force sockets. *See*
  LIF sockets

M

MAC address, 214
manufacturer's disk, installing
  joysticks, 141
master drives, 97
MCI Mail icon, 212
memory, 41. *See also* RAM
  adding, 48-49
  configuration, 47
  flash, 154, 191
  how it operates, 42-43
  proprietary, 47
    determining, 47
  Rambus, 45
  replacing, 48-49
  speed, 45
    determining, 47
  types of, 44-45
    determining, 46
  upgrading, 46-49
memory sockets, 25
  locating, 48
messages, insufficient disk space, 60
metal shield, removable drives, 115
microphones, installing, 186-187
microprocessors, 14. *See also* CPU
Microsoft Diagnostic Utility, 20
Microsoft System Information
  utility, 21
MIDI (musical instrument digital
  interface), 180
mirrors, scanners, 145
MMX (multimedia extensions), 27
modem drivers, installing, 209
modem jacks, 11
modem system settings,
  checking, 212
modems, 205
  connecting
    cable, 238
    phone cords, 209-211
    power cords to, 210
    to cable systems, 214
    to NIC, 215
    to serial port, 210
  drivers, installing, 209-211
  DSL, connecting, 238
  external, 205-206
    installing, 210-211
  how it operates, 206
  inserting into slot, 209

internal, 205-207
  advantages, 210
  installing, 208-209
PCMCIA, 223
phone jacks, 207
phone lines, 206
plugging in, 208
serial ports, 206
setting jumpers, 208
setting up, 208
testing, 212-213
troubleshooting, 212-213
turning on/off, 211
Modems icon, 209
monitor port, 224
monitors, 159
  capabilities, 162
  compatibility with graphics
    cards, verifying, 163
  drivers, installing, 167, 171
  flat panel, 170
    installing, 170
  how it operates, 160
  installation problems, 171
  installing, 166, 170
  multiple
    installation problems, 169
    installing, 168-169
  plugging in, 166-168
  primary, determining, 169
  refresh rate, 162
  resolution, 162
More Info button, 212
motherboard, 52
  batteries, 24
  connecting parallel ports to, 24
  ribbon cables, floppy drives, 75
motherboards, 15, 24
  choosing, 30
  connecting
    serial ports to, 24
    Zip drive to, 119
  installing, 30-31, 34-35
    backing up hard drives, 31
  jumpers, 17
  removing, 32-33
  specifications, 30
mounting screws, floppy
  drives, 75
  removing screws, 77
mouse, 10
  cleaning, 132
  drivers, installing, 133

installing, 130-132
plugging in, 132
unplugging, 132
upgrading, 132
mouse port, 224
MP3 players, 189
  ARM processors, 191
  DAC converter, 191
  flash memory, 191
  how it operates, 190
  installing, 192-193
  software, installing, 192
  USB cable, 190
  USB controller, 190
multiple graphics cards,
  installing, 168
multiple monitors
  installation problems, 169
  installing, 168-169
multiple SCSI drives, installing,
  110-111
musical instrument digital
  interface. *See* MIDI
My Computer icon context
  menu commands,
  Properties, 198

N

nanoseconds, 45
needlenose pliers, 7
NetCam
  connecting to cards, 177
  focusing, 177
NetCam cards, 174
NetCam software, installing, 177
netcams, 173
  how it operates, 174-175
  image sensors, 175
  installing, 176-177
  lens, 174
  USB interface, 175
  video driver, 174
  video processing unit, 175
  video software, 175
network cards, 233-234
  installing, 214, 234-235
  PCMCIA, 223, 225
network hub/router, 232
networks
  home, 231
    Ethernet cable, 233
    file sharing, 233

firewall, 232
how they work, 232
installing, 236-239
network cards, 233-235
planning, 236
printer sharing, 232
TCP/IP address sharing, 232
troubleshooting, 238
notebook computers, 223
  docking stations, 224
    installing, 228
  expansion bays, 224
  how it works, 224-225
  keyboard port, 224
  monitor port, 224
  mouse port, 224
  parallel port, 224
  PCMCIA cards, 225
    installing, 226-227
  PCMCIA slots, 225
  serial port, 224
nutdrivers, 6

O

on/off switch, 8
opening cases, 12-15
operating systems, reinstalling, 71
overclocking, 27

P-Q

page description language, 219
page-fed scanners, 143
parallel cables, connecting, 146
parallel port, 224
parallel port scanners
  calibrating, 147
  installing, 146-147
parallel ports, 10, 218
  connecting to motherboard, 24
parity chips, 45
  determining need for, 46
partitioning hard drives, 70
PC transfer, 155
PCI slot, 163
  installing USB cards, 202
  removing backplate, 202
PCMCIA cards, 223-225
  installing, 226-227
PCMCIA hard disks, 223
PCMCIA modems, 223
PCMCIA network cards, 223

PCMCIA ports, 223
PCMCIA slots, 225-226
Pentium OverDrive processors, 27
Pentium processors, 27
phone cords
    checking, 213
    connecting to modems, 209-211
phone jacks, 207, 211
    checking, 213
phone lines, 206
    checking, 213
pickup tools, 6
pixels, 155
planning home networks, 236
Plug and Play (PnP), 208
plugging in
    keyboards, 135
    modems, 208
    monitors, 166-168
    mouse, 132
plugs
    power cords, 11
    speakers, connecting, 186
PnP (Plug and Play), 208
port size, verifying, 132
ports, 15, 138
    COM, 208
    communications, 208
    game, 10
    keyboards, 10, 224
    monitor, 224
    mouse, 224
    parallel, 10, 218, 224
        connecting to motherboard, 24
    PCMCIA, 223
    PS/2, 132
    serial, 11, 132, 206-208, 224
        16550 UART, 208
        connecting modem to, 210
        connecting to motherboard, 24
    USB, 10, 132, 196-198
        compatibility with Windows, 198
    video, 10, 160
position sensors, 138
power cables
    attaching, tape drives, 127
    connecting, 35, 109

floppy drives, removing cables, 77
power connections, IDE hard drive, 59
power connectors, 83
    DVD drives, 93
    free, 84
    reconnecting, 55
    tape drives, 123-125
power cord plugs, 11
power cords, 12
    connecting to modems, 210
    unplugging, 12
power supplies, 51
    AC current, 52
    DC current, 52
    fans, 52
    installing, 54
    LED indicators, 53
    motherboard, 52
    power switch, 53
power supply, 15
    connecting to Zip drive, 117
    floppy drives, 74
power supply cables, 119
power switch, 53
precautions
    before installing hard drives, 62
        backing up data, 62
        checking BIOS settings, 62
        checking drive bay, 63
        ribbon cables, 63
primary drives, 97
primary graphics card, determining, 169
primary monitor, determining, 169
print head, 218
Print Test Page option (General tab), 221
printer cables, 218-220
printer drivers, 219
printer sharing, 232
printers
    how it operates, 218-219
    ink cartridges, installing, 221
    installing, 220
    parallel ports, 218
    print heads, 218
    printer cable, 218

printer drivers, 219
processors, 218
toner cartridges, installing, 221
printing test sheets, 221
priorities, USB data transfer, 197
processors, 218
    ARM, 191
    Pentium, 27
    Pentium OverDrive, 27
Programs menu commands, Accessories, 21, 212
Properties command (My Computer icon context menu), 198
proprietary controller cards, installing, 126
proprietary memory, 47
    determining, 47
PS/2 port, 132
purchasing
    graphics cards, 163
    hard drives, 61

R

RAM (random access memory), 14, 25, 41. See also memory; SIMMs
    DIMMs, 45
        parity chips, 45-46
    DIPs, 44
    ECC, 45
    installing, 34
    Rambus, 45
    removing, 33
    SDRAM, 45
    SIMMs, 44
        parity chips, 45-46
    upgrading, 41
RAM cache, 14
Rambus memory, 45
random access memory. See RAM
read/write heads
    floppy drives, 75
    removable drives, 115
Real JukeBox software, 189
reconnecting power connectors, 55
refresh rate, 162
reinstalling operating systems, 71

removable drives, 15, 113. *See also* Zip drives
  connectors, 114
  cookie, 114
  metal shield, 115
  read/write heads, 115
  zip disks, 114
removing
  batteries, 37
  cards, 32
  cases, 13
  connectors, 32
  CPU from LIF socket, 28
  CPU from type 1 slot, 29
  devices, 32
  DIMMs, 49
  drives, floppy, 76-77
  motherboards, 32-33
  mounting screws, floppy drives, 77
  PCI slot backplate, 202
  power cables, floppy drives, 77
  RAM, 33
  ribbon cables, floppy drives, 76
  RIMMs, 49
  screws, 13
  SDRAM, 49
  SIMM Modules, 48
  SIMMs, 33
  sound cards, 182-183
  static electricity, 12
replacing
  batteries, 36-37
  drives, CD, 88-89
  hard drives, 57-61, 68-69
  memory, 48-49
requirements
  tools, 6-7
    chip puller, 7
    flathead screwdrivers, 6
    grounding wrist strap, 7
    needlenose pliers, 7
    nutdrivers, 6
    pickup tools, 6
    screwdrivers, 6
    tweezers, 7
reset switch, 9
resolution, 162
restoring CMOS settings, 37
ribbon cables, 63, 83
  attaching tape drives, 127
  DVD drives, 93

floppy drives, 75
  removing cables, 76
IDE hard drive, 58
length, checking, 85
  tape drives, 125
tape drives, 123
RIMMs
  installing, 49
  removing, 49
ROM BIOS chip, 14
rotational movements, 139
routers, network, 232

S

satellites, connecting wire to, 186
scan heads, 145
scanners
  analog-to-digital converters, 145
  calibrating
    parallel port, 147
    SCSI, 151
    USB, 149
  connections, 144
  diodes, 144
  flatbed, 143
  handheld, 143
  images, 144
  installing, 143
  mirrors, 145
  page-fed, 143
  parallel port, installing, 146-147
  scan heads, 145
  SCSI
    ID number, setting, 150
    installing, 150-151
  USB
    installing, 148-149
    installing software, 148
screens, CMOS, 21
  BIOS settings, 105
screwdrivers, 6
  flathead, 6
screws, cases, 13
  removing, 13
SCSI
  determining need, 104
  how it operates, 102-103
SCSI (small computer system interface), 101

SCSI cables, 103
  connecting, 150
SCSI controller card, 106
  installing, 106-107
SCSI devices
  installing, precautions, 104-105
  terminating
    external, 111
    internal, 111
SCSI drives
  installing, 108-109
    multiple, 110-111
  terminating, 108
SCSI ID number, 103
  determining, 110
  setting, 108
SCSI scanners
  calibrating, 151
  ID number, setting, 150
  installing, 150-151
SDRAM (Synchronous DRAM), 45
  installing, 49
  removing, 49
secondary drives, 97
sensors, image, 155, 175
serial ports, 11, 132, 206, 224. *See also* COM port; communications ports
  16550 UART, 208
  connecting modem to, 210
  connecting to motherboard, 24
setting
  drive switches, 86-88
  ID number, SCSI scanners, 150
  jumpers
    hard drive, 67
    modems, 208
    tape drives, 126
  SCSI ID, 108
setting up modems, 208
settings
  BIOS, 105
  CMOS
    accessing, 36
    changing, 69
    restoring, 37
  modem system, checking, 212
Settings tab, 169

sharing
  file, 233
  printer, 232
  TCP/IP address, 232
shutter, 154
SIMM Modules, removing, 48
SIMMs (single inline memory
  modules), 25, 44. *See also* RAM
  installing, 48
  parity chips, 45-46
  removing, 33
single inline memory modules.
  See SIMMs
slave drives, 97
slots, 24
  AGP, 163
  determining type, 163
  EISA, 163
  expansion, 15
  ISA, 163
  PCI, 163
    installing USB cards, 202
    removing backplate, 202
  PCMCIA, 225
    determining type, 226
  type 1, removing CPU
    from, 29
slow hard drives, 60
small computer system interface.
  See SCSI
socket types, CPU, 27
sockets
  CPU, 25
  LIF (low-insertion force), 27
    removing CPU from, 28
  memory, 25
    locating, 48
  ZIF, 27
software
  devices, installing, 198
  JukeBox, 189
  MP3 players, installing, 192
  Real JukeBox, 189
  USB scanners, installing, 148
  video, 175
software drivers, installing,
  87-89, 99
sound, MIDI, 180
sound card cables, connecting, 96
sound cards, 179
  checking for, 85
  connecting CD audio cable
    to, 185

DAC chips, 180
disconnecting cables from, 183
disconnecting devices
  from, 182
DSP chips, 181
electromagnetic current, 180
how it operates, 180-181
inserting, 184
installing, 184-185
MIDI sound, 180
removing, 182-183
wavetable synthesis, 181
spacers, 35. *See also* standoffs
speaker cables, connecting, 98
speaker plugs, connecting, 186
speakers, installing, 186-187
specifications
  CPU, 31
  motherboards, 30
speed
  CPU, determining, 26
  memory, 45
    determining, 47
SPP, 147
standoffs, 24. *See also* spacers
static electricity, 12
  removing, 12
storage devices, 25. *See also*
  CD-ROM drives; floppy drives;
  hard drives
subwoofers, installing, 186
switches
  DIP, 16
  drives, setting, 86
  on/off, 8
  reset, 9
Synchronous SDRAM.
  See SDRAM
synthesis, wavetable, 181
system information, accessing, 20
System Information command
  (System Tools menu), 21
System Tools menu commands
  Backup, 243
  System Information, 21
systems, overclocking, 27

T

tabs
  Device Manager, 198, 245
  Diagnostics, 212
  General, Print Test Page
    option, 221

IP Address, 239
  Settings, 169
tape drives
  controller, 122-124
  drive bays, 123
  drivers, installing, 127
  external drives, 122
  free bays, 124
  how it operates, 123
  installing, 124-127
    setting jumpers, 126
  power cables, 127
  power connectors, 123-125
  ribbon cables, 123-127
TCP/IP address sharing, 232
terminating
  SCSI devices
    external, 111
    internal, 111
  SCSI drives, 108
terminators, 102
test sheets, printing, 221
testing
  CPU, 29
  drives, floppy, 79
  modems, 212-213
toner cartridges
  installing, 221
tools
  requirements, 6-7
    chip puller, 7
    flathead screwdrivers, 6
    grounding wrist strap, 7
    needlenose pliers, 7
    nutdrivers, 6
    pickup tools, 6
    screwdrivers, 6
    tweezers, 7
top hat, 139
transfer, PC, 155
triggers, 139
troubleshooting, 244
  checking for overheating, 245
  Device Manager, 245
  hardware, 245
  home networks, 238
  modems, 212-213
  monitor installation, 167
turning on/off
  modems, 211
  scanners, USB, 148
TV-out cables, connecting, 98
tweezers, 7

type 1 slot, removing CPU
from, 29
types
controllers, determining, 85
CPU, 26
memory, 44-45
determining, 46

U

Universal Serial Bus. *See* USB
Universal Serial Port. *See* USB
unplugging
cables, 33
connectors, 33
keyboards, 134
mouse, 132
power cords, 12
updating drivers, 243
upgrading
BIOS, 27, 38-39
flash, 38
chips, BIOS, 21
CPU, 26-27
memory, 46-49
mouse, 132
RAM, 41
USB (Universal Serial Bus),
10, 195
automatic configuration, 197
compatibility with
Windows, 198
daisy-chained devices, 196
data transfer priorities, 197
enabling, 203
how it operates, 196-197
USB cables, 196
USB devices as hubs, 197

USB hubs, 196
USB ports, 196
USB cables, 190, 196
connecting, 199
to hubs, 201
to PCs, 149, 193, 200
to scanners, 148
MP3, 192
USB cards, installing, 202
PCI slot, 202
USB controller, 190
USB devices
as hubs, 197
connecting to, 201
installing, 198-199, 203
USB drivers, installing, 203
USB hubs, 149, 196
AC adapters, 200
installing, 200-201
USB interface, 175
USB ports, 10, 132, 196-198
USB scanners
calibrating, 149
installing, 148-149
software, 148
turning on/off, 148
utilities, Microsoft System
Information, 21

V

verifying
compatibility, graphics cards
and monitors, 163
port size, 132
video driver, 174
video ports, 10, 160
video processing unit, 175
video software, 175

W

wavetable synthesis, 181
Windows Device Manager, 20
Windows Media Format
(WMA), 189
Windows support of USB, 198
wizards
Add New Hardware
wizard, 185
Home Networking, 237
WMA (Windows Media
Format), 189

X-Y

X-Y coordinates, 138

Y-adapter, 138
yoke, 138

Z

ZIF (zero-insertion force)
sockets, 27
zip disks, removable drives, 114
Zip drives, 113
connecting to
motherboard, 119
installation software, 119
installing, internal, 118-119
power supply, connecting
to, 117

Hey, you've got enough worries.

Don't let IT training be one of them.

Get on the fast track to IT training at InformIT,
your total Information Technology training network.

 | **www.informit.com** |

■ Hundreds of timely articles on dozens of topics ■ Discounts on IT books from all our publishing partners, including Que Publishing ■ Free, unabridged books from the InformIT Free Library ■ "Expert Q&A"—our live, online chat with IT experts ■ Faster, easier certification and training from our Web- or classroom-based training programs ■ Current IT news ■ Software downloads ■ Career-enhancing resources